LONELY GIRLS with BURNING EYES

LONELY
GIRLS
with
BURNING
EYES

*A Wife Recalls
Her Husband's Journey
Home from Vietnam*

MARIAN FAYE NOVAK

LITTLE, BROWN AND COMPANY
BOSTON   TORONTO   LONDON

First Edition

Many of the names of people
in this book, and identifying details,
have been changed for reasons of privacy.

Portions of this book originally appeared, in different form,
in the *New York Times Magazine,* December 4, 1988.

Copyright acknowledgments appear on page 278.

Library of Congress Cataloging-in-Publication Data

Novak, Marian Faye, 1944–
    Lonely girls with burning eyes: a wife recalls her husband's
journey home from Vietnam/ Marian Faye Novak.–1st ed.
      p. cm.
    ISBN 0-316-61323-1
    1. Novak, Marian Faye, 1944–. 2. Vietnamese conflict,
1961–1975 — Women — United States. 3. Marine Corps wives
— United States — Biography. I. Title.
DS559.8.W68 1991
959.704'3'0922 — dc20
[B]   90-40883

10 9 8 7 6 5 4 3 2 1

Book design by Robert G. Lowe

BP

*Published simultaneously in Canada
by Little, Brown & Company (Canada) Limited*

Printed in the United States of America

For those who also served

I wish to thank Andre Dubus, Bruce Weber, Joe Vallely, and my darling Dave.

LONELY GIRLS with BURNING EYES

At every window stand lonely girls whose burning eyes
are bright with tears. . . .

— Yvan Goll, "Recitative I,"
from *Requiem for the Dead of Europe*

One

I AM THE WIFE of a man who went to
war. I watched my husband train for war; I waited thirteen months for him to return from it; and then I waited
another fifteen years for him truly to come home. The
war my husband went to, in Vietnam, has turned out to
be the central event of the 1960s and 1970s in America.
It has certainly been the central event of my life. If I were
a veteran of that war in any of the usual ways — a warrior, a nurse, or even a protester — this fact would not
be surprising. Today, many bookstores and libraries have
sections on Vietnam, with book after book detailing the
vivid and powerful experiences of veterans of that war.
But my story is not there.

There must be thousands of women like me — wives
who waited, who in some sense are still waiting. But we
have been silent. Many of us are widowed, many more
divorced, left to remember bitter memories made even

more bitter by loneliness and loss. Many of us are still married to the men we sent off, but often we are so consumed with holding our men and our families together, there is no time or energy left to tell the story. Worst of all, we have been quietly condemned to silence because of who and what we are or were: wives. What could we possibly have to say about war? We weren't "there," we did not see its horrors or feel its terrors in the field.

And so our experiences have been relegated to the back room of memory, where they have remained, meaningless to everyone but ourselves; but in our most honest, our most doubting, our most frightened and courageous moments, we visit them, alone.

Item: An ad for a bronze replica of the statue at the Wall in Washington, the one of the three warriors. It appears from time to time in a magazine that comes to our house. "[They were] our sons . . . our brothers . . . our friends," it says. *No. Not always. Sometimes they were our husbands.*

Scene: In a used-book store, a woman I know waits on me. Her husband is a Vietnam veteran, and she is a wife who waited. "Why do you want to write about all that?" she says to me. "Why bring it up again?"

"Because," I answer, "I think what happened to us is important. I think some of us were wounded, too." Tears come to her eyes and she turns away from me.

Dream: At first it was a dream, a nightmare. A rainy day, a green-striped awning, and underneath it a bank of fresh dirt on the wet, shiny grass beside a rectangular hole in the earth. Poised over this chasm, held by two ropes — one on each end — is a silver coffin. In this dream I see no one — not me, or the grave diggers, or anyone else — but as the ropes begin to give and the coffin descends into the dark earth, I know that it is my world going into the grave. I know it is my husband inside the silver box.

This was first a nightmare, and then a vision. During the months my husband was away at war, I saw it again and again: in front of my windshield when I drove; on the pages of the books I read; in the dark before my face as I lay at night fighting for sleep.

In this story I have changed names and personal descriptions to protect the privacy of those I love, but the truth is here. These things happened. I am writing this story as I lived it.

I do not claim to speak for anyone except me, but in a sense, I mean to write for all of us — wives, husbands, children, parents, and friends.

I am writing because I can't stand the silence any longer.

Like many girls of my generation, when I was young, I looked forward to getting married and having a rather ordinary life as someone's wife. When I was young, girls often thought that the prefix "Mrs." was a sign of success, a key to their future, a symbol of pride. Such thoughts may have turned out to be unrealistic; but that was the way it was. We thought a girl got married and went off into the golden, happy haze of her future.

Time has shown that the reality for women of my generation more often than not involved divorce, aborted or truncated talents, choppy careers, and the trauma of raising children in postsixties America. Support groups exist for women who have experienced these aspects of American life.

But for some women from the generation that came of age in the late sixties and early seventies, there is yet another element of reality to be considered, one that for many has been the worst, the most powerful of all: the pain that comes from waiting for a man who has gone to war and that comes from living with what happens afterward.

For many of us it has been a pain that does not go away; and it has been more devastating for some than for others, because some women waited in vain, and others waited for men who came back to them profoundly and forever changed in ways that made their lives and the lives of those who loved them tragic. In a country at war, we waited at home among peers who often opposed what our husbands were doing, or who simply didn't care, or who even wanted victory for the enemy: our husbands' enemy.

I married Second Lieutenant William David Novak, United States Marine Corps, in August of 1966 and less than a week later went with my new husband to the Marine base at Quantico, Virginia, where the Basic School for new officers was (and is today) located. There we began our married life, like so many others at the time, with the cloud of war over us, yet with our eyes on the bright and shining future we felt in our hearts was just beyond the time of war. After all, we were young and knew nothing but the future.

The time at Quantico was so important, in retrospect, so crucial to what Dave and I were and have since become, that when I look at the snapshots from the late summer of 1966 to the early spring of 1967 — the first seven months of our marriage — I am amazed that there are so few. I have searched through albums, into the backs of desk drawers, and in boxes in the attic, and I can find fewer than a dozen. But it is not really surprising that we took few pictures. We accepted, as youth does, that the general things in our lives would not change: the landscapes, the buildings, our faces. So the photos are (or were meant to be) of special occasions and things tangential to us, though in a special way.

In the small stack there is a picture of Dave, my husband, with a pumpkin whose surface is carved out to reveal an awkward and incomplete Marine Corps insignia — the eagle, globe, and anchor — instead of a face. The room in the picture, the living room of our small, off-base apartment, is dark, and the pumpkin is blurry and bright from the light of the candle inside. Dave's face, barely perceptible, leans into its glow. The photographer, probably me, meant to feature the offbeat jack-o'-lantern, but what I look at now, nearly twenty-five years later, past the obscuring, frayed brightness of the pumpkin's light, is Dave's face. There is a picture of me here, too, standing in the fall sunlight, squinting against its glare. This shot was taken to immortalize my suit — a green-and-blue-plaid wool, an early gift from Dave for my twenty-second birthday. But it is the vaguely familiar young face of the girl I was that I stare at.

I lay the rest of the pictures on the desk in front of me. A small, square picture curled at the edges and slightly cracked on the surface shows Dave in a green twill uniform and me in a gold satin gown, our arms around each other's waist. The date on the back, in my handwriting, is November 1966. This is a picture of us dressed for the Marine Corps Birthday Ball.

I pick up a water-damaged picture of two Marines in winter gear playing in the snow: boys from Dave's Basic School class, Jon and Ken — or is the second one, the smaller one, Dennie? The boy's face is hidden beneath the helmet, behind the laughing mouth, and for a moment I am bothered because I cannot tell who it is in my hand. *No matter*, I finally tell myself. *They are both dead, and it is only a picture.*

There is another photo of some of the boys from Dave's company. They are in their dress blues, deep blue-black tops and bright cobalt blue pants. They are in our kitchen and hatless — or, as they taught me to say, without covers — sprawling across the photograph in various poses of joyful arrogance. Scott has one arm on Matt's shoulder, and he raises a plastic champagne glass in his free hand in a toast to the camera. He grins around a cigar clenched in his teeth. Dave watches in the background.

And there is a picture of the wives, our floor-length gowns in pink, blue, and green, white gloves in our laps. Our hair — shades of blond, brunet, and red — is teased and puffed into the stiff dress-up styles popular in the sixties. Our eyes focus on the camera; our smiles are shy. In contrast to the exuberance of our young husbands, we seem subdued. We sit closely, side by side, on a long, red couch. On the back I have written: "Quantico — New Year's Eve at our house, 1966."

Looking at the photos now, I want to cry for the girls we were, for the brave young women we had to become so quickly, and for all the brave men, too.

The events and feelings I write about in these pages are from my memory and my point of view, but they tell a story that belongs to us all. In the end, what happened to any one of us happened to every one of us. We were not alone after all.

Tales of great war and strong hearts wrung,
Of clash of arms, of council's brawl,
Of beauty that must early fall,
Of battle hate and battle joy. . . .
And now the fight begins again,
The old war-joy, the old war-pain.

— Charles Hamilton Sorley, untitled poem

Two

THE COLD, MURDEROUS WINTER
OF 1944 began with the news of fighting in forests and
small towns in Germany with names like Hürtgen and
Aachen. Three of my uncles — one my mother's brother,
one my father's, one the husband of my mother's sister —
fought in these places. Two of them, in different units,
were surprised to find themselves both in the Battle of
the Bulge. I was five years old when I first heard my
uncles talk about the war, in my grandmother's tiny
kitchen in Reydon, Oklahoma. The room was crowded
with relatives — my grandmother, my mother, various
uncles and aunts — but seated at the little kitchen table
with its blue-and-white oilcloth cover, my uncles spoke
only to one another. I sat quietly at the table, trying to be
invisible; noticed, I would be sent out of the room, into
the dirt yard to play with my cousins. I stared at the blue
windmills and Dutch shoes and tulips against the white

background of the shiny, slick cloth, and I listened. It was, my uncles would say, telling much in their reluctant few words, a terrible winter, a winter of horrors.

My aunts and my mother and my grandmother, crowding one another at the sink or the stove, went about their kitchen work and listened, too. They murmured to one another now and then, but I knew they were listening. Every once in a while I noticed one of my aunts looking at her husband, and I saw the look in her eyes — a look I would later come to understand was from pain and sorrow and pride. My uncles were heroes to the folks back home in towns like Amarillo, Texas, and Cheyenne, Oklahoma, for having fought in Germany in the winter of 1944.

That was the winter I was born. And it was clearly understood that my uncles' sacrifices helped ensure that I could grow up in a quiet, peaceful, and prosperous America. Yes, I remember the air raid drills — crouching under my blond-wood-and-beige-metal desk at grade school — and the Cold War, and the Bomb. I also remember thinking that we Americans were a good people who would prevail. I trusted the grown-ups in charge of my world. It was a good time — a lull in the century.

It turned out to be a good time for my family, too. My parents had been born and raised poor, in the dust bowl of Oklahoma. During the worst of the Depression, my father migrated to California, to pick fruit, because that was the only hope of a job. He sent his money home, and later, when FDR made things better, Dad went back to Oklahoma, back to those acres of blowing dust that were his family's homestead. When he married my mother, herself off a dust bowl farm — he twenty-one, she seventeen — they became sharecroppers, living in a tent and struggling to work someone else's land.

The first spring of my parents' marriage, a flooding rain ruined most of their possessions. They ended up picking

cotton for another landowner. I think that was the low
point of my father's life. He was intelligent, handsome,
and ambitious. And he could not bear being within hearing distance of the "boss." "He was a stupid man," my
father told me when I was old enough to hear the story,
"and when I realized that your mother and I were at least
as smart as he, I said to her, 'We're going to school.' "

And they did. My father worked three jobs at once —
morning, afternoon, and evening — to send my mother
to a teachers' college. Then she went to work using her
degree to put him through. By the end of the 1930s, they
both had teaching jobs. They had three children in the
forties, and my father bought his first new car in 1946 —
a maroon Ford, I think. That year he became superintendent of schools in a hot and dry southwestern county in
Kansas.

From there he went on to graduate work and, at the
turn of the decade, into school administration. Those
were hard, lean years, with all the family's resources going into my father's career. But by the late fifties, we
were in California, where he was teaching college and my
mother was teaching sixth grade. We had a small but nice
tract home, and both my parents had cars.

No one had given my parents any encouragement for
what they had done. College, degrees, career ambitions —
none of these things were understood back on the farm.
But my parents encouraged me, making it clear from my
earliest memory that I would go to college. They wanted
me to be educated for education's sake, and to have a
degree, "just in case." Equally important, college was a
good place to meet suitable young men. We all understood what my real goal should be, that when all was
said and done, I should marry and have a peaceful and
ordinary life as someone's wife.

> And ye shall hear of wars and rumours of wars. . . .
>
> — Matthew 24:6

Three

  I HAVE a dark, uncomfortable memory. The year is 1965, a few weeks before my twenty-first birthday. It is a pretty fall morning, and the air is cool but edged with sunlight. Blue sky, fall leaves, football weather. In this memory, I am in a noisy, crowded student union at the university in Pullman, in the rolling eastern hills of Washington State they call the Palouse. The sun streams through a large window next to the gray Formica table where I sit playing bridge, and it falls on my back and onto the table in front of me. I triumphantly take a winning trick just as my partner, a boy whose name and face I do not recall, mentions that someone he knew, a boy from his hometown, has been killed in a place called Vietnam.

  I remember feeling confused and irritated with myself, because my interest in the game at the table was uninterrupted, even though I knew then that something awful had happened, something more terrible even than the death of a boy.

I can still see my hands moving from my cards to the table. I can still hear the casual, offhand tone of my partner's announcement. I can remember knowing that something had changed forever. And I remember playing on, *wanting* to play on.

At the bridge table, we quickly began to talk about other things. There was no more talk about the dead boy or why he had died in that strange-sounding place. I am sure that I had read about Madame Nhu's visit to the United States. I am sure I saw the news photos of the Buddhist monks on fire in Saigon. But I am also sure that hearing my bridge partner talk about that American soldier's death was the first time I knew, really *knew*, about Vietnam.

The moment sticks with me the way certain moments do — for no logical reason. It haunts me still, that fall morning in the student union. It is as though something wants to remind me that no one instance of our lives can ever be taken lightly.

When I was a senior in high school, in 1961, my parents, idealistic New Deal Democrats, took seriously JFK's admonition to "ask not what your country can do for you, ask what you can do for your country." They went to Africa then, to the Sudan, as part of the US government's Aid for International Development program. My mother taught at the American Embassy School while my father worked to expand the school system in the Sudan. The time was a good time for the family, an enlightening, maturing time for us all, but perhaps for me especially; for to my mother's delight, the government helped to send me first to Geneva, Switzerland, for my last year of high school, and then to Beirut, Lebanon, for my first year of college.

During the long school breaks, I visited my parents in Khartoum, Sudan's capital. The strict Muslim atmosphere of the city prevented my having a usual Western social life among the Sudanese. The girls my age were very protected and for the most part were confined to their homes and yards. For me to mix with Sudanese boys my age would have been, for them, unthinkable. The rules of behavior and dress were very different and sometimes hard for me to remember. Once, I was stopped by an armed guard for stepping into the street outside our compound in slacks to say good-bye to a friend.

I fought boredom with tennis games in the afternoon at the British Club, where I was allowed on the courts as a guest, though never in the water at the pool. And most wonderful, during summer and holiday school breaks I volunteered at the Harper Nursing Home, a British hospital that boasted six patient rooms (three of them airconditioned) with a total of nine beds. In high school I had volunteered at the VA hospital in Fresno, running the autoclave and preparing blood agar petri dishes for experiments in valley fever. I had loved that work; but this was even better, for working at the Harper meant working directly with the one doctor and nurse who were the staff, and seeing patients. It meant learning exciting things every day.

The nurse, Sister Twissleton, showed me how to lay out instruments for surgery and assist in minor operations. She taught me how to dress wounds and how to treat patients for various ingested poisons. Dr. Jones took me on house calls and to the large Civil Hospital downtown, where I saw diseases many full-fledged medical people in the United States never see, diseases like bilharzia and elephantiasis.

At the same time, paradoxically to me, Dr. Jones and Sister Twissleton were very protective of certain of my sensibilities. I could see bloody surgeries and horrible illnesses, yes, but they drew the line at birth and death. I could not go near the dying patients, and I was forbidden even to listen to discussions about the obstetric and gynecology patients. We used to have morning coffee and afternoon tea sitting in wicker chairs on the broad veranda overlooking the lush backyard of the Harper, and I particularly looked forward to these times because every once in a while, in a relaxed, unguarded moment, the doctor and nurse would forget me and speak of things I was not supposed to hear about. I once heard them talking about a woman who had come to the Harper after walking all night in active labor from her tribe in the desert to reach the help she knew she desperately needed, for one leg of her baby had been born even before she set out on her journey. It was an amazing story, one whose power has never left me. I could not — still cannot — imagine such strength and will.

In Lebanon, at the American University of Beirut, I decided early in my freshman year that I would major in premed. That seemed natural in the environment of North Africa and the Middle East, where, I had come to understand, doctors are seen as nurturers and a career in medicine is therefore considered very appropriate work for women. I thrived in the introductory biological lab courses, where the instructors saw me as just as valid and important as my male lab partner. I wore my white lab coat to and from class, hoping someone might confuse me with the students from the School of Medicine. I decorated my dorm room with a white cotton surgical mask and cap, which Sister had given me, and a picture of the Harper Nursing Home, where one day I hoped to practice medicine.

I enjoyed my studies and my social life in Beirut my freshman year; but by the summer of 1963, I had been away from the United States for most of two years, and I was homesick for my native land. I remember the fall of

1962, sitting at my desk in Jewett Hall, the freshman women's dorm at the American University of Beirut, trying to tune my portable radio past the static so I could hear the clipped-voice BBC announcer talk about Soviet missiles heading for Cuba and the American blockade meant to stop the ships carrying them. Two of my girlfriends, black-haired Arabs whose dark eyes always seemed to have light in them, stopped outside my open doorway and asked if I wanted to go for ice cream.

No one in the halls of the dorm seemed concerned, no one on the campus seemed worried; nor did anyone on the Rue Hamra, where we went to sit on the sidewalk patio of one of the French cafés. I ate my dish of ice cream and tried not to think about what I'd managed to learn from the radio. But still I did. My country seemed to be in some sort of danger, and I was far away, in a place where it didn't seem to matter to anyone but me.

I loved traveling and living in foreign countries. I had seen the brilliant quilt the red and yellow fields of tulips make in Holland; I had had lunches of cheese and wine in the hot shade of dusty olive trees in Greece. Awestruck, I had roamed the ancient ruins at Byblos and Baalbek. But I wanted to be in my own country again. I wanted to go home.

I was happy when my parents agreed to let me return to the United States for my sophomore year. Because it was a reasonably priced university, because I had friends there, and because the town of Pullman was a small college town, I decided to attend Washington State University.

Washington State University was (and still is) a profoundly middle-class place. It is a land grant university, part of a system of rural colleges established by the government and supported by public funds in order to provide quality education cheaply. Still, there was a class system there. In the Chi Omega sorority, where I went to live my sophomore year, I saw this system at work.

Most of the girls in the sororities at WSU then were the daughters of teachers, farmers, and owners of small businesses. These parents saw college and the social life that went with it as something they wanted to give to their children. We sorority girls sat down to dinner in prim rows on both sides of long tables in a dining room lit with chandeliers. During dinner we talked in low voices, or, after the song leader clinged her knife against her water glass to get our attention, we sang old-fashioned, sentimental love songs like "Sweetheart of Sigma Chi" and "Down by the Old Mill Stream."

All the while, houseboys moved among us, silent and unnoticed in their black pants and short, white jackets, easing up and down the narrow aisles between the white-clothed tables, bringing dishes and taking them away again. Many of the houseboys who worked in the sorority were the sons of men and women who struggled to survive, people whose children were often left to find their own way to college.

Dave was one of these boys who waited on tables and washed dishes at the Chi Omega sorority. He was one of the boys who mopped our kitchen floors, took our garbage out, and carried our trunks to the basement. He had dark hair and dark eyes and wide shoulders. And he was very, very quiet. I don't think we spoke more than a few words to one another the first semester I lived in the Chi Omega house. I knew that in spite of the fact that we sorority girls were not supposed to date the houseboys, an attractive maverick in the house named Meg used to go out with Dave. But this bit of gossip was all I knew about him. That, and the fact he was not my type.

My mother was raised on a farm so poor she could never bear to talk about her childhood. Once, I brought home from college James Agee and Walker Evans's *Let Us Now Praise Famous Men*, and I asked her if her life had been like that of the poor documented in the book. She opened the paperback and solemnly turned a few pages, looking carefully at the pictures. Then she closed it and handed it back to me. "Nothing in there is as bad as it was," she said, and she walked away. Still, in spite of having had nothing, or perhaps more correctly, *because* of having had nothing, she had some romantic notions about my future. I learned to play the piano (not too badly) and the violin (badly), and I learned to speak French and German. She called these skills "accomplishments," and she set a lot of store by them. Above all, my mother wanted me to be accomplished. Accomplishments became advantages in the world. Advantages led to a good marriage.

In my mother's mind, I would not succeed through a career, especially not a career in medicine — both my parents had made it clear that this was neither appropriate nor possible. I would succeed by marrying, and I could excel by marrying well — that is, by marrying a professional, preferably from a professional family. "We came this far," she used to tell me, "so you wouldn't have so far to go." " 'From shirt-sleeves to shirt-sleeves in a generation,' " she ruefully quoted to me once when she heard that the daughter of a professor who worked with my father had married an auto mechanic.

Dave's father was a housepainter on the west coast of the state, in Tacoma. He was laid off every December when it got too cold to paint outdoors, and he was rehired every March, when the warm weather came. Dave's mother sold Tupperware. I did not know any of this then, but I did know that Dave was earning his own way, that he was someone whose parents would have had great difficulty paying for their son's education.

My mother and father were egalitarian in most ways.

In fact, in the fifties my father refused a job offer at the University of Virginia because it was not yet integrated. But having fought their way "up," they had little sympathy or real respect for workers and farmers. If it's true you hate what you fear, then my parents were afraid of the kind of life they left behind when they drove those dusty miles out of Oklahoma. They were afraid of it for themselves and spent their life escaping it, though it always haunted them no matter how far they fled. They were even more afraid of it for their daughter — the kind of life the son of a housepainter might have to offer. I knew that without being told. No, David Novak was not my type.

Softness he had and hours and nights reserved
For thinking. . . .
His laugh was real, his manners were homemade.

— Karl Shapiro, "Elegy for a Dead Soldier"

Four

BY JUNE OF 1964, at the end of my sopho-
more year at WSU, I knew I would not be a doctor after
all. Not only were my parents unenthusiastic (to put it
mildly, I might as well have told them I wanted to help
colonize the moon), but I was so poor in math that I had
begun to understand my capabilities would limit me, as
well. And the dean of science had led me to believe — he
seated at his desk, I standing before it with my academic-
record folder in my hand — that he was not in favor of
admitting women to the premed program. Added to these
disappointing drawbacks was the joyful stumbling block
of the family I hoped to have one day. But a restlessness
filled the void left by my vanished hopes of being a doctor.

In late June, when the wheat is tall enough to wave in
soft, summer winds, the hills around Pullman look like
green oceans. Looking out across the quiet, broad Palouse
from the top floor of College Hall one day, I had an over-

whelming urge to travel again, to go someplace far away and exciting. My parents agreed. My mother was particularly happy about this decision, of course. Travel was broadening — and in those days it wasn't every other person you met who had had that experience. A girl who had traveled was definitely advantaged.

My junior year wasn't a sponsored, proper year abroad like the ones most juniors who study overseas experience. Mine was a fragmented, wonderful year of trains crisscrossing Europe, a Greek freighter to Port Said and Alexandria, a fall semester at the American University of Beirut, where red hibiscus grew wild covering a hillside that ran into the Mediterranean Sea. In the spring I left Beirut and sailed to France, where I studied French civilization at the Sorbonne in Paris and lived with three other students in a fourth-floor walk-up in a three-hundred-year-old building with two bathrooms for the eleven apartments.

By the summer of 1965, I had walked through the same corridors in Paris as Abelard, and sunned on the same corniche in Alexandria as Cleopatra. I had often been almost dizzy with excitement — dancing in bistros in Rome and Florence, walking hour after hour through the great museums and churches of Europe — dulled after a while only by so much so beautiful.

The tone of my letters home must have reflected the unfocused tone of my life, because the letters my parents wrote back were about earning a degree appropriate for a woman and about being responsible, and my need to do both. And so I went back to Washington State for my senior year.

The campus had not changed. I had changed, though, and it was hard to adjust to the rules and the curfews in the sorority after my year of freedom. There was a new crop of freshman girls in the house; the cook and three of the five houseboys were new, too. Dave was one of those no longer working there. He was still on campus, though — a teaching assistant working toward an MA in mathematics. We often ran into each other on the steps of Todd Hall, where he arrived to teach his algebra class as I was leaving the building after having spent a frustrating, horrible hour in the clutches of new math, a requirement then for the teaching certificate I had decided to earn to go with a degree in foreign languages. He remembered me, always smiled when he saw me, and one day in September he asked me to go to a movie with him.

In the fall of 1965 on the campus of WSU, boys going on casual dates wore something like a pastel oxford shirt, a brown wide-wale corduroy suit, and wing tip shoes. Girls wore sweaters and skirts or a simple dress. For my first date with Dave, I wore a black-and-white tweed skirt, a red sweater, a necklace of cultured pearls, and black patent leather shoes with a small heel. I was ready, waiting on the edge of a chair in my room, when the girl on duty buzzed me. I hurried down the wide, curved staircase into the white-tiled entry hall where the boys waited to pick up their dates and where they left them at the end of the evening, with a quick kiss — on the lips, if they were daring.

Dave was standing by the sign-out desk. He stood with his arms folded over his chest and his legs wide apart, leaning back on his heels. Two other boys, hair slicked, both wearing slacks and V-neck sweaters over oxford shirts, waited near him stiff and straight. When Dave saw me, he dropped his arms to his sides, shifted his weight forward, and smiled a wide smile.

I stared back at him, up and down. His hair was neatly combed and his clothes were clean. But he was not wearing a corduroy suit or slacks and sweater. He wore jeans, faded from age and use — this was before stone-washed jeans had even been dreamed of — and the jeans were torn — unheard of — a small, white-edged hole in one of the knees. No one wore jeans on movie dates then, certainly not ragged jeans. To make it all as bad as possible, his shirt was nothing but a blue-and-white striped T-shirt, and his shoes were really only very worn moccasins.

We drove downtown in silence. Dave didn't seem to have the courage to overcome his shyness for even the smallest conversation. As soon as we took our seats in the theater, even before the movie began, he faced the screen squarely and, except to ask me once if I wanted popcorn, he did not speak to me until the lights had gone on in the theater and we got up to leave. He told me then he wanted to take me back to his place. "For a drink," he said, "and maybe to talk."

Dave and five other boys, some of them also former houseboys from various sororities around campus, lived in an old frame house with broken windows, half a chimney, a sagging porch, and tall weeds in the yard. This wreck sat wedged beside a stately, tall-columned fraternity house on one of the small side streets near the university.

Dave led the way through the dark yard up the walk to the house. A sign made of movie marquee letters spelled out its name: WHITE TRASH. We stepped up onto the wooden porch, where empty beer cases marked "Lucky Lager," "Rainier," and "Olympia" were stacked almost to the ceiling against the front wall of the house.

Inside, broken pieces of furniture cluttered the living room. All of the chairs — a large, overstuffed armchair and three or four dented and torn chrome-and-plastic kitchen chairs — faced a large black-and-white TV in the middle of the room. Like the chairs, the TV was broken. Its smashed tube lay on the floor in front of it. A big fieldstone fireplace and two bookcases whose shelves were lined with empty beer bottles made up the far wall behind the TV. A pair of mounted deer antlers hung over the mantel.

Dave proudly pointed out the fishnet curtains draped across the front windows, the street signs and the stop sign hanging on the wall above the broken-down couch. He showed me the kitchen. Each cabinet door was painted a garish shade of purple, pink, or orange. Then he turned to me and said, "Would you like to go up to my room now, for that drink?"

His question startled me — this was long ago, in another world and time — and I hesitated for a moment. But I could hear records playing and voices in other parts of the house, so I agreed and followed him up the dusty stairs, across a small, dark hallway, and into his room.

A gray wool blanket with bits of straw stuck to it hung over the single window. On the left side of the room sat a narrow, steel cot, sagging badly and covered with a thin, army green spread. Straight ahead a poster hung above a simple table shoved against the wall. The poster showed a Marine in green-brown battle dress. It said VALOR in large block letters. And then, in smaller letters, "The United States Marine Corps Builds Men." A sort of bookshelf made from a wooden apple crate sat on top of the table, underneath the poster.

A closet with its door off its hinges, two rifles mounted on the wall, and a homemade bar with a small wall shelf behind it were on the right side of the room. The shelf held three bottles: a bottle of blackberry brandy, something orange without a label, and a small, green bottle of lime juice. These liquids were the only bright color in the room. Next to the bottles, three or four glasses gleamed in the dim light. A neat, square stack of white paper napkins sat on the bar itself.

It was awkward. There was no place to sit, not even a chair at the table, so I sat on the firm edge of the army cot while Dave leaned against the wooden plank of the bar. We drank blackberry brandy and talked. That is, I talked. I talked about the football team, about my year overseas, about the new cook in the sorority house. I spoke with the front of my mind while the back of my mind watched this boy, and noted and felt sorry for his lack of everything. Even the closet was almost empty. Two or three garments hung on hangers from the rod, and a pair of jeans dangled from a hook at the back. The whole room had an empty, hard look to it that seemed to fit what I saw then were Dave's sad, hard limitations.

He was not like the boys I was used to, the ones from the fraternities whose promise — potential professional men like professors, lawyers, and doctors — appealed to my dreams of the future. He was not charming, was not good at small talk, and did not possess anything of material value, not even decent clothes. Hardest for me to comprehend, he didn't seem to care — or even to notice.

I was glad when he finally took me home. It was a relief to hang my clothes in my crowded closet, to climb into my bed with its pretty pink spread, to lie there with the lights out and remind myself how lucky I was to have my kind of life.

Dave and I still passed each other on the steps of Todd Hall. And we still spoke. As hard as I tried not to, I felt some strange combination of obligation and attraction whenever I saw him. He was always the same, sweet and friendly and apparently unaware that our date had been a disaster. He continued to ask me out, but I always declined as gently as I could, and he seemed unaware of what that meant, too.

One February afternoon, I faced him from underneath my yellow umbrella and listened while he asked me once again to a movie. A cold rain poured onto the old cowboy hat he always wore in bad weather. Water ran over the brim, onto the shoulders of his coat. The rain pounded on my umbrella. A little surprised, but not really — I admired his persistence and I liked the way it made me feel — I heard myself say yes.

Our date was for the following Saturday, and the cold winter rain had turned to snow by then. I had been baby-sitting all day, filling in for a classmate, a girl named Anne, and my charge was Nina, the five-year-old daughter of a university professor and his wife who had gone skiing for the weekend at Snoqualmie Pass. Anne was due back to put the little girl to bed so that Dave and I would not be late for the show.

Nina had insisted on eating her dinner on the porch, and even as cold as it was, I had let her. She was a lonely, withdrawn child who had no sisters or brothers and few friends, and I felt sorry for her. She was on the swing, finished with her dinner, and I was trying to coax her indoors when Dave walked up to the porch, his breath like steam in the chilled air. "Ready?" he said.

I shook my head. "We have to wait for Anne." I looked at Nina, perched on the swing. She was so bundled up she looked like a penguin, her arms short and high in her dark blue snowsuit, her mittened hands hanging there like flippers. We had played in the snow most of the afternoon, and I knew she was tired. It was getting late, too, already dark, but Nina begged to wait on the porch. I looked at Dave. "Now that you're here," I said, "I can take care of the dishes, if you don't mind."

Without a word, Dave sat down on the swing by Nina, who looked up, raised up on her knees, and scooted away from him, toward a corner, never once even blinking. I balanced the dishes in one hand and opened the door to go inside. When I turned to close it behind me, I glanced over at Dave and Nina. Dave was smiling at the little girl, an awkward, self-conscious smile. Nina was still staring back at him, her eyes as fully wide as they would open, her cheeks flushed. From the cold, I hoped. I had forgotten how shy Dave could be, and I felt bad that I had left that strange, timid little girl with him. I hurried to clean the kitchen.

I spent only a few minutes on the whole job, from throwing my coat off to washing the dishes, putting them in the drainer, and wiping the counter and stove tops. I was sure I would rush back to the porch to find Dave stoically, silently sitting beside an equally stoical but frightened Nina. I dried my hands, tossed the dish towel onto the kitchen table, and grabbed my coat. I think I ran down the entry hall to the front door.

When I opened it, I was surprised to hear the soft, gentle voice of a storyteller — Dave's voice melting the icy air. I moved away from the door then and went to the window of the library. From there I could see the back of Dave's dark head and the top of his dark jacket on one end of the porch swing and all of Nina still in her opposite corner, but no longer drawn up into a stiff little ball. Her legs jutted over the edge of the seat; her thin shoulders — thick in the snowsuit — leaned against the swing's back; her face was lifted toward Dave's. And her eyes were the steady, happy eyes of a child being told magic.

Inside the house, I smiled. And at the movie that night, I sat at peace in Dave's silence.

What, then, was war? No mere discord of flags
But an infection of the common sky
That sagged ominously upon the earth
Even when the season was the airiest May.

— Robert Graves, "Recalling War"

Five

SOMETIMES ON SUNDAYS Dave and I drove to a little town called Dusty, where there was a corner café that served huge pieces of homemade apple pie. On Saturday nights we went to dances and parties together where the air in rooms packed with people got so hot and muggy we found ourselves outside, in the snow, in our shirt-sleeves, gasping for air. When spring came, we took picnic lunches down to the Snake River or up to Kamiak Butte. But most of the time we just went downtown, to Rico's Pub, where we ordered Coke or beer and they brought it to the tables along with popcorn served in pie tins. At Rico's, we sat in one of the old wooden booths with initials carved all over the tables and the backs of the benches, and we talked.

I learned a lot about Dave then. I learned that he had a younger brother named Dennis, that part of Dave's shyness came from his having had severe speech problems

from the time he was a baby until he was almost a teen-
ager. Years of speech therapy had made speech easy, but
years of not being understood had made speaking, especially in groups or to strangers, difficult. I learned that
Dave's best friend since junior high was one of his house-
mates at White Trash — Bob Aaby, a boy also from Tacoma, also making his own way as a houseboy in a
campus sorority. Bob was brusque, stocky, muscular, and
fair-haired. He had a happy, ready smile, a rough charm,
and a good wit. He found most things in life amusing, if
not downright funny, and he could tell wonderful stories
from the thinnest material of everyday experiences. Later,
when I got to know Bob, he told me more about Dave:
that Dave had paid every penny of his way through
school, and that he had earned a Phi Beta Kappa key
while doing it. Bob also told me that he and Dave were
both Marines, that soon both of them would be called to
active duty. They had gone to kindergarten, elementary,
and high school together, had lived together at college,
and would be Marines at the same time, too.

In my twenty-one years, I had moved eleven times —
sometimes from country to country, sometimes from state
to state, sometimes only from neighborhood to neighborhood. I had never known anyone my entire life outside
of family members. I envied Bob and Dave for having
such a long friendship, for having shared so much, and
for expecting to share more. And I came to see that Bob's
easy manner — his ability to articulate, to laugh readily,
to tell a good story, and not only to get along in crowds
but to charm an audience — made him a good companion
for Dave. Bob was as loud as Dave was quiet; he was as
assertive as Dave was reticent. But Dave was comfortable
with Bob. He did not have to tell him how he felt about
things or who he was. Bob understood.

One thing I learned that Dave and I had in common
was that the Depression and its effects on our parents had

marked our paths early in life. They were very different paths, but their making had the same source. Dave's mother had spent the Depression years with her family in the rich forests of western Washington State, where her father and brothers fished in the rivers and lakes and hunted game, and where she and her mother and sisters planted and tended huge gardens in the rich, rained-on earth, all to put food on the family's table.

Dave's father, left homeless in Nebraska to find his own way when he was only thirteen years old, joined the Army as soon as he could pass for seventeen, and there he found a home — a place to sleep, a job, and enough to eat. In these ways Dave's parents survived the Depression, not through the New Deal policies designed to help the hopeless or through education, as in the case of my parents. His mother took from the land what it provided when it was able to keep its promise, and his father bartered his services for his keep.

Respect for hard manual work, for the outdoors, for making your own way, and for military service — all had been instilled in Dave since birth. And so his path to the Marine Corps was much more inevitable than his path toward college.

In 1961, Dave and Bob drove across Washington State to enroll at WSU. Like all boys enrolling at land grant universities, they had to join a branch of the Reserve Officer Training Corps during their freshman and sophomore years. ROTC probably never had two more enthusiastic members.

It's not surprising that Dave liked the marching and the outdoor drills. In many ways this outdoor, physical world was much more familiar to him, much more to his liking, than the confined, mostly passive world of the classroom. He was a boy who liked music — he played clarinet in the high-school and college concert bands — a boy who collected flowered china teacups and stamps from around the world; but his spirit had been formed in the outdoors, hiking on the mountainsides around Tacoma, hunting in the forests, and fishing in the waters of western Washington.

Dave and Bob had fulfilled their ROTC requirement by the summer of 1963, but neither of them had any intention of abandoning the military. They would have probably chosen army officer's training through the ROTC program, but one day that spring they had stopped at a recruiters' table in the student union. There, two handsome, well-built young men in neat crew cuts and sharp, blue uniforms trimmed with red piping stood almost as though at attention and talked about the Marine Corps. "Bob and I were going to go in the service," Dave told me during one of those long evenings at Rico's, "no matter what. And someone told us the Marines were the toughest. We wanted to see if we could make it there."

In the summer of 1963, they went to Platoon Leaders' Class (PLC), the boot camp for officer trainees in the Marine Corps, held at Quantico, Virginia. They returned to Quantico for more PLC the following summer, after their junior year at WSU. Dave was commissioned in the spring of 1965, the spring I had spent roaming Europe. In February he had asked for and received a "deferment from assignment to active duty" so that he could work toward his master's degree in mathematics. Not incidentally, this also meant he would begin active duty with Bob, who had added a major and needed another year before he could graduate and be commissioned.

In March, the first full Marine units waded ashore in Vietnam.

It made me feel close to Dave to hear him talk about his family, about where he grew up and what was important to him. But I did not love him. Although he had stopped seeing other girls, including Meg, I still went out with other boys and was even serious about one of them.

Tom Williams was a senior at the University of Washington in Seattle, a boy I had known since high school, and my mother's wish for her daughter; he was intelligent, good-looking, charming, and popular — obviously born to be a success in life. We had dated off and on all through high school, going to parties, movies, and proms. Since graduation, though, our relationship had been a long-distance one, and we had only seen each other a little in the summers, at spring break, and at Christmas — when we could manage to be in the same place at the same time. When we were apart, which was most of the time, we wrote each other love letters.

But as the winter of 1965 left and the spring of 1966 took its place, I found that at the same time I was looking forward to a weekend date with Dave, I was dreading a weekend call from Tom. Talking to him made me feel guilty. His letters, which appeared in my mail slot regularly, made me feel even worse. His thick, rounded scrawl on the envelopes and paper was as familiar to me as my own, but the letters made me sad, like outgrown friends.

Even though boys at Washington State University were required to belong to ROTC in their freshman and sophomore years, for the most part they took the training seriously and performed well. They drilled outdoors when the weather was nice, and in the Hollingbery Field House when it wasn't. On Fridays, ROTC members wore their uniforms to classes, and in full view of anyone passing by, the cadres marched in review and stood for inspection on the parade ground. At WSU the military was a presence so familiar in the early and middle years of the sixties as to be almost invisible. It was associated with the field house, the "uniforms" of the boys in ROTC, and the Friday marching on the drill fields. Incredibly, neither I nor anyone I knew associated it with war then.

Girls were not allowed to take part in ROTC officially, but I did belong to a small group of females who were attached to the Air Force ROTC program in a cadre called Angel Flight. We dressed up in blue skirts, blue caps, black heels, and off-white woolen capes, which we threw over our right shoulder so that we could salute — and so the cape's striking gold satin lining showed. We hosted at official social functions, performed special abbreviated short-order drills, and marched in parades. A few of the girls, me included, also belonged to the AFROTC rifle team. I enjoyed all of it: the drills, rifle practice, the dress dinners — even the graduation teas, hot, sweaty affairs in a room crowded with proud parents and nervous boys drenching their new dress uniforms with sweat while trying to look like officers and act like gentlemen.

In 1966 Washington State University had a student population of almost eight thousand, and since more than half of these students were males, there was a large ROTC at the school. Every spring the members held a military ball. As a member of Angel Flight, I was going to this dance, and I had asked Dave to be my date. He had been a commissioned second lieutenant in the Marine Corps for almost a year by the spring of 1966, so I knew he had a uniform, that he had something appropriate to wear.

The dance was held on a warm spring evening in early May. I came down to the foyer and waited there for Dave. We always had a girl "on duty," someone to answer the door, greet visitors, and summon the girls to come to the entrance. But I came down early, dressed in a fitted, gold satin, beaded gown. I did not want to wait for my date in the overheated, cramped room I shared with three other girls, so I had left them upstairs throwing clothes around and filling the air with mists of hair spray and perfume. The entry hall was cool, and I waited standing by the sign-out desk, afraid to sit for fear I would wrinkle my dress before my date had even arrived.

I first glimpsed Dave through the narrow lengths of glass that lined the sides of the front entrance of the house. He came up the sidewalk from the parking lot and stepped up onto the porch, and I opened the front door wide for him. The thick, green linden trees that lined both sides of the street in front of the sorority house framed him there. Even in the twilight, the green of the grass on the lawn and of the lindens shone. And the white of Dave's uniform was startling. The purity of the white of the uniform he wore — against the glowing trees and the darkening blue of the sky — made him beautiful. I had not known before that he was beautiful, but suddenly, from the open door, I knew it, and I have never forgotten. His coat and pants, his hat, his gloves, his shoes and socks — everything but the gold emblem on his hat, the gold bars on his shoulders, and the brass buttons on his coat — were all white, white on white, blinding like shining armor.

I have not wanted to be apart from Dave from the moment I first saw him in his dress whites on the night of the Military Ball. This happened at Washington State University in the spring of 1966, at about six-thirty on a warm evening in May.

I saw Tom Williams one more time. I had written to him about Dave, and Tom wanted to "straighten things out." I agreed to meet him in Pullman, in the bar of the local Chinese restaurant, at that time located on Main Street. Even at four o'clock on a Friday afternoon, the Ming Room was crowded in those days, full of students from the university just up the hill. The restaurant was dark, smoke-filled, and jumbled. Bodies clustered around the small tables that were crowded close together in the back room of the restaurant. It smelled like cigarette smoke, beer, and sweat.

The tile floor had been laid in a large checkered pattern of what probably had once been red and white, but dirt and cigarette ashes had so dimmed the colors that they were dead shades of light and dark gray. A jukebox against the back wall stood out in the dusk. Its slim, curved blue and yellow neon lights flashed the outlines of its form while it blared a Beatles song, one of their slow, soft tunes whose names I can never remember.

Tom had not arrived yet, so I picked out a small, empty table in a corner and struggled through the crowd toward it. When I sat down, I slid my chair around so that I could watch the doorway. A waitress came over and I ordered two drinks, wanting her to know that I had not come to drink alone. Almost as soon as she turned away, Tom sat down. I had not seen him come through the door. He leaned over and kissed me on the cheek, and I smelled the clean, fresh smell of his after-shave.

"Did you order for me, too?" he said.

"A red beer," I said. "For both of us."

"What the hell is a red beer?" He had settled back into his chair and was smiling at me.

"Red beer is beer with tomato juice. A speciality in Pullman, and you'll love it."

"Look," he said leaning forward, suddenly serious, his dark eyebrows hiding his eyes in the murky room. "I haven't come hundreds of miles to talk about local drinking habits. What's going on? Who is this guy you wrote about?" And he took both of my hands in his across the top of the table. I looked away then, off into the main dining room, and for a moment I wished I hadn't agreed to meet him at all, not even in a public place.

"His name is David Novak," I said, turning toward Tom. "He's from Tacoma. He's getting a master's degree in mathematics, and he's a second lieutenant in the Marine Corps. He loves me, and I love him, Tom. And I want to marry him someday. I'm sorry." The waitress appeared with our mugs of rust-colored beer and set them on the table in front of us. Tom released my hands and grabbed the handle of his mug.

"A Marine?" he said. "Are you joking, or what? You're hooked up with a Marine? Don't you have any idea what those people are up to these days?"

"They're up to what you'll be up to as soon as you get called," I said. I was sure that Tom, like every other young man in the country whose draft deferment would be running out upon June graduation, more than half-expected a short military career. The country was fighting in Southeast Asia, and American boys were going to the war. That much I had learned at the bridge table in the student union the year before. Now I was about to learn something else.

"I'm not going to be called up," Tom said. "No one has to be called up. And I'm not talking about running off to Canada, either." He pulled his draft card from his wallet, laid it in front of me, and pointed at the classification: IV-F.

I looked from the card to his face. "What's the matter with you?" I asked. "What's wrong?" The Tom sitting across from me had run cross-country in college and had served his two years of ROTC, too. He hiked in the mountains and went white-water rafting during the summers. He was one of the healthiest boys I knew. Being classified IV-F indicated a health problem, didn't it? I was confused. "I had an allergy to cats when I was seven years old," Tom said. He was smiling again. "You can take a health record even that old to Seattle and there's a draft board there that'll call it OK. I'm home free." He took the small, white card from the table and slipped it back into his billfold. "I'm opposed to our involvement in Vietnam,

Marian," he said. "It's wrong, and I'm not going to fight there. And I'm disappointed you'd even date a Marine, never mind wanting to marry one."

On the way back to campus in Tom's rented car, I couldn't think of much to say to him. Our relationship, all the shared times, had suddenly melted to a hard, nameless core in the crucible of an issue I didn't fully understand. I saw my lack of understanding Tom's position as a truly sad intellectual failing. Dave's position was so clear to me. He would serve his country. But I did not know what Tom was thinking, though I tried to find out.

"If you don't go," I said to him, "someone will go in your place. Doesn't that bother you?" I was getting out of the car when I said that.

Tom only glared at me. "Go back to your safe, smug little world," he said. "You'll never understand anything." And he reached over and pulled the car door closed in my face.

I never saw him again in person, though I have followed him over the years in the news, first in his role as an antiwar activist and later as he took part in minor politics.

Is it a purblind prank, O think you,
Friend with the musing eye? . . .

Nay. We well see what we are doing,
Though some may not see —

— Thomas Hardy, "Men Who March Away"

Six

DAVE AND I TALKED A LOT about getting married. Our marriage talk was that vague sort of conversation people resort to when they know the inevitable but have not faced it head on yet. We knew we wanted to be together, and in 1966 at WSU that meant married. We also knew we had to wait. We would be married — after. After Dave got out of the service. People around us were getting married almost every day — friends from all over campus were having spring weddings and planning summer ones. Marriage would be a part of our world, too — later. We knew that "later" and "after" would come. It was just a matter of time.

I had hoped for a real proposal before graduation, a proper down-on-one-knee, satin-ring-box, "Will-you-marry-me?" proposal. Not that Dave's plainly asking me could have made things any more certain. But I wanted to announce my engagement in the sorority during one of the formal dinners we had twice a week, on Thursday evening and Sunday afternoon. In the Chi Omega house we announced engagements during a ceremony that marked, in the sixties anyway, what we saw as the triumphant conclusion of one important part of a girl's life and the joyful beginning of another.

All spring the girls in the house had been making these announcements. As soon as a girl got her ring, usually a small diamond on a thin circle of gold bought on time at Foss's Jewelry Store, she took it to Neil's Florist Shop. There it was tied with a fancy satin bow to a candle decorated with a cluster of flowers at its base. Only the engaged couple's closest friends knew about any of this. So gasps of surprise greeted the houseboy who brought the burning candle into the darkened dining room during dress dinner. The houseboy, who always seemed to me to be half embarrassed and half amused, handed the candle with its ribbons and flowers to the housemother, who sat at the head of the first table. The housemother then handed it to the house president, who sat next to her. And so it passed from hand to hand, once, twice around the room, while we all whispered, admiring the ring, or, if we were not close to the lucky girl and not in the know, trying to guess whose it was. When the new bride-to-be finally blew out the candle, untied the satin ribbon, and slipped the ring onto her own finger, the rest of us smiled and clapped. A diamond ring on a girl's left hand was a wonderful, lovely thing, for marriage in that age was a respectable, desired career for a woman. For most of us girl-women at WSU in 1966, it was the most respectable, the most desired.

In late May, I went to the basement of the sorority house to take my red-and-black-plaid suitcases from the trunk room for the last time, and I packed my clothes and my books. Graduation was only days away. The ring ceremony was a moment of glory I would have to miss.

Dave and I had three years to wait before he would be out of the service and we could marry, and we both agreed that we would not like a long engagement. So the engagement ring became one more thing for me to wait for, one more thing for later.

My parents did not come to my graduation. My mother and father were both home from Africa, back in California, but my mother was teaching grade school, and my father was teaching college, and the schools where they taught were still in session. They wrote me that they could not get away so close to the end of the school year. But Dave put on his brown high-school suit — the seams strained across his shoulders and chest, and the sleeves were too short — borrowed some Sunday shoes, and came to be my audience. Afterward, he took me for a hamburger and a Coke at the Cougar Cottage. I still wore my black cap and gown and carried the white orchid he had bought for me.

In the small, crowded café just off campus, we hid in a back booth and talked about the future while the jukebox blared. For a while we were going to have separate futures. Dave would be staying in Pullman for the summer to take the last two courses required for his master's degree, and in the fall he would go on active duty with the Marines. Meanwhile, my parents expected me home. Their house had been emptied of children — my older brother was on his own in graduate school; my younger sister was married — but I was supposed to move back to the bedroom I had shared with a zoo of stuffed animals while I took summer courses at Fresno State College to complete teacher-certification requirements for the state of California.

I don't remember exactly how all this was decided, but I do know my part was simply to agree. I was twenty-one, a college graduate, and I had traveled alone in Europe, the

Middle East, and North Africa. But I was an unmarried daughter, now out of college, and I belonged at home.

Because Dave had to be in school for the summer, he would miss the Basic School sessions that began at Quantico in June and August, and would have to begin in October. He explained this to me on my graduation day over our hamburgers at the Cougar Cottage. None of it meant much to me. I did not know what he meant when he said "Basic School," or where Quantico was, or that the letters MOS stood for "military occupational specialty." None of what the handsome, earnest young man in the too-small brown suit talked about that day had anything to do with anything real as far as I was concerned. His talk was not connected to marriage, or a job, or anything I had planned for my life. But I listened. What Dave said did not make sense, but I loved him, and I would wait, wait for a time past all of these things I did not understand. I would wait for him to do what he had to do.

We had two free weeks after graduation before summer school started. I was packed and ready to go, but had to stay in Pullman to be a bridesmaid in a wedding to take place the week after graduation. When Dave learned that, he pointed out that we had time for a trip across the mountains to Tacoma. Would I, he wanted to know, like to meet his family? I would.

On a bright Saturday we drove for six hours, first across the desert and then over the mountains of Washington State, to the coast. Dave's father, mother, and younger brother lived on a dead-end street in a modest but quiet and pretty neighborhood in Tacoma, two blocks from the water of Puget Sound. Their home was small and plain, but freshly painted a bright barn red with brilliant white trim. The lawn was mowed short and neatly trimmed; there were fresh dirt V's cut around the edges of the concrete drive and along all the walks and curbs. A large bush full of small, pink roses was in full bloom in the middle of the front yard, and bushy red and white fuchsias spilled over the sides of white plastic pots that hung from the wide, low eaves of the house.

We parked the car in the driveway, and almost before we could open the car doors, Dave's parents were coming down the front walk toward us. His father took my suitcase from me. He was short and thick, and his eyes were a light and almost transparent blue that surprised me. Then his mother shook my hand, and I saw in her Dave's medium height and dark brown eyes. Her hair was silver-gray, but I knew without anyone telling me that it had once been black, like Dave's. They were friendly, Dave's mother and father, but reserved. I understood. Their elder son had brought home a stranger.

They did try to make me feel at home, though. Dave wasn't a boy who brought many girls home, and my being brought all the way from Pullman to meet the family was a sign that things were to be taken seriously. I knew this for certain when, the day after my arrival, Dave took me to meet his grandmother, his mother's mother who lived in a little red house behind Dave's parents' home. "Gram" was a neat and pleasant lady in her mideighties. She had white-white hair and quick, dark brown eyes.

The three of us — Dave, Gram, and I — sat in her small living room, and Gram talked. "I love all my grandchildren very much," she said, "but Dave is special, because when he was small I helped take care of him for a while. His father was overseas with the Army during the war, not in combat — far behind the lines in Hawaii — but he was gone for almost two and a half years."

Gram and I were sitting next to each other in matching upholstered rockers. On the wall next to my chair, an old pendulum wall clock quietly ticktocked, a steady, reassuring sound. Dave sat on a couch across from us. On the

wall above his head a large Victorian needlework pro-
claimed that "Prayer Changes Things." Outside the large
front window behind Gram and me, pink rhododendrons
brightened the small, undefined yard and the dusty alley-
way beyond.

"I suppose you find David quiet," she said. "Maybe too
quiet."

The perceptiveness of her statement startled and embarrassed me. "Yes," I said, "sometimes I do."

"Well," she said, "for years he made sounds that were
supposed to be speech, but which no one but one of his
aunts could really understand. I think he must have been
very frustrated and lonely. It's awful not to be understood.
Some of his teachers even thought he was retarded, you
know. But he's not stupid — he's very smart."

"I know," I said, and I looked at Dave, who had been
sitting silently, listening to his grandmother. She smiled
at him and then at me, a satisfied smile. She had wanted
me to understand, and I think she felt I had. And she was
right. What she told me brought into clear focus Dave
and the strange, lonely little girl on the swing he had been
able to talk to so easily that cold night in Pullman.

On the third day of the five-day visit, Dave, his mother,
father, and I were talking in the living room when Dave
suddenly asked me if I would like to show his family my
pictures of Europe and Africa. He was talking about the
red box that held my collection of colored slides, black-
and-white photos, and postcards of the places I had been.
Dave knew I carried the red box everywhere, and that I
loved to show its contents. I liked to talk about the places
I had been, to think about going to see them again.

I found the box where I had put it, in a corner of my
suitcase. I brought it back to the living room, sat down
next to Dave, and opened the lid. Sitting on top of the
pictures was a small, gold diamond ring. I looked up at
Dave. "Will you marry me?" he said.

I flew back to California the following week, engaged, a diamond on my left hand.

We had decided to marry as soon as Dave came home from Vietnam, where he was sure by now he would be sent after his five months of officer training in Virginia. We did not want to wait three years, and Dave had promised the Marines Corps at least that much time.

Beauty, strength, youth are flowers fading seen;
Duty, faith, love, are roots, and ever green.

— George Peele, "Farewell to Arms"

Seven

MY PARENTS were not happy about my being engaged. Or, more honestly, they were unhappy about my choice of a future husband. "Who is this boy, anyway?" my mother asked. It was a hot June afternoon, hot as it can be I think only in the waterless valleys of California in the summer, and we were in the kitchen washing the supper dishes. I had been telling her about Dave and talking about our engagement; I had even laid some pictures of him on the counter. My mother dried her hands on a small, cotton towel, picked up one of the snapshots, and tilted it to the light. She looked at it a while, and then she put it down on the counter and turned back to her sink of dishes. "He looks nice enough," she said. "Pleasant. But I simply can't understand what you see in him."

My father's reaction was pretty much the same, though he was less willing to say to my face what he felt. But I knew. My parents had never met Dave, and that he was honest, hardworking, and decent did not matter. He was from a working-class family, and even worse, he was a Marine. I still cannot understand exactly why, but even before the summer of 1966 my parents disapproved of everything and everyone military. They were not peace activists or conscientious objectors, and since they were FDR Democrats who followed his lead on all other issues, it seems unlikely that they were true isolationists; but there it was: they simply did not accept the idea of military service. Other men on both sides of the family served in WW II. But my father had somehow, someway, stayed out of the armed services then, though he was physically fit and of draft age.

No, I have never understood it. But both he and my mother were firm in their beliefs, and they wanted me to believe, too.

I had not been home in Fresno very long before an old classmate of mine, one who had also been one of my mother's former students, came by our house on his way to safety in Canada. After he left, my mother spoke to me about what she saw as this young man's honor, courage, and sacrifice. His self-exile, she pointed out, meant he was giving up friends, family, and home so that he would not have to fight in Vietnam. Couldn't I see that Dave was wrong to want to wear a uniform? How could I marry a boy who was so obviously morally empty?

My father made his point more quietly, without directly attacking Dave. He spread a map of Southeast Asia over the kitchen table — I have no idea where he got it, but it was new, with bright shades of pink, blue, yellow, and orange on stiff paper — and he patiently and carefully explained to me what he called the "disaster" that was the Tonkin Resolution, which gave congressional authorization for presidential action in Vietnam. I bent my head with his over the map and listened. I was torn. I agreed with him that war as an idea is fundamentally tragic, that President Johnson may well have been wrong in how he reacted after North Vietnamese boats reportedly attacked two US destroyers in the Gulf of Tonkin two summers before. But I could not really make a connection between any of that and the boy I loved.

I could not accept then, still cannot accept, that my parents did not understand my love for Dave, that they could not care for my feelings at least as much as they cared for their political ideals. Their reaction, it turned out, paled in light of those that the country in general later had toward its native sons in uniform.

That summer, the boys Dave lived with in White Trash were forced to vacate their house. The building had been condemned and the fraternity that owned it wanted it torn down to make room for a parking lot. Dave moved to the other side of town, to a basement room in the home of an elderly widow. The campus was almost deserted by this time, peopled by the relatively few summer-school students and the small faculty and staff needed to teach the classes and keep the offices open during the short summer term.

Pullman itself was hot, desolate, and quiet. The wheat fields all around it had turned dry and yellow, and the earth visible along the edges of the highways had baked brown and dusty. If the Palouse was not your home, it was a lonely place to be in July. Dave could not really afford long-distance telephone calls, but he called me anyway. And I looked forward to his calls, because they were almost the only reality in my world.

In Fresno, I was student-teaching in a junior high school on the outskirts of town, and my students, many poor, many from Mexican immigrant families, were also real to me. I enjoyed their company and I enjoyed teaching them. At home I shared my classroom experiences with my teacher parents, but I could not share with them those feelings and thoughts that overpowered even my love for teaching and my affection for my students. They did not want to hear about Dave.

Both Dave and I were lonely and isolated that summer — he on a large university campus, I in the middle of my family. So when he called one night and told me he did not want to be alone anymore, that he wanted me to marry him and go with him to Quantico, I said, "Yes, I'll go."

My parents had been hoping that I would end my engagement to Dave, and they thought they had every reason to believe this would happen. For one thing, I had had serious boyfriends before, and I had broken off these relationships, sometimes for no reason apparent to my father and my mother. And they had believed, too, that the Marine Corps would eventually separate Dave and me and that time would do the rest. My inconsistency and the fates of war had made them certain that I would never marry the young lieutenant.

But we did marry, on a warm August evening in 1966. The simple religious ceremony offered no hint that the bride who walked down the aisle was walking into bitter memory, that in a few months' time the shy groom in the white tuxedo coat and black pants would join the ranks of warriors, while his bride joined the invisible regiment of waiting wives.

There's never a bond, old friend, like this —
We have drunk from the same canteen!

— Charles Graham Halpine [Miles O'Reilly],
"The Canteen"

Eight

WHEN DAVE AND I drove eastward from Washington state to Virginia three days after our August 1966 wedding, our life together was made of six months of steady dating, two days of marriage, and suppressed hopes and dreams. Dave had sold most of his stamp collection to pay for our trip to the Marine Corps base at Quantico and to set up housekeeping there. We had nothing but the three hundred dollars from the stamps, some wedding presents, a 1959 black Chevrolet Impala, and each other. We had truly meant to wait and marry when Dave got back ("to get back": to return alive from war). But we moved the wedding date forward almost two years, not only because Dave was lonely, or because I was isolated in Fresno, or because we were in love. It was also because we knew, through nothing more than instinct — we were not wise — that we had rough terrain to cover, and we might survive better together. We felt from some-

where deep down and almost unconscious that the ceremony, the legality and the public nature of the commitment, might hold us together if our selves, our physical
or spiritual selves, failed us. The idea of me as "wife"
comforted Dave, I know, and I readily and happily accepted the title.

We drove for five days to get to Quantico, and as soon
as we arrived, even before we found a motel room for the
night, Dave wanted me to see the base. He wanted me
to see the place he had spent the summers between his
sophomore-and-junior and his junior-and-senior years of
college.

We had a lunch of sandwiches and Cokes at a small
café in a little town called Triangle, just outside Quantico's main gate, on the north side of the base. I was a
proud young bride. I tried to move my left hand so that
the gold band and diamond showed; I sat close to my
new husband in the front seat of the old Impala; when
we cashed a wedding check at a bank in Detroit on the
way to Virginia, I had been thrilled to sign "Mrs. David
Novak" on the back.

But from the first moment we drove past the MPs at
the main gate to the Quantico Marine base, I began to
feel the weight of the burden that was, and surely still is,
part of being a military wife. There is a replica of the Iwo
Jima Memorial by the guard post, the one of battle-weary
Marines struggling to raise the American flag. And over
the road leading into the base is a large sign: CROSSROADS
OF THE MARINE CORPS.

I saw the statue and the sign and the Marines in uniform at the gate, I saw their pistols and their serious ex-
pressions, and I felt a slight pressing on my soul, something worrisome.

In August Quantico is a hot and humid place. "Quantico Town," just east of the base, toward the water, is
little more than a main street with small cafés, bars, and

uniform shops. It is not a pretty town. The base itself, though, is lovely and peaceful. Many of its brick buildings are old and attractive, and they provide charm and a sense of stability. The low hills are covered with trees whose green does not fade until the leaves change colors in late fall. The large parade grounds are green, too, and everywhere you look you see strong young men in uniforms; in those days — before the adoption of regulation camouflage — most of those uniforms were a shade of solid green, too.

We had come to Quantico so that Dave, a new officer, could learn the things officers need to know. In this almost serene place, he would study military tactics, military law, and weaponry. He would practice leadership.

From Mainside, at that time the core of the base, we drove over the blacktop roads lined with trees to the Quonset huts and wood buildings of Camp Upshur, where Dave had spent those summers of his college years he had told me about so often. A man in a pair of red shorts and a yellow T-shirt with usmc in red on the front ran past us going the other way on the gravel by the side of the road.

At the camp, I saw men everywhere in dark olive green pants, shirts, and visored caps. They walked across wide lawns and down cement walkways with purpose, going somewhere to do something. A dozen or so of these young men in the green uniforms sat in the dirt in front of one of the corrugated-steel huts, swiping at the barrels and stocks of their rifles with white, oil-stained cloths. Some of the rifles were in pieces, spread on what looked to me like small blankets on the ground. In the bright sun reflected off the steel hut, the men squinted and sweated over their weapons. It is ominous when weapons are cared for with such devotion. I knew that even then.

We drove back over a winding road to Camp Barrett, to the concrete Bachelor Officers Quarters there, the BOQ.

We went to find Dave's friend Bob Aaby, who had come to Basic School at the beginning of summer while Dave finished his MA. For the first time since the two had started elementary school, they had been separated.

Dave went into the gray building. Soon after, both Bob and Dave came out to the car. Bob, Dave's loud, blue-eyed opposite, was a mass of muscled thickness in green fatigues. When he hugged me, I thought he would crush me. Then he disappeared into the BOQ and in a very few minutes he was back again, in civilian clothes, carrying a little leather case and a small bag. It was Saturday afternoon, and Bob was desperate to get off base.

Dave threw the trunk of the car open, and Bob and he pushed and shoved things to one side so they could, just barely, fit in Bob's small canvas bag and leather shaving kit. Then we drove off, the three of us crowded in the front seat. We drove south down Highway 1, toward Fredericksburg. We passed forests of pine and the small creeks they call runs and more of those gentle hills covered with oaks and maples and beeches. Auto-body-repair shops, gas stations, and small motels broke through the natural scenery every mile or so.

The car windows were open, and the air that rushed in through them cooled the late afternoon sun that made the water in the runs twinkle and the leaves of the tree-tops shine. I sat, silent, and looked hard at this new place I had come to, wondering what kind of a home it would be, while the boys talked back and forth over the top of my head, about Tacoma, about the boys who had lived with them at White Trash — places and people they had known.

In Fredericksburg, we paid for a room at the lovely, old General Washington Inn. I settled into a red brocade chair in the air-conditioned lobby to wait while Dave and Bob went off to buy beer. When they came back a good thirty minutes later, they were each carrying a six-pack and smoking a cigar, and it was clear they had had something to drink already, somewhere between the package store and the hotel. I put the magazine I had been glancing through back on the coffee table in front of me and followed the boys up the wide, carpeted stairs to our room. It was the first nice room we had had on our entire "honeymoon" trip. There was a bed with a high, polished headboard, a large dresser with brass pulls, a thick rug on the floor, a small side table, and two wing chairs like the ones in the lobby. I was thrilled. Dave and Bob did not seem to care where they were. They were still talking, excited and happy to be together again. They were not talking to me, though. They were not even talking about places and things I knew anything about. Strange names and unfamiliar words dropped into the conversation and faded away without being explained: "Fort Sill," "artillery," "MOS." Nothing made any sense to me, and I soon lost interest and grew sleepy.

It got late — I could see that it was dark outside the windows — and still Bob made no move to leave. Dave didn't offer to take him back to the base, either. My husband and his best friend just sat back deep in the armchairs, and they talked, more quietly as the evening got tired and old, and they smoked, and they drank. I sat on the edge of the bed and tried to stay awake. I tried again to understand what I heard. But I simply couldn't follow it. A lot of it was about the Corps, and they seemed to talk in some sort of slang about things like weapons and tactics.

I watched Bob and Dave together, and I began to see the love that men can have for one another that has nothing to do with sex or romance. It is a kind of love that has to do with caring, and loyalty, and even the special sharing of knowledge about certain things.

The room was warm and smoky, and it smelled terrible.

I was worn out, my head ached, and all I wanted to do was rest, but I was too excited about being at Quantico, about seeing Bob again, about what lay ahead of us — our own apartment, new friends, and married life. Suddenly, Bob set his beer on the little round table by his chair, put his cigar in the ashtray, lay down on the floor at the foot of the bed, and promptly fell asleep. As fast and as easily as that. Dave looked at me, and I shrugged. There was obviously nothing for us to do but to turn out the light and go to sleep, too. So we took off our shoes and lay down on top of the bedspread, where, like Bob, Dave immediately slept.

I wanted more than anything to sleep, too, but my nervous excitement made sleep impossible, and so for a long time I lay wide awake in the dark next to Dave and watched the top of the hotel's blue neon sign, mounted on a large board in the parking lot below, flash outside the window.

At breakfast, Bob and Dave ate like starved men — eggs, pancakes, hash browns, orange juice. I suppose I was probably hungry, too — none of us had eaten supper the night before — but I was too tired to eat. I slumped in the orange plastic booth and sipped a cup of black coffee. All night I had watched the blue flashes from the hotel's sign hit the interior of the room with the beat of a pulse. I had lain in bed until dawn and listened to Bob's and Dave's steady breathing, and I had begun to wonder and worry. It had come to me in the night like one of those bright neon flashes that I had to find a job, and we had to find an apartment we could afford. I had had an unpleasant shock: grown-up, married life was full of awesome responsibilities.

If love of money were the mainspring of all American action, the officer corps long since would have disintegrated.

— *The Armed Forces Officer*

Nine

WE FOUND A CHEAP APARTMENT in a small, rundown complex of buildings at the top of a hill in the little town of Falmouth, nineteen miles south of the base at Quantico. A small sign at the bottom of the hill said "Green Wood." A narrow brick road, badly in need of repair, curved upward around the hillside and came to an end in an open dirt parking area in front of a white, frame, two-story building. Our apartment was on the ground floor. There was one just like it directly over us on the second floor, and one more off to the side in another wooden structure, separated from our building by a few yards.

The place deserved its name. What we saw from our front windows were the woods and the hillsides, woods that ran up away from the small parking area and down to the main road. Green trees everywhere.

The married couple who owned and managed Green

Wood in those days lived in a large, white colonial about fifty feet beyond the apartments. He was old and ill, and she was young and obese. She spent most of her days lying in an antique four-poster with carved pineapple-knobs at the tops of the posts, staring at a little TV on top of the highboy at the foot of the bed. Once, she called me on her bedside phone to come over and change the channel for her. I went, though to this day I can't say why.

The apartment we moved into at Green Wood was furnished with worn, fake-oriental carpets; thin organdy curtains gray and heavy with dust; an enamel-topped table, a bed, a chest of drawers, and a dresser — all varnished almost black; a red couch and armchair upholstered in one of those nubby, scratchy fabrics popular in the fifties. A large Quaker gas heater took up much of the space in the cramped living room. Our rent was sixty-eight dollars a month, and in these few small rooms, I began to unpack our wedding gifts and make a home.

We had rushed our wedding, gone without a real honeymoon, and hurried to Virginia so that I could be there in time to find a teaching job, our best hope for an income before Dave went on active duty at the end of October. I had not even finished unpacking when I went to the main office of the county school department to see the county superintendent. I had been trained to teach high-school German, French, and English, but I told the solid, fiftyish man in the black-leather executive chair that I would be willing to teach any high-school subject except mathematics. I would even attempt to teach chemistry, if necessary. But not math.

"How about a first grade?" the superintendent asked. "What I really need right now is someone to teach the first grade." I stared out the window above his head. The heat was making little waves in the air above the blacktop parking lot, and the trees and the buildings on the other side were distorted. I fixed my eyes on the squiggling trees and tried to make myself stop blushing. I could feel my face burning even in the air-conditioned office.

I needed a job badly — Dave and I had no income. But I could not teach first grade, either. To teach first grade, you had to teach children, babies almost, how to read — how to do as well as they possibly could one of the most important things they would ever learn to do. I had had classmates who had majored in early elementary education. They took special courses and worked very hard so they would know how to teach a child to read. I had taken none of these courses.

"No," I said, "thank you. I couldn't possibly do right by a first grade. But I'll try anything else, except math. I have no useful background in math."

"Well," the superintendent said, sitting back and gingerly touching the tips of his fingers together, "I'll have the secretary give you some forms to fill out and we'll see what we can do."

I left the superintendent's office discouraged. Dave was waiting for me in the reception room, and when he saw me, his eyes became slightly worried — calm but mildly inquisitive — though he did not say anything. I filled out the forms, gave them back to the secretary, and Dave and I walked out into the heat. "It doesn't look good," I told him.

"Never mind," he said. "We'll manage." It was a Thursday morning. School was scheduled to open the following Monday.

The day after my visit to the main office, on Friday, the superintendent's secretary called to ask if I would substitute for a sixth-grade math teacher — only for the first day of classes — at a middle school in the northern part of the county. She said "math," and I tried to say no into the phone, but I could not get the word out. Dave and I had twenty dollars in one-dollar bills and some odd change we kept hidden on our dresser in a milk-glass vase, a wedding present. Twenty dollars would not go far — certainly not until the end of October. I needed a job.

As the secretary waited for an answer, I reasoned that I could manage a math class for one day. We could play word games, or I could read to them something from the classics, maybe. There must be some way to avoid the math and still not waste class time. My mind soothed my conscience. I said, "Yes, I'll be there." She gave me directions to the school, a room number, and the time I was to be in the classroom; then she quickly hung up.

Monday morning, I drove myself to the modern, tan-brick building. The day was beautiful, the sky blue and even, the air not heavy yet, still light from night cooling. It was exciting to be going to work. Dave had fixed breakfast because I was taking my time getting dressed, and he had made sure there was enough gas in the car to get me to the school and back with some to spare in case I got lost. I took with me a notebook in which I had written out word games that involved mathematical terms Dave had helped me with, and I also took along a book of short stories to read from. I hoped to do a good job, to be asked to work again. To have the $68-per-month rent and $25 for the next month's groceries, I would need to substitute-teach, at $15 per day, for at least seven days. I was as organized and ready as I could make myself.

But at the school it was clear, even in the parking lot, that something was not right. Cars were arriving and leaving with their tires squealing, and people were herding children off of buses and into and out of cars. There were a lot of raised voices, even some yelling. I wedged the car into a space and after checking in at the office and asking up and down the crowded corridors, I finally found room 26.

Parents bunched in front of the door there, shoving and talking loudly. I held my books tightly to my chest, pushed my way through the crowd, and struggled to pull the door open. Just then a short, red-faced man with wild eyes held his clenched fist in front of my face and screamed at me. "You're not the teacher — they say the teacher in room 26 is a nigger! My kid's not going to school with niggers and she's not going to have any goddam nigger teacher, either — you hear me?" I took my eyes from his face and looked around me.

Then I saw it. I had known it vaguely, in the back of my mind, from the newspapers or something I'd heard on the radio, but I had not really absorbed its meaning until that moment. This was the first day of complete school integration in the area. Obviously, the administrators had worked out a plan to ease the confrontations they knew would come when parents brought their children to school for opening day, and I was part of that plan.

The red-faced man had meant his angry, frustrated, hateful words for the absent black teacher. His words frightened me and made me almost physically ill, but they did not personally hurt. They fell flat and empty, as harmless as words like that can ever be, at the feet of a white girl.

I opened the heavy, metal door and entered the classroom. Two or three children followed me in and sat down while I waited by the open door until I was sure no more would be coming in. About a dozen children were already in their seats. They were white children mostly, but three of them were black, and all of them were looking at me, waiting. I shut the door and walked to the front of the room, where a stack of math books towered on the teacher's desk. I handed each child a book and told the class to open the books to chapter 1. And I began a math lesson.

The day seemed to go on forever. By eleven o'clock, I had "taught" two classes of math that I did not understand myself but tried to explain. Then a free hour, followed by lunch; I did not rest or eat, but instead read over the math book and tried to make sense of it. Then three more classes, which went a little better, but not much. My head pounded horribly from noon on. At last the final bell rang, I erased the board for the last time that day, and it was time to go home.

Sitting in the car, driving down the highway, I was troubled to leave that troubled place but glad to get away. The pounding in my brain slowed down to a throb and the ache behind my eyes stopped; and as I began to relax, I found myself going over in my head the teaching I had done that day. And then I started to feel guilty about the job I had done. I worried about it almost all the way home, until it came to me suddenly that whoever the teacher was whose classes I had led that day, I had more than anything done him a favor. He was going to look really good tomorrow.

That evening, just as Dave and I were sitting down to supper, the superintendent himself called. He was desperate for a first-grade teacher. Would I reconsider? By then, first grade did not seem so impossible after all. I reconsidered.

I began my teaching career at a first-through-fourth-grade school two miles south of our apartment, down the main road, Highway 1. The district was poor, the people middle- and low-income. The school itself was an old, brick, square building with a large, worn, grass-and-dirt playground in back where children played on monkey bars, slides, swings, and seesaws. A small gravel parking lot took up most of the space in front, and off to the right was a cemetery full of very old headstones, small, broken wrought-iron fences, huge trees, and that green Virginia grass, thick everywhere.

Deep within the cemetery, almost all the way to the other side, I could see a tiny, one-room log cabin. It looked empty and abandoned. I learned later that this cemetery was the site of the oldest existing grave in Virginia, and that the little log cabin was the schoolhouse where George Washington had gone to first grade, sent there from his home at Ferry Farms on a little pony that knew the way.

Teaching first grade, even a first grade of fifty students, turned out not to be as difficult as I had imagined, for in the case of this first grade, even though there were fifty children in the class — rows and rows of little children in little chairs — the class was not mine alone. I team-taught it with another teacher.

Her name was Elizabeth Thorburn — a slight, delicate, powdered, gray-haired southerner who was someplace in her seventies. She had taught in the district for more than fifty years and had taught first grade in that little brick elementary school in Falmouth for several generations. She had taught some of the children's mothers and fathers and grandmothers and grandfathers, and in the case of one child, she had even taught the generation before that. She taught me more about teaching in one school year than I had learned in all of my education courses. When I told Dave what had happened, how they had hired an ignorant new graduate with no experience to speak of to work with what must have been one of the wisest, most experienced teachers in the country, he laughed. "A first sergeant," he said. "Pay attention — you're going to learn a lot."

For my nine-hour-a-day, five-day workweek, I was promised $333 a month take-home pay. Dave had finally

found work, too, a part-time job in Fredericksburg, something he could do while he waited to go on active duty.
He was employed by the city, taking surveys house-to-
house, questioning people about their road use so the city
could plan its street improvements.

Dave and I were relieved. Our money problems were
over — or so we thought: at the end of my first day at
work, I took home the news that I was not going to be
paid until the end of the month instead of at the beginning. By the middle of the month, we were short of not
only money but food as well. I was scared. I thought
briefly about calling home.

But we had a few dollars left in the white vase, and
every two or three days Dave went to the commissary on
the base and bought cans of soup and a box of rice or
spaghetti. It was enough, and since we were both working, I knew things would be OK. Then, one Saturday
morning when there was about a week left to the month,
we ran out of food. There was not a can or a box of
anything in the cupboards. "Why don't you pick up some
soup and a box of crackers," I said to Dave. I was standing
in front of the open cabinet doors. Dave went to the bedroom and came back carrying the white vase. He turned
it upside down into his palm and held his open hand out
to me. On it lay a nickel and two pennies.

I looked at the three coins, and then at Dave, waiting
for him to solve the problem. After all, we had to eat, and
he was supposed to be the provider. He was strong and
smart; he could solve complicated mathematical equa-
tions. Surely he would know what to do now.

He only sighed, sat down in a kitchen chair, and looked
back at me. He seemed paralyzed. I was frozen, too, waiting to see what he was going to do.

He spoke first. "What do we do now?" he said, dropping the three coins on the table.

As soon as his words sunk in, I suddenly felt very old

and very tired. I loved Dave, but it was hard to accept that my knight had a flaw in his shining armor, that my intelligent husband did not have all the solutions. It took me a minute to answer. Finally, I said quietly, "I don't know what you're going to do, but I'm going for a walk." I took the nickel from the table, leaving the two pennies, and I left the house, letting the screen door slam shut behind me.

I walked to the bottom of the hill, stumbling over the broken bricks in the pavement, and crossed the highway to get to the old 1930s, silver, art deco diner on the other side. The diner had two doors, one at each end; the door toward the front end had a sign that said "Whites Only," and the door at the back had a sign that said "Coloreds Only." The signs did not mean anything anymore — everyone went in the "Whites Only" entrance.

Inside, next to the old, clangy cash register were several open boxes of candy bars — five cents apiece. I picked out a Milky Way and put my nickel — our last nickel — on the counter. I flashed a small wave at the cook-waiter-owner at the grill, who was dressed in grease-and-catsup-stained white. Then I crossed back over the highway, stopping by the side of the pavement long enough to peel back the brown, wax-paper wrapper of the candy bar, and as I climbed up the road to the apartment, I ate the Milky Way and tried to think what to do. By the time I got to the top of the hill, I had thought of something.

Dave was sitting in the living room when I got home, and without a word I passed by him to the telephone and picked up the telephone book. I turned to the yellow pages, found the heading LOAN COMPANIES, and read down the list. There were five or six in the Fredericksburg area. I read the names out loud, not for Dave to hear, but so I could judge them. I finished the list, then went back to the second name: Colonial Friendly Loan Company. I liked the way it sounded.

We drove down to the mall on Highway 1 in Fredericksburg where the loan company had its office. Fredericksburg has many malls now, but I remember only the one then, and it was small. The loan company was next to the La Vogue Dress Shop, and I stopped in front of its large window, drawn there by a bright green-and-blue-plaid wool suit with a double row of big, round, brass buttons down the front of the jacket. I thought wistfully for a moment about having that instead of my drab beige. Then I remembered what I had come to the mall for, and I followed Dave into the loan office.

I had to sign the papers for the loan, because Dave was a part-time temporary worker while I, on the other hand, had a year's contract for full-time work. We borrowed twenty-five dollars on my signature and paid it back a week later when I finally brought a paycheck home. We had excellent credit with the Colonial Friendly Loan Company for years. They finally lost track of us, and we stopped getting their fantastic loan offers in the mail.

Marriage is good for nothing in the military profession.

— Napoléon I

Ten

SCOTT BARNES and his wife Melinda were our neighbors; they had the apartment above us at Green Wood. They came from someplace in Arizona — Phoenix, or Tucson, perhaps. If they told me exactly where, I have forgotten, but I suspect they never told me. They were vague about the details of their life, and though polite, they were cool toward us, especially Scott; I began to think I did not like him.

By the time we moved into the apartment below theirs, Scott was already busy at the base, because first he had to complete the equivalent of the basic training that Dave had completed during his summers at college. And Melinda was busy with her job as a receptionist in a law firm in Fredericksburg.

But their jobs didn't explain their distance. We were all young people away from home, we were close neighbors, and Scott and Dave were both Marines, so it seemed natural to me that we should try to become friends. Still, during our first few weeks as neighbors, though Dave and I asked Scott and Melinda down to our place several times, our hellos on our way in and out of the parking lot at the apartment complex were practically all of the contact we had with one another — the exception being the couple of times when Dave helped Scott tune his car.

Working on the car with Scott one weekend, Dave discovered that we all shared the same exact wedding anniversary. I thought it was a happy coincidence of fate and said so to Melinda the next time I saw her. She turned pale and walked away.

One Saturday afternoon a few weeks later, I was working in the kitchen and looking out the window above the sink when I saw Melinda coming up the walk. She carried a large box with the name of a dress shop in Fredericksburg on it. When she passed my window, she saw me and waved. I waved back. Instead of going on up to her place as she had always done before, Melinda came to my back door.

"Would you like to see what I've bought for myself?" she asked.

"A new dress?" I said, moving quickly to open the screen door. She nodded and stepped through the doorway. I was surprised that Melinda wanted to visit, but inside the kitchen, she surprised me even more by saying she wanted to put the dress on, to model it for me. I showed her the bedroom and closed the door behind her, mystified.

I was sitting on the arm of the couch in the living room, still wondering, when Melinda came out of the bedroom. Her dress was very nice. It looked like it was made of wool flannel, and it was in a small, black-and-brown houndstooth pattern. The sleeves were long, and they buttoned at the cuffs. The collar was like those on a man's shirt. The dress was belted at the waist with a matching cloth tie, and the skirt hung in full gathers. I thought Melinda was lucky to have found such a pretty dress.

"It's beautiful, Melinda," I said.

"It's versatile. You can wear it without the belt." She untied the tie at her waist, and the folds sprang out so that they fell from the shoulders.

"It's nice that way, too," I said. "But I like it better with the belt."

She stood in the middle of the room, looking at me, the belt dangling from her hand, and the dress billowing around her.

"You still don't get it, do you?" she said.

I didn't know how to answer. Get what? What was I supposed to get? I sat and stared, stupidly, I suppose.

"I'm pregnant," Melinda said at last. "Scott and I were only married in August, and I'm already showing. See?" And she smoothed the folds of the dress tightly over her shallow bowl of a stomach.

"Scott joined the Marines for one reason only," Melinda said. "So we'd have a good excuse to leave town. No one at home knows, not even my parents. We just told them Scott had joined the Marines and we had to be out here by the end of August. We had a small wedding, but I was afraid someone would notice something and be able to tell." Melinda sat on the couch and looked at me. "It would kill my mother if she knew."

Melinda's cheeks were flushed and her eyes were sad. I stared back at her and tried to imagine what it must be like to be sick with worry at your own wedding. To think that you might ruin your mother's life.

"We didn't intend to tell anybody here," Melinda said. "Then Scott let it slip to Dave about our weddings being on the same day, and I've been wondering just how long it would take you to put two and two together."

I had known a girl in high school named Cynthia who had dropped out in her junior year; we were told she was ill. I saw her two years later, in front of a movie house where a Disney movie was playing, and she introduced the small, blond child with her as her little sister. I knew then what had happened to Cynthia.

Later, in college, one of the girls in the sorority had suddenly married and moved into a depressing, linoleum-floored basement apartment near the sorority house. There was furtive whispering among her close friends. When they gave her a surprise baby shower, I went.

Her name was Carol, and she was pretty big by the time of the party. When she came to the door, she was wearing an unflattering, yellow-flowered smock and black stretch pants. Dirty dishes lined the counter and filled the sink of her small kitchen. She tried to be nice about our coming to her door without warning, us in our trim skirts and pretty sweaters, smiling, single, and free, offering her neatly wrapped boxes in pink and blue papers. But I knew she was not glad to see us.

And now, in Virginia, Melinda was in my living room, worried about what I would think. What I was thinking was that she was lucky to have Scott, lucky that she didn't have to drop out of high school and pretend her baby was her baby sister. I was thinking how happy I was that Melinda did not have to be confined in a basement apartment while she watched her friends go about college life. I was simply happy for Melinda. I was happy about Scott, and I suddenly liked him, for marrying Melinda, for bringing her out of her community intact, at the risk of his own life. I would never think of him as cool and distant again.

Melinda was still waiting for me to say something. "I think babies are wonderful," I said. And I meant it.

Dave had been a member of the active reserves during his last two years of college, so he had an ID card, a military ID, even before he went on active duty with the Marine

Corps. Having this ID meant he could use the base facilities, and since everything cost less there than it did in the stores in Fredericksburg, Dave shopped in the commissary for groceries and got his haircuts in the barbershop at Mainside. I think the best deal of all was the movies — thirty-five cents admission to feature films — a third of what we were used to paying.

Feeling rich because we had grocery money and some to spare, we drove to Mainside, to the movie theater at Little Hall. We had a hot dog at the snack bar in the basement, then we went into the theater for the 8:30 show. We saw a western, *Shane,* starring Alan Ladd as an unwilling gunfighter in the Old West who is driven to violence in the name of justice. Dave loved the character of Shane, even though at the end of the movie Shane remains an outsider to the very people he has risked his life to defend.

"If we ever have a son," Dave told me halfway through the show, "I'd like to call him Shane."

It was late, almost eleven o'clock, when we crossed Bartlett Avenue to the parking lot. The night was warm even for early fall in Virginia, and very dark. The streetlights and the lights in the lot were only faint glows high above the ground. I could see the tops of the cars shining in the dark, but I couldn't distinguish their colors or their makes. And the lot was crowded from one end to the other. After all, it was Saturday night, and the lot bordered both the enlisted-men's club and the base MP station, and across the street was Mainside, swarming with Marines. Adding to all this, less than a block away, was the main street of Quantico Town, with its bars and cafés.

We couldn't find our car in the dark, crowded parking lot. We looked for it where we thought we had left it, then, as I stood looking around me dazed, confused, and a little frightened, too, Dave said, "You start at that end and I'll start at the other, and the first one to find the car will just call out." We met in the middle, face to face, and neither one of us had seen the black, flaring-finned Impala.

Another search had the same results. Our car was gone. Stolen. I felt hollow inside, and I began to feel a kind of sweating desperation, too. It seemed that everything was going wrong. I was used to a life of carefree dependency; even when I traveled alone in Europe and the Middle East, I had felt taken care of. Now it seemed I had entered a life of troubled independence that was beginning to seem a lot more trouble than it was worth. I knew without asking, this time, that Dave had no more solutions than I did.

I still don't know what weakness overtook me in that parking lot as I looked hopelessly around me. But I wanted someone to deal with this — anyone, as long as it didn't have to be me. We went back to Little Hall, and I went straight to the pay phone and called home, collect.

My father answered. "Dad," I said, trying hard not to cry, "our car's been stolen. What are we supposed to do now?"

"Where are you?" my father's maddeningly calm Oklahoma drawl responded.

"On the base — at Quantico."

"Do you know anyone who can come get you?"

"Yes. I think so. The couple who live above us. They probably can."

"Then call them and get a ride home. You're three thousand miles away, Marian, and I'm afraid that's all I can suggest."

I put a coin in the pay phone and dialed. Melinda answered. "How awful!" she said. "Stolen?" And then Scott talked to Dave, and soon Melinda and Scott drove up in front of the building, though it seemed forever to us sitting on the steps in front of Little Hall looking out toward the street, waiting for them, but hoping also that meanwhile whoever took our car would by some small miracle decide to return it.

Because the early fall was so beautiful, I didn't really mind the walk to and from school, though sometimes, at the end of a long day when I faced the climb up the hillside to the apartment, I really missed the car. Being without it was even harder on Dave. He had to walk three miles to Fredericksburg, where he was taking the surveys, and once there he walked through neighborhoods all morning with his questionnaires, and then he had the three miles home to walk again when he was through for the day. On the weekends, we walked together to the local grocery store and carried the bags home in our arms — a total of five miles.

Dave went on active duty on October 29, 1966. He brought his travel reimbursement home, and we walked to a used-car lot near my school and bought a white, 1953 Plymouth with a fairly decent paint job and four very bald tires. We paid $300 for it and drove it our five remaining months at Quantico, and it did not give us a moment's engine trouble the whole time. When we left, we sold it for $200 to a newly arrived student lieutenant and his wife.

I thought I was growing up fast. Keeping house, cooking, working on my lesson plans, worrying about the children at school, worrying about Dave. Wife. Teacher. Housekeeper. And I was only twenty-one years old.

The days at school were long, for both the children and me. The teachers at the Falmouth Elementary were supposed to be at school when the first bus arrived at seven-thirty, to watch the children on the playground in the milder weather, and to let them into the building and supervise them there when the weather was bad. And we were not to go home until the last bus had left, around

four forty-five. We were with the children at recess three
times a day, five days a week. We had no teacher's aides,
interns, or student teachers that year. We even ate lunch
with our classes. When we ate together, we talked to the
children about things that did not seem to fit into regular
schoolwork, about manners and being nice to one another. And we could make sure that all the children had
a lunch — an important responsibility in that community.
Early on I discovered that Mrs. Thorburn often paid for
the lunch or snack of one child or another. She did this
so quietly and matter-of-fact efficiently that nothing was
made of it, and even as canny as children usually are
about such things, I'm sure they never caught on. I knew
about these lunch payments because I managed the meal
counts and the money.

Mrs. Thorburn also gave little talks about good eating
habits. I remember her more than once explaining to our
rows of skeptical faces the importance of collard greens.
They made healthy skin. Did they want faces full of pim-
ples like some of those poor high-school boys and girls?
No? Well, then, eat the greens. They might not look so
good or taste so good, but we all must sacrifice for the
good of the body that is the Lord's temple. Mrs. Thorburn
got a lot of mileage out of collard greens.

Some days at lunch or during rest time, she would tell
stories that her grandfather had told her about fighting in
the Civil War when he was little more than a boy himself.
One day, as we were getting ready to go outside for recess,
we looked out the windows and saw fat flakes of snow
scattering down past the panes. Should we go out? The
children were complaining about the cold and asking to
stay in and play games. I looked at Mrs. Thorburn. She
did not answer the question on my face, but instead told
a story about her grandfather, who had left home at seventeen to join the Confederate army in the winter of
1863.

"One afternoon," she began, "my grandfather fell asleep after a long, cold morning's march." The children, who had been reluctantly pulling their jackets and hats from the coat racks, stopped, listening. "He was hungry and shivering, because the army, in fact everybody in the South, was short of food and clothing. He fell asleep in a grove of bare trees, but he dreamed he was in his father's peach orchard at home, and the peach blossoms were falling off the trees so thickly they covered him and he was warm under a blanket of white petals. He was happy because he knew that soon there would be peaches to eat, warm and juicy and sweet. And then he woke up, and he was lying on the ground covered with snow." The children did not move their eyes from Mrs. Thorburn's face, but her story was finished. "Now you all go on outside," she said. "You all have fun in that old snow. You've got warm jackets and nice hats, and there'll be a good, hot lunch waiting for you at noon."

Let the young Roman study how to bear
Rigorous difficulties without complaining
And camp with danger in the open air,

And with his sword and lance become the scourge of
Wild Parthians. . . .

— Horace, *The Odes*
(translated by James Michie)

Eleven

DAVE ENTERED BASIC CLASS 3-67, where he was assigned, alphabetically, to the third platoon of Company E with other men whose last names began with the letters *L* through *P*.

The Basic School at Quantico was, as it is now, a group of modern-looking brick and concrete buildings about twelve miles from the main part of the base, surrounded by the trees and hills that are everywhere in that part of Virginia. The main buildings face a large, flat, grassy drill field. In the middle of that field, from a flagpole, flies the Stars and Stripes. Every morning, the lieutenants at Basic School hold a ceremony to raise the flag, and every evening the companies gather again to take it down to the recorded strains of the national anthem; the phonograph record is so worn that static drowns out half the notes. This ceremony has not changed. It was there in our time as it is now.

At Basic School, Dave and his classmates — all of them already commissioned, some of them months before, some of them only days before the course started — were taught those things men need to know to wage war. That is, they were taught those things that can be learned about war in such a short time and so far from the fields of battle.

Our lives soon revolved around the world of Basic School. Dave's olive green uniforms hung in our closet; his heavy, black boots stood in the hallway with his shoe-shine kit; a blue-and-white-striped can of brass polish sat on our kitchen table next to the sugar bowl and the ceramic-corncob salt and pepper shakers. I wrote out lesson plans as soon as the supper dishes were put away, while Dave studied military manuals.

We watched television when our homework was done: "The Ed Sullivan Show," "Bonanza," "The Beverly Hill-billies." And sometimes "Gomer Pyle, USMC." Dave hated that show, but I loved it, seeing in it some reflection of us and our situation. Later, I saw how unrealistic the show was — not for its inattention to getting details right, but because it was an absurdity that people could watch a show about Marines in 1966 and 1967 that, as far as I can remember, never showed war. But, of course, the show was a comedy, and it was supposed to make people laugh.

While we watched TV, Dave polished the brass of his web belt and shined his boots, and I ironed his heavy, green cotton utilities for the next day, soaked his cap in hot liquid starch, and baked it slowly in the oven over an empty five-pound coffee tin.

Dave left our apartment early in the morning, before dawn, when the frost was still on the ground and the stars were still white frost in the sky, his heavy boots crunching over the frozen grass on the way to the car. He carried his manuals and always wore the fresh uniform I had washed and ready for him, with crisp, sharp creases ironed in the blouse the way he had shown me. At the BOQ, he "shared" a room with two of the bachelor officers and one other married man. The bachelors lived and slept in the room. Dave and the fourth lieutenant only had lockers there.

In the classroom, captains and majors, many just returned from Vietnam, lectured about infantry weapons and supporting arms, patrolling, tank-infantry operations, amphibious operations, military history, first aid, military law, map reading, and infantry tactics. It was advanced, intensive schooling to augment what the young officers had learned during the summer camps. The instructors kept an emotional distance that Dave has told me since he understood only after coming back from the war himself. "They had already learned the price of getting close to men who might die," he said. The young lieutenants at Quantico would learn about this in their own time.

Classroom work was only the smallest part of the training at Basic School. The command at Quantico intended to make the men platoon commanders, to give them the deepest, richest knowledge of weapons and tactics they could, but, more important, to give them some practical idea of how to use this knowledge. The student officers ran over the hills, mile after mile in full gear. They did push-ups and sit-ups — typical workouts carried out on the wide lawn, the obstacle course, and the roads marked for the conditioning marches. This physical preparation was followed by days — and nights, too — in the woods, setting ambushes, patrolling, practicing vertical envelopment, and experiencing every other field situation their trainers could simulate.

Somewhere in those woods of Quantico there was, and still may be, a replica of a Vietnamese village — four or five "hootches," a "canal," footbridges, storage areas. It was built in August of 1966, and it was named Xa Viet Thang — "Village of Vietnamese Victory."

A bank of benches covered a small rise above the "village." There the new lieutenants sat and listened to their instructors talk about mines and booby traps, about how to search a village, where the dangers were. On the bright, crisp, red-and-gold fall days at Quantico, it must have been hard to look down at that peaceful setting, those mute wooden houses among the beautiful, brilliant trees by that quiet, clear water, and imagine the sounds and smells and dangers the lecturers described.

When the field exercise went on through the night, Dave stayed at the base two and sometimes three days at a time, coming home the evening of the last day exhausted, dirty, and hungry, but strangely spirited.

I don't know how truly helpful that starlit training was when these young officers found themselves leading men in the pitch-blackness of a jungle night, but I do know that the exercises were useful to Dave in at least one important, practical way. On one of these night maneuvers, the low branch of a sapling, bent forward by the man walking in front of Dave, swung back and knocked one of his contact lenses out of his eye. Dave fell to his knees and tried to do the impossible — find the missing lens in the dark, in a bed of molding, broken leaves on the floor of the woods.

It was clearly a hopeless task, and he did not look long. He had to function as best he could the rest of the night and all of the next day, for all practical purposes half-blind, without depth perception. As soon as he could, he put in for three pairs of prescription eyeglasses — one pair of sunglasses, one pair of regular glasses to wear instead of contacts, and one to keep in his pack — just in case.

Dave had been so determined to join the military — and to serve in the Marine Corps, where he saw the biggest challenge — that he passed his physical for the Marines only because the Navy doctors who examined him did not know how bad his eyesight was. He wore contact lenses then, and he had worn them for his physical, of course. Because contact lenses were seldom worn in those days, especially by boys, no one thought to ask if he had them. And Dave didn't tell.

The first, slight nod paid to the wives by the base command was an invitation to a morning coffee held by the wives of the officers in charge of the platoons at the Basic School. We, the wives of the lieutenants in Echo Company, were invited to the home of the major who was the company commander. The coffee was going to be on a weekday morning the first week of November; I would have to take the day off. The idea was to meet and talk with one another and the senior officers' wives, too.

I was excited. Although I saw Melinda once in a while, liked working with the other teachers at school, and sometimes was summoned to sit and watch TV with our landlady, Mrs. Ledbetter, in her bedroom, I missed having a lot of girlfriends my own age. I wanted to meet the other wives and couldn't wait for the day of the coffee.

That morning, I dressed in my green-and-blue-plaid wool suit with eight round, brass buttons on the jacket — the suit that I had seen in the dress shop at the mall. The outfit was an early present for my twenty-second birthday from Dave. He had remembered that I'd admired it the day we'd gone to borrow the twenty-five dollars from the Colonial Friendly Loan Company, and when he went to pay off the loan, he bought the suit for me.

I was thrilled that he'd noticed and remembered, and I thought the outfit made me look pretty and sophisticated. I was glad, because I wanted Dave to be proud of me. My hair, shoes, purse, earrings — everything — was in place, and I stuffed an extra pair of nylons in my bag

in case I got a run in the pair I was wearing. Dave had
been spending hours spreading brass polish on buckles
and wiping soft cloths endlessly back and forth across the
tops of his boots. His sense of military spit-and-polish
was rubbing off on me. We had crowded each other that
morning, at the bathroom sink and the ironing board set
up in the kitchen. It was his first day of classes, my first
chance to meet the other wives.

Every time I looked in the rearview mirror on the way
to the base, I took a split second to check my hair and
face. What I saw satisfied me; and what a beautiful morning it was all the way around.

Officers who lived on the base lived in a variety of
housing. Neville Road, which ran from Mainside up
through the trees to the top of the hill behind Little Hall,
was a curving street of single units and duplexes — gracious, white frame-and-stucco, slightly southern in style,
with small-paned glassed porches. These officers' houses
at Quantico looked as if they belonged off-campus in a
pleasant college town or near the golf course of a small
suburban community. They did not seem to belong to a
military base. The streets of houses wound slowly around
and up; trees shaded the backyards and flowers still
bloomed, even in early November, in black window boxes
and small beds in the fronts.

The major's home was farther up the hill, toward the
top, in one of the half-dozen 1930s brick apartment
houses around Harry Lee Hall, the officers' mess. It wasn't
hard to find the right building: I could see several young
women going up its walk. I parked the car and followed
their path through the front doors, up the staircase, and
into an apartment on the second floor.

An older woman, in her thirties, thin and all sharp
angles, met us just inside the door and asked us to make
out our own name tags at a little table beside her. I stood
in a small line with three or four other young wives near

the table and waited for my turn. From where I stood, I could see the living room past the entry hall and beyond that, through a large archway, into the dining room. The rooms were full of women, some older like the one at the door, but many my age.

The women stood in small groups, talking. Now and then I could hear a soft laugh or a slightly raised voice. Everyone seemed to be having a good time, or, at least, everyone was determined to make it seem that way. The line at the name-tag table inched forward, and I got more and more excited. I could see the tea table in the dining room, a white cloth, a silver service, some yellow and white flowers, probably chrysanthemums, in a crystal bowl, plates of food, delicate-looking things. I could hear the faint, ringing clink of china cups being set on china saucers, and, softly, a record playing light classical music. The smell in the room was the mixed women's-party smell of fresh-brewed coffee, sweet perfumes, hair spray, cigarettes, and new clothes.

At last it was my turn at the name table. I wrote out my name with the black pen, pinned the tag on the right lapel of my jacket, and turned to the party.

But something went wrong. Several older women walked toward me, smiled vaguely in my direction, and went on. Once in a while one of the younger wives looked at me and smiled. But no one came to lead me through the refreshment line or to one of the small groups that chattered quietly around me, as I saw them doing for the others. I went alone to the table where coffee was served, holding the fragile, flowered cup and saucer and the crumbling cookie in my damp hands, forcing a smile at the perfectly coiffured, gracious woman who poured from the silver coffeepot.

I managed to smile, too, at the other women in the room when they passed me and smiled in a vague, unnerving way that made me wish I had not come.

The morning dragged long minutes into long hours. *So this is how it is going to be?* I thought. *Five months of strangers in a strange place?* I was not going to belong, and worst of all, I couldn't understand why. I moved toward a wall in the living room where there was a space between a sofa and a library table, too small for one of the groups, but a safe spot for me.

I was trying to drink my coffee, eat my cookie, and look unconcerned and not as hopelessly awkward as I felt, when a woman with a sweet smile on a small, round face came up to me and introduced herself as the major's wife. "I'm sorry that no one has introduced you," she said, "but" — and she put her hands palms up and shrugged — "we can't locate your husband's platoon." She paused. "We don't seem to have a lieutenant with your last name on any of our lists."

For a moment I stared at her blankly, then I lowered my chin quickly toward my name tag. I set my cup on the table next to me and turned the tag up into my face. Even reading upside down, I could see clearly that I had printed in big, black letters my maiden name.

Embarrassed, stammering, I told the major's wife my "real" name, and she led me across the room toward the doorway and introduced me to Joan Wilder, the wife of the captain commanding Dave's platoon, letters *L–P*. Mrs. Wilder was saying good-bye to a beautiful woman with the reddest hair I had ever seen on an adult. "Welcome to Quantico," Mrs. Wilder said, "and Marian Novak, meet Bonnie Parker." Then she added: "I'm afraid Bonnie's the only wife from the platoon who hasn't yet left for home. You've missed meeting the others."

"I hope I see more of you soon," Bonnie said just before she stepped out into the hallway. "Maybe at the Birthday Ball this weekend."

Her voice was as friendly as her words. She seemed to mean it, about wanting to know me. But I wondered. I

had been married nearly three months already, and I was
so nervous over a silly coffee I had forgotten who I was.
I had thought that I was truly and solidly married, but I
guess it takes a restructuring of the psyche to really absorb
a new identity. Whoever I was, I was sure Bonnie Parker
thought I was a fool.

My own active duty began with adjusting — nothing
more and nothing less seemed required of me. When I
married Dave, I had agreed to accept whatever it was that
had to be done, no matter how inconvenient or unpleasant. This was my service. I have often wondered whether
I would have been able to agree to it if I had known how
difficult that service would eventually turn out to be.

Basic School, especially during the war years, was in-
tense and difficult for the boys who attended. It left very
little time for sleep, or study, or even to be with your
wife, if you had one. I understood the obligations Dave
was under, and acquired a patience and an acceptance I
have not known since. It was that kind of life.

As soon as Dave went on active duty, I went to the
base, to Little Hall at Mainside. I climbed the broad, concrete stairs, entered the glass doors, and turned down a
wide, waxed terrazzo corridor to the right. In a little office
there, a corporal took my photograph and then issued me
a tannish-orange military ID with the picture laminated
to it. This was my passport to all the places that mattered
then: the PX, the commissary, the officers' club, the base
clinic. I left the office clutching the small plastic card and
walked a few steps down the hall to the base shoe store.
All the walking I had done after our car was stolen had
ruined my work shoes.

The store was very small, perhaps twenty feet by twenty
feet. But it had a good selection of shoes, mostly women's
and children's, and I had never seen such reasonable
prices. I picked out a pair of brown leather, low-heeled

pumps and showed my ID to the clerk when I paid at the counter. I left Little Hall feeling happy and secure. I still remember the strange, comforting thrill of that first use of privilege. I began at that moment on the wide steps of Little Hall at Mainside, Quantico, Virginia, in the sunshine of a fall day in 1966, to appreciate the trade-off, the service you got for service.

Driving off the base, things looked different to me. The men on the sidewalks and going in and out of the buildings in their dark olive utilities and Marine green uniforms looked different, and the buildings themselves did, too. I looked up toward the hill where Waller Hall, the officers' club, sat overlooking the small town of Quantico. The rambling, dilapidated Victorian building did not seem so formidable now that I was welcome there on my own.

Down the street was the big and blocky commissary, with its large parking lot packed with cars and women wheeling shopping carts loaded with brown paper bags. Small children tagged behind their mothers or waited in the cars with their faces pressed to the windows. None of it was off limits to me anymore. Dave had shopped here for us until today, but now it was my commissary, too. I could go there alone, under my own auspices. The same for the PX, filled with sheets, towels, dishes, brooms, watches, clothes, and all sorts of other things. And the chapel, where the chaplain had his office. Officially my chaplain now. Everything on the base was now an official part of my life.

The Marine Corps saw this differently, I know. As far as those in command were concerned, I was not an integral part of the Corps. They did not bother with too many provisions for the wives of new lieutenants. For one thing, we were rare to begin with. In a platoon of about forty-five men, seven or eight might have wives. So these wives were not welcomed with a lot of fanfare at Quantico. In fact, looking back, I can see now that the Marine Corps may not have even wanted us there — the only concern was to train new officers, and very quickly, too. I noticed early on that the bachelor officers in training had housing, airy "dorm" rooms in a modern building at the Basic School, while the married second lieutenants had to scramble to find something they could afford off-base in nearby Triangle or farther south on Highway 1 where apartments were less expensive than they were north-ward toward Washington, DC. The small housing allow-ance did not begin to cover the costs of food, rent, utilities, and gasoline and upkeep of a car to get you home and back.

I don't think the Marine Corps had the slightest idea what to do with the wives of these young, war-bound junior officers. But by issuing us the military ID, they did recognize us as their own. When I got my ID card, it did not matter whether the Corps wanted or welcomed me or not. Emotionally, I began to feel that I belonged.

We're marching off in company with death.
I only wish my girl would hold her breath.

— Alfred Lichtenstein,
    "Leaving for the Front"

Twelve

IN THOSE EARLY DAYS at Quantico, Dave and I saw a lot of Bob Aaby, his old friend from Tacoma. Once we were settled into the apartment at the top of the hill, Bob spent many of his Saturday afternoons there with us. He was in his last weeks at Basic School, Dave was working two part-time jobs, and I was teaching long hours, so we were all tired by Saturday. The Saturday afternoons Bob spent with us were quiet and slow hours, and for both him and Dave, I think, they were pleasant and comforting as well.

Dave and Bob tuned in the little Magnavox TV to a sports broadcast of some sort, football usually, and settled down for the afternoon. Bob sat in the overstuffed easy chair, his elbows resting on the rough upholstery of its wide arms. He drank beer and smoked cigarette after cigarette, filling the room with a gray haze of smoke while he and Dave, his arms behind his head and his body stretched out on the red sofa at a right angle to Bob, talked about college and old friends and watched the football games on TV.

If the weather was nice, I took long, solitary walks in the woods behind the apartment complex. If I stayed inside, I folded laundry, flipped through women's magazines — *Seventeen* was still my favorite — and prepared lessons for school. Or I made ham sandwiches and bowls of buttered popcorn and brought them with beers to the living room for Dave and Bob. Once in a while I stayed there a moment or two, standing between the two boys — between the chair and the sofa — and I pretended to like watching the football game on TV. I really had liked football games at WSU — sitting in the stands on chilly, bright Saturday afternoons, bundled up in soft wool and crushed among cheering friends. But the little black-and-white figures jumbled across the screen in that small, choked room did not represent football or fun to me.

For the most part, I did not share these afternoons with Dave and Bob. I did not share their long history, and I was not (or so we all thought then) a real part of where they were at the present. Dave and Bob were comfortable together; each was a reassuring presence from the past for the other, and they were determined, I think, that their old friendship *would* not change. But I knew things had changed. And I had seen the picture of a sinking ship Bob had sent Dave when he heard about our engagement, so I knew that Bob knew that things had changed. Dave was just a little slow to realize it.

The only fight Dave and I had the whole time we were at Quantico was connected to this issue. It took place because we were awakened in the middle of the night by a phone call from Bob: Bob was downtown, Dave told me, putting the receiver down and reaching for his jeans. He needed a ride.

Fredericksburg was only ten minutes by car at the most,

but by dawn, more than three hours later, Dave was still not home. I had decided he must be lying dead somewhere between our house and downtown Fredericksburg, in a wrecked car by the side of the highway, or in the woods, stabbed through the heart. I was hysterical, waiting by the phone, when I heard the car coming up the road. I ran to the kitchen window and saw Dave get out of the car, alone, and walk — safe and sound — to the apartment door.

"Where were you?" I screamed.

"In DC," he said, looking at me as though I'd lost my mind. "I told you. I had to pick Bob up and take him to the base. He got into a brawl over a girl and his ride took off."

I did lose control then. I attacked Dave's forearm with my fingernails and left two wounds about four inches long where the skin pulled back in furrows that slowly and steadily oozed first a clear plasma and then blood. Dave wrapped a dish towel around his arm and then tried to calm me, making me sit down at the kitchen table while he brewed tea.

That night changed things between Dave and me, and between Dave and Bob, too. I don't know why, but Dave never held the attack against me, as violent as it was, but instead seemed to gain a deeper understanding of our relationship from it. He saw the hurt behind my anger, and he was sorry for it and for his part in it, as unintended as it was. I think that night I truly became Dave's wife, because after that he was a more caring and thoughtful husband; Bob was often a guest in my home afterward, but he was never again my rival.

Though tempered by Dave's understanding, it was still a male, Marine world I inhabited. Quantico and all it meant in the way of training Marine officers in warfare seeped into every corner of my life but, in the beginning, anyway,

not with any connection to me. And not with any connection to the war in Vietnam, either — not then. That is the
strangest part. In those early days at Quantico, we did not
watch the news or read about the war in the papers except in passing, and we did not discuss it or what it might
mean to us, even among ourselves.

It was as though war, the Vietnam War in particular,
were a forbidden subject. How oddly impossible that ex-
quisite self-protection of the last days of my youth seems
to me now.

After his session of Basic School started, Dave and I
had the same weekday hours. Like me, he left the apartment early in the morning and did not get home until
after dark. Between Dave's basic training and my school
teaching both of us kept very busy during the week. The
intensity and long hours of our work made play important, and gradually we began to find things we enjoyed
doing together on the weekends. Bob still joined us now
and then, but we didn't stay in the apartment as we had;
we went to movies on base or to the officers' club, and
once, the three of us went to DC, where we visited the
Smithsonian, heard a Marine Corps Band concert, and
saw the evening parade at the Marine Barracks at Eighth
and I streets. I enjoyed those times with Dave and Bob,
but I had spent years living with girlfriends, and I missed
talking with girls my own age, about clothes, or hairstyles,
or even about teaching. It did not help matters that we
had rented a place so isolated, far from the base and on
the edge of town. We had few neighbors — just Melinda
and Scott and the Ledbetters — and I didn't see much of
them; Melinda came home from work and rested, and
Mrs. Ledbetter rarely left her bedroom to begin with. For
the first time in my life, I was lonely.

I had learned from Dave that several of the other wives
from the platoon lived near one another in Triangle, one

of the little towns just off the base. It made me even lonelier to imagine them and their husbands all spending their Saturday afternoons together, visiting Williamsburg or the museums in Washington.

Years later one of them told me this had not happened. Her husband would meet some of the other boys from the platoon during those precious spare hours for pickup games of basketball while she sat alone in their apartment, into the evening, waiting for him to get home. It seems that boys gathering courage for a death-defying leap into manhood do not turn to needy girl-wives.

Since the coffee had turned out so badly for me, I looked forward to the Marine Corps Birthday Ball with both hope and dread. According to Marine Corps tradition, the Marine Corps' birthday, November 10, is celebrated everywhere in the world where there are two or more Marines. It is also traditionally the most formal and festive affair of the year for Marines, for it marks the beginning of the Marine Corps at the Tun Tavern in Philadelphia in 1775, the first gathering for service of those "few good men."

Dave and I had both looked forward to the ball for weeks. It was too late in the season to wear dress whites, so Dave had ordered his dress blues and our calling cards, a set for each of us, from Bolognese's Tailor Shop soon after we had come to Quantico. Dave wanted the dress blues not only for the ball, but also because he had a uniform allowance of three hundred dollars coming to him, though only on the condition that he purchase all of the uniform requirements, calling cards included; he was lacking those and the dress blues.

But in the rush of all the orders the lone tailor shop had to fill in the fall of 1966, Dave's had not been completed yet, and so he had to accept wearing his class-A winter greens, a heavy, dark green twill, to the dance. Of course, I had my gold satin gown, the same one I had worn in May to the Military Ball in Pullman.

Bob's class at Basic School had graduated the day Dave went on active duty, but Bob was staying on, to spend part of his leave at Quantico with Dave and me. He wanted to go with us to the Birthday Ball, but he didn't have a date. There were very few single girls around Quantico, but I knew a nice, rather pretty girl in Washington, DC. We had both attended the American University of Beirut in 1964, and we had spent Christmas of that year together in Turkey. Her name was Marcia. I called her, and after a few minutes of excited talking — most of it both of us at the same time — she said, "Yes, I'd love to go with your friend." I knew for certain that Bob and Marcia had little in common; Marcia was shy and prim. Bob was not even close to being either. But that didn't matter to me. I wanted Marcia with me, someone connected to my past — the kind of connection that Bob and Dave had. I was determined that this one time I would not settle for our eternal triangle, not for the Marine Corps Birthday Ball.

On the morning of the ball, Bob, Dave, and I drove north to Washington to bring Marcia back to Falmouth. The day was bright and warm, and I remember that we were relaxed and happy. Dave had the morning off — it would be his last free Saturday morning until Christmas — and Bob was enjoying his first real break in months. Their good mood was catching. We told jokes and sang along with the car radio all the way to Marcia's house, which, it turned out, was actually in a "desired-neighborhood" suburb just south of Washington. I sat between Bob and Dave in the front seat of the old Plymouth, new to us then, and I remember the clean smell of a black cardboard air freshener shaped like the Playboy Bunny that hung in front of me from the rearview mirror, and how the smell of it mixed with the smells of Bob's cigarette smoke and my White Shoulders perfume.

Driving back down the highway to Falmouth, Marcia and I sat in the backseat of the car and told each other stories that we both already knew — stories we had lived through together, the kind that begin, "Remember when . . . ?" She told me about her job with the foreign service. She wanted to make it a career and was excited that she had a good chance of being sent back to the Middle East soon. She missed the excitement of travel.

The boys sat in the front seat, square-shouldered, eyes straight ahead. Every mole and mark on their scalps was visible through their unforgiving, short haircuts.

Marcia and I spent the rest of the day washing and setting our hair, taking turns sitting under my blue plastic hair dryer, combing our hair out, putting on makeup, and pressing our gowns and the boys' uniforms. Bob and Dave watched TV until it was almost time to leave. While Marcia and I put on our dresses, they took turns showering in the already steamy bathroom. Then they dressed, too. Bob took a picture of Dave and me, I took one of him and Marcia, and we all headed for the car.

Early, winterlike darkness made it hard to see on the base, but the lights in front of Larson Gymnasium lit the parking lot in front, and I saw couples entering the double front doors. In their dark uniforms, the men were like shadows, but the women sparkled. The night was very cool and clear and moonlit, and the shiny materials of the dresses shimmered below the ladies' short evening wraps.

Just inside, warm air rushed at our faces while the cold air from the open doorway hit our backs. Beyond the crowded entrance, we could hear the loud noises of people and music and see the bright red of the regimental flags hanging from the ceiling over the dance floor — and ahead of us, the swirl of the bright colors of uniforms and dresses. The large room was crowded with hundreds of people, most of the men dressed in the deep blues of dress blues, the women in the light and bright shades of evening dresses — pinks, lavenders, greens, yellows, golds. The white coats of the waiters mixed with the black short dress jackets and bright red cummerbunds of the majors, colonels, and generals. The brass of their buttons and insignia and the gold of their epaulets glittered in the dim light of the dance floor. The colored lace and satins, the graceful velvets, and the rustling taffetas of the ladies' gowns made me think of the dresses of those beautiful women who glide around Austrian ballrooms in movies set in the age of Strauss.

But standing in the doorway, awestruck, I saw that in spite of all the bright and different colors, the hall belonged to the young men — to all those young lieutenants in their dark Prussian-blue coats and bright blue trousers with the blood red stripes.

Marcia and I left our wraps with Dave's and Bob's covers at the hatcheck, and we all squeezed our way to one of the linen-covered tables off to the side of the dance floor. We were the only four at the eight-place table. The white tablecloth was dotted with small, red coasters on which the Marine Corps globe, anchor, and eagle, and the dates "1775–1966," were printed in gold. While Bob and Dave went to the bar to order drinks, I looked around the room. It was full of people, but I did not recognize any of them. I peered through the haze of warm air and smoke looking for Joan Wilder, the captain's wife, or Bonnie Parker, the student wife I had met at the coffee. Except that it was pretty, I could not remember anything distinctive about Bonnie's face. But I was sure I would spot her red head.

Shortly after the boys came back with our drinks, the lights in the ballroom dimmed, and the crowd hushed. The band struck up the national anthem, and then a color guard marched to the center of the dance floor and presented the red-white-and-blue flag of the United States and the red-and-gold flag of the United States Marine Corps. An honor guard followed, accompanying a large cake iced in white and decorated with gold-icing piping and red sugar roses, a cake big enough to allow everybody in the room a piece. Then there was singing, "The Marine Corps Hymn," and toasts — to the guest of honor, to the oldest Marine present, and to the youngest Marine present.

The base commandant gave a speech. The cake was rolled away, followed by the honor and color guards. And the band began to play again, this time a mix of songs, from "The Anniversary Waltz" to "Louie, Louie." Something for everyone. While the crowd on the dance floor got larger, the four of us at the table talked and watched.

Bob and Marcia looked uneasy and their conversation sounded a little strained. I understood. They had just met that afternoon; and besides, Dave and I probably seemed awkward to them, too. We were surrounded by the elegant trappings of almost two hundred years of Marine Corps tradition. There was all that intimidating brass, and then there was also the uncomfortable feeling that because we were naive and new in the service, we were missing important steps in a sophisticated but invisible protocol.

All around us, other young people did seem to be managing, though. They were not only dancing or lining up at the silver chafing dishes on the long hors d'oeuvres buffet, they were mingling in bunches on the edges of the dance floor and at the tables. I heard raised voices and laughter on all sides of me.

We finally left the table to dance, first Dave and I, and then Bob following with Marcia to the center of the floor. I saw them circle away from us to the beat of a fast waltz, first Bob's face toward me, then a turn and I saw Marcia's.

Neither of them was smiling. Suddenly, a tall lieutenant
with a broad and handsome face and a pleasant smile
tapped Dave on the shoulder. "Hey, Novak, why don't
you and your wife join us?" he said. He gestured with a
nod toward a crowded table on the other side of the room.
"A bunch of us from the platoon are over there."

Dave and I looked at each other; then Dave said,
"Sure," to the lieutenant and, "Is that OK with you?" to
me.

"If that's what Bob and Marcia want to do, too," I said.

Dave grabbed Bob as he and Marcia danced by and
talked into his ear for a moment; then we all squeezed
through the milling and dancing people, following Dave's
friend to the other side of the room.

"That's Jon Parker," Dave yelled to me over the noise.
"We have lockers in the same room at the BOQ." Just
then I saw Jon walk over to the crowded table to a stun-
ning redhead, who was smiling at me. There was the red
head — the hair piled in curls — I had been looking for
all evening: Bonnie's. How could I have forgotten the
clear, chiseled beauty of that face? Or the way she talked
and moved, with the calm assurance that she was a
woman who pleased?

There was a scramble while extra chairs were brought
to the table and shifted into place, displacing everybody.
When people settled again, Jon gave the four of us a
general introduction. Besides Jon and Bonnie, there was
Ken Ouelette and his wife, Libby. Ken's locker in the
BOQ was in a room next door to the one where Dave
and Jon stored their gear. Ken and Libby were from Louisiana and had soft, singing accents. Ken was dark-
complexioned and had black hair and dark eyes; Libby
was pale — even her eyes were a light gray — and her
short, blond hair was teased into a caplike bubble. She
looked fragile, somehow.

And there were the Melansons. They were from De-

troit — Sam and Leah. When I looked at them, I thought
twins. They had the same shade of dark hair, the same
narrow features, and the same thin eyebrows. They
seemed quiet to me — not shy, but sedate and withdrawn.
Leah nodded in my direction when Libby introduced us,
but she did not speak.

Sam had a locker in the room on the other side of Dave
and Jon's, along with Raymond "Matt" Matthews. When
Matt and his wife, Diane, were introduced, she said, "It's
great to finally meet you." Her white teeth punctuated a
pretty smile marred only a little by a slight overbite. Matt
and Diane were both tall and blond, but Diane had fair
skin and blue eyes; Matt's blondness was "muddy" — he
was brown-eyed and freckled and fadingly tan. He stood
up from the table and shook my hand and then waved at
Dave. Matt had been clowning around with empty bar
glasses, balancing them on the table in front of him by
placing a red plastic coaster on top of one to serve as a
platform for the next. A stack of about half a dozen looked
ready to topple.

There was a bachelor in the group, too. Dennie Peterson lived in the room in the BOQ in which Ken had a
locker. He was a wiry, small-framed boy from California,
quiet and shy. His demeanor reminded me of Dave's, and
I immediately liked him because of it, without even
knowing him.

For the rest of the evening, we danced and drank and
laughed together. Except for the uniforms the men wore,
anyone seeing us would have thought we were at a dance
on the campus of any college in the United States. But
anyone listening to our conversation would have known
that we were not; the tone and topics were not those of
college kids. Dave and the other lieutenants talked about
the Basic School and their instructors there. The wives
talked about jobs and weddings and honeymoons. All the
couples except Ken and Libby were newlyweds, married

within the year; I was surprised to learn that the delicate, small Libby and the easygoing Ken were the oldest among us and had been married a long time — almost six years. None of us had children. Diane and Leah said they wanted children as soon as possible. The rest of us weren't sure when, but we all wanted them someday.

We talked about ironing uniforms and starching the hats, about shopping at the commissary and the PX — Diane seemed to know where all the best buys were — about plans for Christmas away from home. And we gossiped, too, our tongues loosened by the drink and the good time. Someone mentioned that she had heard that a certain general's wife always wore a hat because she was going bald, and the scuttlebutt was, we would have to wear hats to receptions on base, too. Someone else pointed out a pretty girl across the room, a colonel's daughter attending the ball with a boy from the platoon. Other "news" flew around the table. When the subject was someone I did not know, Bonnie would lean toward me and explain. She seemed to know everybody, and so did her husband, Jon, who, I saw when I searched for Dave's eyes, was the busy, laughing center of the men's huddle on the other side of the table. Dave is by nature shy, and in that company of pretty, bright, and confident women, I felt inhibited, too. But I loved listening to the others, and it didn't really matter what they talked about; it was enough for me to be with them. We were, I saw with much happiness and relief, all in this strange, new world together.

The band stopped playing, and we knew the evening was over. We got up reluctantly and drifted away from the table by twos to retrieve our wraps and covers from the coatroom attendant while the band packed up and the waiters removed the empty chafing dishes from the serving tables.

Outside, in the chilly air of the middle of the night,

Dave and I said good-bye to the others while Bob and
Marcia waited for us in the car. It was "Good-bye" and
"We'll see you soon." And we all meant it. We had made
plans for the following Saturday afternoon, plans to meet
at Waller Hall, the officers' club, as soon as the boys got
out of class.

The morning after the dance, we drove Marcia from
our place back to Washington. On our way back to Falmouth, we dropped Bob off at the base, at his quarters in
the BOQ. Soon after, he left for eight weeks of artillery
training at Fort Sill, Oklahoma. I don't know what happened to Marcia.

I spent many hours alone at Green Wood after that
night, but I never felt lonely again during our time at
Quantico. When we joined the men from Dave's platoon
and their wives at the Birthday Ball, I went through an
initiation, a private, silent initiation — something that
made me feel that I belonged, that I still belong, to that
group of Marines and wives of Marines who came together at that long, white-clothed table in Larson Gymnasium. The week before, the corporal at Little Hall had
handed me my ID and I had begun then to feel a part of
something military, though in a vague, unfamiliar way.
The night of the Birthday Ball, I became part of the Marine Corps, in a special, particular way.

That night I began to see myself, and Dave, and the
other wives, and the other men as all of one piece. A kind
of a family. What forged us together in my mind was not
any common background or special compatibility. It was
the uniqueness of what we were that formed our particular connection: the wives of young Marines in wartime.
I imagine the deaf know about bonds such as these, and
people who find themselves in the same compartment on
the train from Milan to Paris, or in the waiting room of
a medical specialist. We knew one another then in a way
our civilian neighbors in Virginia could not, in a way our

friends from college could not, and in a way even our own families could not.

I did not analyze any of this then — none of us analyzed our feelings in those innocent days. I did not say out loud or even admit quietly to myself, not for many years, that I felt "Marine." I never went to war in Vietnam, but that was my war. I did not go to boot camp at Parris Island or to Basic School at Quantico, but the Marine Corps was my home. I was learning to love the Corps the way Marines do, I think: by loving the others who were a part of it. I was beginning to learn what it means to be a Marine wife.

And because we had courage;
Because there was courage and youth
Ready to be wasted; because we endured
And were prepared for all the endurance;
We thought something must come of it:
That the Virgin would raise her Child and smile. . . .

— John Peale Bishop, "In the Dordogne"

Thirteen

SCOTT AND DAVE rode together to the
base, usually taking our Plymouth. Melinda had been
driving Scott the twenty or so miles to Camp Barrett,
dropping him off, then coming back down the highway
to her own job. Now that Dave had to make the same
trip as Scott did, he could save Melinda the long, extra
drive.

Melinda dropped me off on her way to work when the
weather was bad — or when I was not feeling well, which
by the middle of November seemed to be most of the
time. The children came to school sick with the flu, and
I seemed to be catching it all the time. Sometimes staying
at home in bed for a day helped, but the flu medicine the
Navy doctor prescribed for me did not. Still, I kept taking
it.

One Sunday afternoon, I lay on the couch in the living
room and waited for my flu medicine to take effect. I had

taken the last two pills in the bottle together, hoping for the best. I thought if I took the pills and rested, I might be able to go to work in the morning. I didn't want to miss work, so I lay still and tried to convince myself I really was feeling better. But by the time Dave walked in the door with the Sunday papers, I knew I needed to refill my prescription.

"Forget the prescription," he said when I told him. "I think it's about time you see a doctor again."

But the clinic was closed. I went all the way to the base in misery, only to wait there in misery. I lay miserably on a hard, wooden bench in a dark, empty, antiseptic-smelling hallway — a nauseating hallway — while Dave and I tried to figure out what to do next. I didn't want to go to the emergency room; that was for emergencies, people in real trouble. I had the flu — a miserable flu, but not an emergency for a young, otherwise healthy person.

"If I just had more medicine," I said, "I think I'd be OK." Dave stared at me for a minute, biting his lip, and then he reached down and helped me to my feet.

The young corpsman on duty at the dispensary took the empty bottle and read the label. He looked at Dave, then he looked at me, and back at Dave. "How long has your wife been feeling ill?" he asked.

"A couple of weeks," Dave said. "Two, maybe three weeks."

"Sir," the hospitalman said, placing the bottle, still empty, back in Dave's hand, "if it were my wife, I wouldn't let her take any more of these. Sounds to me like she's pregnant, not sick." Dave wheeled around, facing me. I tried to say something, but I was too weak and sick. I needed to find a bathroom — I was about to throw up again.

The diagnosis made at the door of the dispensary was correct. I was pregnant. By December, what had been occasional morning sickness came every day and lasted all day. Sometimes I could not get out of bed. On those days, Dave left me in the early, still-dark morning with a plate of saltines next to my pillow and a bottle of 7-Up on the floor beside the bed. He also left a paper bag there, but I couldn't bear to use it. That meant that sometimes I had to crawl to the bathroom, and once, Dave came home in the early evening to find me lying curled up on the bath mat by the tub. If he forgot to switch on the light in the bedroom before he left, he came home to find me lying in the dark. It wasn't worth it for me to make the effort to turn it on.

I missed the first two weeks of work in December. The days when I was sick at home were dark and very, very long. Dave could not call, Mrs. Ledbetter stayed in her bed in the big house on the other side of the parking lot, and Melinda and Scott were gone to work all day. No one else besides the people at school knew I was "sick." At the top of the hill, Green Wood seemed to be a planet spinning in its own black space, its two bedridden inhabitants staring at life played out on an earth in black-and-white on a TV screen.

One day Mrs. Thorburn came up to the apartment and brought with her dozens of little, handmade get-well notes from the children, colored with crayons and painstakingly printed. The notes made me miss the children almost more than I could bear. The next day, I talked all the willpower I could into my body, and I left the apartment before dawn with Dave and Scott. After they got out of the car at the Basic School, I drove to the base clinic and waited, jaw tight and fists clenched, for a doctor. I left the clinic with a prescription for Bendectin.

The Bendectin controlled the violent nausea. In its place was an ugly but fairly benign queasiness. With the help of the pills, I managed the queasiness pretty well, their only failure resulting in my throwing up in the middle of a county-wide faculty meeting. I have to add that

the teachers, mostly middle-aged women, turned to me
from all sides of the room as though they were parts of
one body, and then in a rush of separate parts moved
toward me, Motherly Sympathy in a mass.

Sometimes the early snows in Virginia are like heavy
frosts. The snow covers the ground in patches then, and
in the uncovered places the grass is still green. Sheep and
cattle graze in the winter fields, moving from clear spot
to clear spot. Snow lies in the furrows of the cornfields
and gathers on the sides of the roads, but there is none
on the roofs or in the trees. The year we were at Quantico,
winter came in gently, with only flurries. Still, it killed
fall. The bright foliage turned dusty and then disappeared
altogether, and the trees were gray and bare against an
often bare, gray sky. The first real snow fell the weekend
before I went back to work, Bendectin in hand. Four
inches covered the ground; it really was beginning to feel
like Christmas.

At school the children had begun to talk excitedly about
Christmas, and we sang carols and colored pictures of
Santa Claus, Christmas trees, and wreaths. Mrs. Thorburn
told stories about a manger and a baby. At home in our
apartment during supper, Dave talked about Christmas,
too. The young officers were being trained very hard at
Basic School, spending long, cold days and nights on the
trails and in the woods of the base.

The postman brought Christmas cards to the apartment,
cards from as far away as Washington State and California
and even Lebanon, and I taped them to the doorjamb
between the living room and the kitchen. All of them, that
is, except one addressed to Dave in feminine handwriting
done in red ink, marked "Please Forward," and sent on
by Dave's mother. The name in the upper left-hand corner was Meg's. Her card came on one of the Saturday
mornings Dave was not at home, and at first I left it on

the kitchen table with the bills, for him to open. But it bothered me there. It taunted me even when I was on the other side of the apartment and it was out of my sight.

When I heard Dave's car climbing the drive, I don't know why, but I grabbed the card, took it to the bedroom, and stuck it into the padded silk box that held silk underwear from my trousseau — a place I knew Dave never looked.

Guilty and embarrassed even after all the years, I finally gave the card to Dave twenty years later, on another Saturday morning, when I was cleaning a closet and came across the padded silk box. Standing in the hallway with a broom in his hand, he read the card out loud, though I knew already what was in it. "I was cleaning out some of my stuff," Meg wrote, "and found one of our dance pictures — made me think back on all the fun we had — and it really was fun . . . I'll be in Seattle for New Year's — are you going to be anywhere near? I sure would like to get together with you. . . . Have a Merry Christmas and the best to you in '67 and all the years to come. — Meg."

Dave put the card back in its envelope and handed it back to me, smiling. "She's probably gathered by now I'm not interested," he said.

On the base at Quantico, at Mainside, the Motor Transport units decorated the lawns in front of their building with a large, plywood sleigh, complete with Santa, reindeer, and gifts. The men at the Ordnance School painted a huge mural showing a Marine helicopter dropping gifts and a landing craft with its ramp open and gifts pouring out. Swags of fake greens decorated the entrance to the PX.

Dave liked to drive down Bartlett Avenue to look at the displays. He had never been away from home for the holidays, and I think he was a little homesick. His mother's large family all loved the holidays and celebrated together, usually at Dave's house, where they played games and ate special dishes, such as Rocky Road Cake and cranberry-orange relish, that were made only this one time of the year.

I would not have blamed him if he had been depressed by the thought of having only me around on the twenty-fifth. My family celebrated holidays very quietly if they celebrated them at all — even Christmas was just another working day on the farms they were raised on — and added to that, I could not cook very well. Even my attempts were doomed, because when I saw raw eggs or meat I was overcome with nausea. Still, I loved Christmas. I had visited Marcia that one December in Istanbul — a bleak place of dirty snows and cold rains in the winter — and I had spent another Christmas in the Sudan, sweating in my coolest sundress and sipping lemonade by an aluminum tree hung with plastic icicles. Both had been wonderful Christmases. I was short on family traditions and know-how, but I was long on spirit.

That year the base commander let Marines cut their own trees on the base reservation. So in the name of Christmas spirit and tradition, the Sunday morning after the snowfall, six of us — Diane and Matt, Scott and Melinda, and Dave and I — drove to the woods at Quantico, parked our cars by the side of a small road, and took our borrowed saw into the trees.

Snow covered the open ground and sat in patches on the packed, curled leaves where the trees were the thickest. By this time, Diane, Melinda, and I were all pregnant. Melinda was the furthest along in her pregnancy, and though lucky in that she was past the usual months of morning sickness, she was entering the last couple of months of pregnancy, those of the worst physical discomfort and the heavy, panting awkwardness. Diane had learned only days before that she was going to have the baby she had been wanting for so long. She was ecstatic, but tense. We pregnant wives were slow in the woods. Our young husbands went on ahead of us — not rude, or even thoughtless, really, just full of the energy and high spirits that are marks of healthy youth. They walked over the rough, snowy ground in long, quick steps, sure of themselves, excited about finding their own Christmas trees to take home.

Melinda, Diane, and I followed, gingerly picking our way over the frozen earth, the snow, and the icy leaves. We steadied ourselves going uphill by holding on to small trees or the ground itself, and often Diane and I gave our hands to Melinda, who seemed to struggle for breath and strength both. I learned that morning in the woods that Diane had miscarried earlier, during the summer when Matt was at Officer Candidate School, and she was desperate to keep this baby. She had found a doctor in Fredericksburg who was giving her a drug called DES to prevent another miscarriage, and she was hopeful. The doctor wasn't sure the drug would work, but he had been encouraging, though cautious and cautioning. Diane was terrified of falling. We could not keep up with the boys, but we kept in sight of them and could see them, or at least their jackets, through the woods. And we heard them. They were talking loudly, and every now and then we heard loud laughter, too. We women spoke softly to one another, and our words were lightly strained with worry: "Do you want to rest, Melinda?" "Do you feel OK, Marian?" "Watch your step, Diane."

I know we must have talked about such things as our work and specials at the PX, but what I recall of that morning is the boys' carefree spirit in the woods and the wives' concerns — for ourselves, for one another, for our babies. And at the base of those concerns, I see now, was our unspoken concern for our husbands. Only months before, we had all three been college girls. In the woods that morning, we were women with worries.

Matt, Scott, and Dave found their trees. In a little gulley whose sides were frozen, snow-dusted clods, they found a grove of fir. They called to us — at first, to hurry, and when we caught up to them, to approve their choices. While they sawed, we wives stood in a little clutch nearby, our hands in our pockets, and watched. I don't know what Diane and Melinda were thinking, but I was glad to see Dave happy and having fun at Christmastime. He had chosen a tall, thin tree, a tree high enough to welcome Christmas, but narrow enough to fit into our small living room.

That night we made a stand for our gangly fir out of two boards nailed together and then nailed to the bottom of the tree trunk. We stood the tree in a corner, and I put a white sheet around its base. We had twelve pink-and-white ornaments, Styrofoam balls one of Dave's cousins had covered with scraps of material and lace left over from the bridesmaids' and flowergirls' dresses from our wedding. We hung the decorations all in front and added some tinsel. It was a beautiful tree.

The second real snow of the season began to fall in the evening two days before Christmas, and it fell for forty-eight hours. Dave and I stayed in the apartment all day Christmas Eve. The oil stove threw out constant, warm blasts, and we listened to Christmas carols on the radio and watched the snow fall to the ground — at first in a gentle, delicate veil, and later in a fury of dense swirls. When we woke in the morning, the morning of our first Christmas together, we looked out at the woods. The world had turned white and pure and still.

Wives and maidens, who are the souls of soldiers, . . .
if you fail to do your part they cannot fulfil theirs.

— John Ruskin, "War,"
from *The Crown of Wild Olive*

Fourteen

IN FRESNO, during the last week of
July — only days before my wedding — my mother had
taken me shopping. We drove downtown in blistering
heat, to a clothing store whose name I no longer recall —
one of those ancient, dependable, outmoded establish-
ments with polished wood floors, pneumatic tubes, ceiling fans to cool the air, and floorwalkers in black suits.
There, in the women's section on the hot mezzanine, under my mother's careful eye, wearily I tried on suits. I
chose two, a pale avocado green linen and a nondescript
beige wool.

In the hat department, a slight, nervous woman about
my mother's age, in my mind far too old to have good
taste, brought stacks of hats — some of them the pillbox
kind Jackie Kennedy had preferred — to the triple-
mirrored dressing table. With a light, practiced touch, and
a surprising and, to me, uncanny ability to choose the

ones I had already decided were the prettiest, she placed
a dozen or so, one after another, on my head. I picked
two to match the suits; and after a few more stops in
various corners of the store, my mother and I circled out
of the heavy revolving door into the thick heat with boxes
that harbored suits, hats, gloves, shoes, and purses, all
coordinated, all in proper good taste.

"These outfits will take you anywhere," my mother
said as we loaded the packages into her Volkswagen
"bug." "To luncheons or teas or receptions. You take care
of them and they'll last for years."

Another afternoon, we drove to one of the newer department stores in the suburbs, this one a big, modern
block of a building surrounded by a row of tall palms.
The heat depressed everything: the fronds of the palm
trees drooped from it, and people dragged heavily across
the parking lot; the air itself seemed weighted down, like
colorless smog.

Inside the air-conditioned store, we rode the escalator
to the second floor, to the china-and-linen department.
My mother led me to a glass counter that was also a
display case filled with gleaming, silver-white pieces sitting on deep blue velvet. Behind it, on the wall, glass
shelves displayed more pieces. Candy dishes, butter
servers like small, silver coffins, goblets, pitchers, trays of
all sizes. There my mother asked me to choose a tea service, which, she said, was to be my parents' wedding gift
to me. "You might need a silver service," she said. "As
the wife of an officer, you'll be expected to entertain — I
think mostly at teas. A nice silver service is an advantage."

This was my mother's one moment of recognition, of
acknowledgment, of what Dave was and what I would
be as his wife, and the gesture, misguided as it turned out
to be, made me happy. I have no idea where my mother
got her ideas about what my life in the military would

be. Perhaps she had seen movies, or maybe she had read something — a book of military etiquette from the library. However she got her idea, she did think I would at some point in the future need a tea service; and in the interest of this future, she meant, as usual — no matter how late in the day she had come to it in this case — that I should have an advantage.

As for me, I had no idea what to expect from military life, not at the glass counter in Rhodes department store in Fresno or, later, at the Marine base in Virginia. At Quantico, throughout the last months of summer and the first months of fall, before Dave began his active duty, I read the base newspaper, the *Quantico Sentry*, and noted the garden parties, the teas, the luncheons. Sometime during my first weeks in Virginia, one item particularly interested me. It was the announcement of a luncheon to be held at Harry Lee Hall around the middle of October. I remember that the article announced not only the lunch, but also, afterward, a panel discussion on protocol for the wives of student officers graduating from Basic School at the end of the month. Panelists were going to discuss the protocol of relocating to a new base — who to call on once there, how to distribute calling cards, when and how to entertain. That all sounded promising to me.

In other issues of the *Sentry*, I read about the activities of the Noncommissioned Officers' Wives' Club, of the Officers' Wives' Club, and the Overseas Officers' Wives' Club: bridge games, visits to the wounded at the naval hospitals in the area, holiday fairs. There seemed to be a club for everybody, and I wondered what club I would belong to and what kinds of friends I would make in it. The one lasting good that had come from my time in the sorority at WSU had been some pleasant, enduring friendships.

As for the tea service, I arranged it on top of a chest of drawers in our apartment at Green Wood: the heavy, fluted tray leaning against the wall; the coffeepot on the right and the teapot on the left, facing each other; and the creamer and sugar bowl in between the two pots. After a few weeks, the oil stove blasting away periodically from the next room aided natural occurrence, and the metallic, brown-pewter shadows of tarnish spread from the deep creases of the fluted edges and curly designs across the open planes of the silver pieces.

Then I packed the set up in its maroon, tarnish-proof flannel and put the box toward the front of one of the bedroom-closet shelves. But I never did need it, and it was only in the way there. The wives of the student lieutenants held no teas that year at Quantico, not at my home or anyone else's. And we had no wives' club.

What I didn't realize until years later was that we had come to Quantico in step with the war in Vietnam. I didn't understand in 1966 that most Marine wives would not be going with their husbands to their new duty station; most Marine husbands would be based in Vietnam. I didn't know then that wives had only recently and suddenly become more than usually a burden to the military and a luxury to the men, and that no one in charge seemed to know what to do about it.

The old command chronologies — the records of the Basic School — tell the story: the time allotted for Basic School was cut, from a peacetime thirty-six weeks to a wartime twenty-one; the workweek was extended from five days to five and a half; overnight training exercises were increased; the workday was extended from eight to ten hours; and student numbers at Basic School rose during 1966 from 1,053 at the beginning of the year to 1,347 at the end — triple what they had been in the early sixties. The number of US troops in Vietnam had risen during the year from 181,000 to 385,000. From January of 1961 through December of 1965, 1,484 American fighting men were killed in Vietnam. During 1966 alone, we lost 5,047. Green lieutenants were falling in disproportionate numbers. The result of this was, according to the chronologies, "a frantic cycle of student training [in which] rough spots appeared. With six student companies on board, activities accelerated around the clock. Things had to be done quickly and smoothly the *first time.*"

Over the weeks, life changed on other parts of the base as well. The war had come to stay and grow. In the *Sentry*, items about clubs and social events and people involved in them dominated the front pages throughout the fall of 1966. By winter, the front pages were full of news about the war. The Overseas Officers' Wives' Club apparently disbanded; I never saw another word about it. Husbands were going to one place overseas — what was called in base terminology the "Western Pacific Area." They were staying thirteen months, and wives weren't waiting on the base at Quantico for them while they were gone. Marines going to Vietnam were based officially with the Fleet Marine Force, FMF, a name that made me think of troops on bleak, gray battleships in the middle of a big, gray ocean. No base at all, in my mind.

Long items about Marine Medal-of-Honor recipients began to appear in the paper. Several pieces were published about the Book of Remembrance, a hand-lettered, parchment, leather-bound book dedicated the year before, in 1965, on the Marine Corps' birthday. It listed the names of all the Marines killed in Vietnam, from the first one who died in the war, on October 8, 1963, to the present. But by the fall of 1966, it was clear the calligrapher could not keep up with the names of the dead, so the script in the Book of Remembrance was converted from hand-lettering by using a semimechanical, silk-screened method. Funds had to be raised to do this, and the base newspaper did its part. By the time the war was over, the one hand-lettered volume with twenty names per page had grown into five printed volumes.

Old-timers must have noticed the change in the pace and the nature of life on base. The normal Basic School class of one company had grown to three, and two classes perpetually overlapped. More than a thousand students crowded into the space equipped for three hundred. You could hardly squeeze your car into the lot at Camp Barrett; classrooms were crowded, barrack space hard to come by. No more the quiet, steady life of former years those officers ranked captain and above could recall. No more time for lessons in military etiquette and tradition. No more time for parades and class pictures. The young officers were pushed, shoved, and hurried through training so they could be sent off as replacements as soon as their short, hectic life as student officers was over.

Frantic, confused, difficult, and necessary: that was the life of the young men at Basic School then. The base struggled as it transformed itself jarringly from its slow, Cold War stride to the fast and frantic cadence that had as its single-minded purpose the preparation of young men to lead other young men in battle. There was a life-or-death intensity to it all, and time itself had one purpose: to be filled with preparation for war.

As for us? Well, Dave and I were inexperienced, ignorant, and new to the military. As far as we knew, everything was normal.

Bid them be brave; — they will be brave for you.

— John Ruskin, "War,"
from *The Crown of Wild Olive*

Fifteen

WE ALL LOOKED FORWARD to New Year's Eve because there was going to be another dance, this one at Harry Lee Hall, one of the older brick buildings up the road from Waller Hall. I didn't think any evening could be as wonderful as the night of the Birthday Ball, but when I read about the decorations the Garden Club was planning, and when we wives talked about what we would wear New Year's Eve, I started to wonder.

Most of us had put away our college formals for one reason or another and were planning to wear more sophisticated, grown-up gowns. No one had money to waste, and there was a lot of talk about where to shop for the best buys. Melinda and I had the added problem of having to wear maternity dresses. Diane was not "showing" yet, but she insisted on helping us shop. It was a challenge to find a dress that was roomy enough and pretty, too.

Melinda was especially big, and she soon gave up looking and settled down to sewing her own dress after work.
I could hear her sewing machine whirring above my head
in the evenings. The rest of us hunted until we found
something we thought was "perfect." Some borrowed,
some bought. Mine was not a real maternity dress but a
"regular" gown, in jade green, two sizes bigger than what
I usually wore.

Dave and I had a little party before the dance, and in
the pictures we took that night the gowns stand out in all
their brightness. In the background behind these dresses,
our apartment, already dingy, fades all the way to dreary
nothingness.

The pictures are all smiles and bright clothes and gaiety.
We were a happy group, though why, I can't say. Time
has shown us we had no reason to be happy — no reason
my middle-aged reasoning can point to, except, of course,
that we were young and beautiful as youth is, and we felt
invincible and eternal. The boys were magnificent in their
dress blues, and we girls were resplendent in our gowns.
We glittered and shone, from our satin shoes to our teased
and sprayed hair. Even our skin glowed. The pictures
show this.

But when I look closely, I can see now that the eyes of
those young wives make liars of their smiles. We knew —
how could we have not? — that we would not have many
more chances to smile for a while. We must have known
that for some of us things would never be the same again,
though I am sure that in the way of the young, we each
anticipated the sorrow of the girl next to us, not our own.

I can remember clearly to this day the laughter and the
music that filled Harry Lee Hall on New Year's Eve, the
last night of 1966. We arrived in our separate cars, but
we found one another in the parking lot, and we drifted
in laughing groups under the awning, through the glass

doors, and into the building. Melinda and Scott soon wandered off over the flowered carpet to find couples from Scott's platoon, and it wasn't long at all until all of the married couples from Dave's platoon — and Dennie, too — had gathered around two or three of the tables that lined the edge of the dance floor.

I wasn't disappointed in the night. New Year's Eve that year was, life has shown me, a rare mix of music, talk, and love. The band, the food, the bright red regimental flags in Harry Lee Hall — they were all the same as those the night of the Birthday Ball in Larson Gymnasium. But we were different. By New Year's Eve we all knew one another and had begun to feel part of the same thing. We knew we would all face the next phase of our lives together. We were bound by ties of friendship, shared experience, and loyalty. Some call this esprit de corps; whatever it is, it comforts and strengthens those who know it.

At midnight the band played "Auld Lang Syne," and we linked arms in our corner of the room and sang. Afterward, in a burst of generosity we could ill afford but that we have never regretted — in fact, that we have been thankful for — Dave bought breakfast for everyone, and we ate together at one long table on the balcony of the hall: Matt and Diane, Sam and Leah, Ken and Libby, Jon and Bonnie, Dennie, and Dave and I. Ken climbed up on the balcony railing next to the end of the table and, clinging to a pillar with one arm, toasted us all with the other, hoisting his glass of champagne out over the room below. "To us, to the Corps, and to the future!" he called out.

We raised our glasses and drank; Libby cautioned Ken about making a scene. "What'll they do to me?" he answered. "Send me to Vietnam?" And we all laughed at his joke, though by then we had heard it already, many times.

The ghosts of that night live on in my heart, and they

dance and laugh even now in my memory. They twirl, young and beautiful, around the room of my imagination in their bright dresses and dress blues. I only have to close my eyes to see their faces, their lovely, loved faces.

Last year on a quiet, sleepy, summer afternoon, I went back to Harry Lee Hall. I walked into the cool and silent ballroom, and I stood in the middle of the empty floor and looked around. I saw the balcony, and without thinking, I instantly moved my eyes along the railing to the spot where Ken had stood, to the very pillar he clung to. I heard him call out again, to us, to the Corps, to the future. I heard the music, and suddenly I saw all of us in the room.

The ghosts that have danced in my mind all these years took to the floor and swept around me, and for a moment the years had not gone by and it was New Year's Eve, 1966. I would have given anything to have been able to step into my memory and dance with the boys that were Dave, and Dennie, and Matt, Jon, Sam, and Ken. It was hard to turn and walk from Harry Lee Hall into the sunshine.

We faced the future in those new days of 1967 with what I think must be called courage. It's true that we were too inexperienced to feel particular fear and too unwise to be afraid of the abstract. But we knew something; I see it in the pictures of the wives. And yet we smiled and danced, and I remember laughter, too. I call that courage. And we had it.

If the war subdued the social life at Basic School in those days, Waller Hall made up for a lot — or, I should say, the hours we spent there did. Waller Hall, the officers'-club building at Quantico, was an old, Victorian, white clapboard perched on the top of Rising Hill, overlooking the main street of the town of Quantico, Quantico Creek, and the Potomac River beyond. It was three-storied, had peaked-roof porches, and a wide, enclosed veranda striped with white columns.

From the night of the Marine Corps Birthday Ball in early November until graduation in late March, the married student lieutenants from Dave's platoon and their wives often met there — once in a while for dinner in the plush dining room on the first floor, or, more likely, for drinks or a snack, bunched together around one or more of the small tables in the basement where the bar was located.

Behind the bar itself, Joe, the bartender — handsome and dignified in his bright white, short jacket — good-naturedly made drinks as he had for Marines since the beginning of WW II. The room was cool and dark in the summer and warm and dark in the winter. It was a good place to meet your friends.

We sat on the benches that lined the walls or in chairs at the tables and listened to the jukebox, or, when there was live music, to the Dick Sherman Quintet or Dave Wilson and the Lucky Seven. We ordered light suppers, or lunches if we met on Saturday afternoons after the men had finished at Camp Barrett for the week. We ordered pitchers of beer, and we talked. Hour after hour of talk.

It was in the basement bar of Waller Hall that we began the quiet sharing of more than circumstances and experiences. That's where we began to share our feelings and history and hopes and dreams, the kind of things you share through talk, the things you can share *only* through talk. The kind of talk that makes people unforgettable even when they have not been a part of your life for a long time — even when they are not a part of the earth anymore. It is my memories of Waller Hall, torn down the year after we left Quantico, that brighten the dark corridors of my past more than anything. The bright lights are the faces of old friends.

What did we women learn about one another during

those long-ago afternoons and evenings in that place? I
think we learned what men facing combat learn about
one another: names, or nicknames; hometowns, perhaps;
a few facts of background; and, most important, that we
understood one another's circumstances, that we trusted
one another, and that we could count on one another.
And it was that knowledge that tied us together — that
still, I think, ties us together in some distant way, even
now, when almost everything else in our lives has
changed.

We went to Waller Hall as often as we could. There,
Dave and I sat and leaned over our small table into the
faces of our friends, straining to see in the poor light and
to hear above the music and the noise of talk and laughter
all around us.

We wives spent other time together, too, without our
husbands; two of us would go shopping, or three of us
to lunch in Fredericksburg or on the base. But whether
we were in pairs or small groups, we remained a unit.
Once, Diane, Bonnie, and I met for lunch at the snack
bar at Mainside before going on to some base function,
and I suddenly became very ill. With Diane on one side
and Bonnie on the other, I managed to reach a bathroom
just in time. Feeling better, but embarrassed and not well
enough to stand yet, I sat on the floor of a toilet stall and
tried to make the others leave me, to go on without me
to the gathering. But they would not. "We'll leave when
you're ready," Diane said. "Together."

We liked being together — not because we were especially compatible or because we enjoyed the specific company of one another, but because we had begun to
depend on one another; we were all we had besides our
husbands, and they were going away.

When the men had free time, though, we spent those
precious hours with them. In the dim, warm light of the
bar in Waller Hall, wives and husbands relaxed in a group

and talked about things that really mattered then, about things that still matter.

That's where Libby, looking like a pale pixie except for her dark and deadly serious gray eyes, told me that she and Ken had fought over his joining the Marines. "He was too old to be drafted," she said. "Twenty-seven. And he had a good job — he was a manager at Sears. He was going places. We'd been married six years, and I thought I knew him like the back of my hand. That it was more or less settled, about his not joining. I thought we'd fight about it a while longer, he'd forget about the idea, and that would be that. But he came home one day and said, like he was telling me he'd taken the car in for a tune-up, 'I joined the Marines today.'"

That Ken had joined, and that he had joined over her protests and without telling her beforehand, was a hurt that gave Libby pain all the time I knew her at Quantico. She sometimes cried about what she was afraid it meant — that she had somehow lost Ken already — breaking what I thought was one of our firmest unwritten, unspoken rules. Ken was stoic and patient with Libby. He had come to his decision to be a Marine from somewhere outside of their marriage. He was willing to pay the price for his one act of betrayal, to be forgiven, and occasionally to be reminded of the pain he had caused.

Libby stayed with Ken and followed him into the Marines because her love for him was stronger than her need to be free of the worry and the pain his joining had caused her. But it was a hard truce they had called in their private war, an uneasy truce; and when the subject came up, as I remember happening at least twice, it made all of us around them uneasy, too.

Libby was very different. We all recognized that. For one thing, the rest of us — Bonnie, Leah, Diane, even Melinda — knew we were marrying Marines. For another, we were younger than Libby and had been married for much shorter times. We had been in a state of flux even before we left for Virginia. We had just left college and entered marriage, with no settled married life to disrupt. And finally, there was this: Libby was not only older than the rest of us, she was wiser. What we were just beginning to learn in the security of our group, she had come to know by herself before coming to Quantico.

I watched uneasily when Libby was upset, but Bonnie could not bear to see her suffer. When Libby cried, Bonnie comforted her, leaning her head full of thick, red hair close to Libby's small, blond one and putting an arm around her shoulder.

Bonnie and her husband, Jon, were special as individuals: Bonnie was lovely and charming and good-natured; Jon was handsome and confident. But together they were golden; heads turned when they entered a room or stepped onto the dance floor. And because of all this, they held a kind of power over the rest of us that they never abused, but instead turned back to us, making us all stronger. I depended on Bonnie, as I think the other wives did, for friendship and encouragement. She gave both easily, and Jon did, too. They were glorious and larger than life, and you felt that since they were one of you, what you were was a fine thing.

When I close my eyes and see Waller Hall, I see Diane, too, late from work again, sliding onto a bench in the bar. Her pale face brightens, her smile widens, her cheeks even flush as she excitedly describes her newest find: a bedspread that "matches exactly" or a "perfect" tablecloth. I have never known anyone with a stronger nesting instinct. Diane's talk was always filled with references to the future home she would have: the house, the furniture that would go inside, and, most of all, the children she would bear to fill it.

The rest of us shifted a little uneasily in our chairs and threw small looks at one another when Diane talked about "when Matt gets back" or "next year, when all of this is behind us." Was such talk bad luck? We weren't sure, but it made us all a little uncomfortable, I think.

Gradually, I got used to Diane's extravagant plans for the years ahead and began to understand that they were her way of coping. She put her eyes on the future, and never, that I ever knew about, did she consciously lose sight of it — not even later, when Matt was actually in Vietnam. It must have taken enormous willpower to ignore the reality of it. I envied her strength, her ability to believe so much that her hopes and dreams would come true, that she could, in a sense, "buy" them. Even after several heartbreaking miscarriages, she bought baby furniture, "for later, when the babies come."

In spite of her miscarriages, Diane was thrilled when she learned about my pregnancy. Even though I did not feel well in the early months and hated the clothes I had to wear and the way I looked in them after I started to get big, I could never bring myself to complain in front of her. She seemed to understand without my having to say anything, and one day she took me to DC, to a small shop — not yet called a boutique in those days — she'd found that specialized in lovely but expensive dresses that could be worn both as regular and as maternity clothes. She pulled from the racks a few dresses she had somehow decided were "right," held them up to me, then chose two for me to try on. From those I picked one, a sleeveless cotton shift in a shocking-pink and bright-orange abstract pattern. It fell straight from the shoulders in billowing folds, and it had a huge ruffled collar that almost hid my chin. It came with a small matching triangle scarf for the head. It was dramatic, and I didn't feel pregnant in it. I loved it, scarf and all — never mind that it would be weeks before the weather was warm enough to wear it. But it was forty dollars, more than half a month's rent, and far too expensive.

"Use the grocery money," Diane said, taking the dress from me and handing it to the clerk with a "we'll-take-it" look. "Serve pasta and tuna for a while. Keep the dress in the trunk of the car until you have to pick up stuff at the cleaner's, then sneak it into the house with the rest of the cleaning. It works every time."

I didn't doubt "it" worked for Diane. But I didn't dare try it. I bought the dress and told Dave what I paid for it. He laughed when he saw the dress on, and he told me I had paid too much for it no matter how much it was. I kept the dress for fifteen years and felt guilty and a little foolish, too, every time I put it on. And it always made me think of Diane.

Sam and Leah were regulars at Waller Hall, too, but they came early and left after only an hour or two; I suppose Leah's pregnancy left her exhausted. I recall her vibrant smile, but I don't remember talking with her as much as I did with the other wives, and I know that if it were not for the platoon connection, we probably would not have chosen to be friends. But the connection did exist; my fate was Leah's, and I felt deeply for her, as I think she did for me. That was, and is, one of the precious mysteries of my life: at a time when everything was tinged with fear and sadness or longing and foreboding, we had without question the solace of one another.

I didn't get to know Sam well, either, or Dennie, the quiet bachelor who often joined our group. When Sam and Dennie were at Waller Hall, they spent their time huddling over a pitcher of beer with the other men, talking about Basic School, the instructors, or what was coming up in the way of new training the following week.

It was the wives who told histories — and if the others were like me, at home that night, they shared what they had learned. Dave and I talked, over a fried-egg sandwich at the kitchen table or maybe even later in bed with the lights out: "Did you know that Leah and Bonnie were both beauty queens? Diane told me that Bonnie has a closet full of trophies from fraternities. . . . Did Matt tell you that he was on his way to join the Navy when a friend dared him to join the Marines and that's why he did? . . . Diane's still taking those hormones to stay pregnant. She says if Matt goes off without leaving at least that much of him behind she'll go crazy. . . . I'm glad I'm having a baby, Dave. . . ."

It was at Waller Hall that we wives of the young men from the third platoon, E Company, Basic School 3-67, began our silent sharing, a sharing of fear and worry that would become the hallmark of our friendship. It was a quiet, seemingly delicate connection, but it was all we had, and in the end it was enough. In the end it was strong. Except when Libby spoke her pain and fear out loud, we did not talk with one another about war and death. But we all knew what we had come to Quantico for, and this knowledge forged from our fragile connection the bands of a sympathetic sisterhood that survived in some way the war, the destruction of marriages, and the death of young husbands.

O envy the peace of women
giving birth and love like toys
into the hands of men!

— Laurie Lee, "A Moment of War"

Sixteen

ONE FROZEN, SNOWY SATURDAY
MORNING in February, the telephone rang. I had spent
the night before alone, because Dave was on one of those
overnight field exercises, practicing war in the woods
around Quantico. I ran to answer: *Maybe one of the girls
wants to come over.*

It was Melinda — alone, too, because Scott's platoon
was also away on weekend exercises. She was not, she
said, feeling well. Would I mind coming up and fixing
her a cup of tea? "Don't knock. Just come on in."

I was still in my nightgown, but I dressed quickly. Melinda was by this time the most pregnant woman I had
ever seen, and although she had never told me exactly
when her baby was due, I suspected it was very soon.

I climbed the icy outside wooden staircase to the upstairs apartment as fast as I could, holding tightly to the

painted two-by-four that was the handrail. I was five months pregnant myself.

When I opened the door at the top of the stairs, Melinda called out, "Back here." I walked to the end of the little hallway and looked into the bedroom. Melinda, a large, mounded heap, lay in her bed on her side, facing me where I stood in the doorway. Her face was white and tiny dots of perspiration lined her upper lip. Her hair looked limp and uncombed, and it was damp where it stuck to her cheeks and forehead. She was lying very still, but her eyes moved with me as I came into the room. "I have a terrible backache," she said. "I thought maybe I'd feel better if I ate something — maybe some tea and toast."

In the kitchen, I found a box of matches and lit a burner on the gas range. I found tea bags and bread, and when the tea and toast were ready I took everything back to the bedroom. Melinda had turned onto her back and was rocking from side to side and moaning. Her eyes were squeezed shut, her eyebrows drawn together, and her upper teeth bit her lower lip. "Melinda," I said, setting the tray on the dresser, trying to move calmly and sound calm, as you do around hurt animals, "do you think you might be in labor?"

She opened her eyes and looked at me. "No," she said. "My back hurts. I've never had such a bad backache, but I don't think this is labor."

"When is your baby due?" I asked.

"Not today. And besides, I'm not having contractions, just pain in my back."

I stood for a moment looking at the bed and the woman in it. I knew something was not right, but I wasn't exactly sure how it was supposed to be, either. This was in the time before "natural childbirth," Lamaze classes — a time when medical people told pregnant women not much of anything except to take vitamins and not to gain weight. In the obstetric clinic at the base, you lined up in the hall and were seen by the first available doctor, much like waiting for a teller at the bank. I doubt that in her nine months of pregnancy Melinda had even seen the same doctor more than two or three times. In my own five months of pregnancy, I had been examined three times, each time by a different doctor, who asked me the same questions and told me the same things.

In short, Melinda and I knew very little about having babies. But my instincts told me that she was about to deliver, and that she was going to do it soon. In my mind, I went through the possibilities for help. I looked out the window and crossed our landlords off the short list. Their car was not parked out front. There was no way to reach Dave or Scott in time for them to really help. And how did a person get an ambulance from the base? No one had ever told me — and, besides, there didn't seem enough time for that. I would have to take Melinda by myself.

The problem was that Dave had warned me not to drive the Plymouth on the iced-over roads. The tires were so smooth they had no traction. In fact, those bald tires were the reason he and Scott had ridden to the base with Matt the morning before. Since Dave had decided our car was not safe and Scott wanted to leave theirs for Melinda, Matt had come up the hill to get them.

"Your car is running OK, isn't it, Melinda?" I asked.

"Yes," she said. "And Scott filled the tank a couple of days ago."

"Good," I said, relieved. "I'm going to drive you to the hospital, just as soon as I can get you put together. Where's your overnight bag?"

While Melinda struggled to sit up on the edge of the bed, I opened her drawers and picked out a nightgown, some underwear, some socks. I found her toothbrush, a bar of soap, and toothpaste in the bathroom. Back in the bedroom, I took her hairbrush from the top of the dresser, and a small bottle of perfume, too, and put them all in the small, brown bag I'd found in the closet.

Melinda managed to get into the clothes I put on the bed beside her, and she succeeded in shoving her feet into some old loafers, though I noticed she had not been able to put her socks on. I pulled her coat off its hanger in the closet and held it while she tunneled her arms through the sleeves, one at a time so she could still hold on to the bed.

She leaned on me, and I guided her to the living room and lowered her onto the couch. I went back to the bedroom and stripped a blanket from the bed, gathered it bunched in one arm, and picked up the overnight bag with my free hand. Melinda was bent over on the couch when I came back. Her head was almost resting on her big stomach; her hands were clenched to her sides, white knots at the ends of her black sleeves. She scared me.

"Where are the car keys, Melinda?" I asked, dropping the blanket and her bag at her feet.

She looked up, swallowed, and said, "In the kitchen — on a little hook by the door."

The hook was where she said it was, but it was empty. I looked on the windowsill above the sink and along the countertops. I opened all the kitchen drawers, one at a time, and felt in the backs of them where I could not see. There was no car key in that kitchen.

"Melinda" — I was trying to sound unworried — "the keys must be someplace else. I can't find them in the kitchen."

She looked at me, but did not seem to see me; she didn't seem to be with her body in that room anymore. Finally, she said, "My purse," and looked toward a card table piled with books and papers in the corner of the room. Melinda's black purse was there, too, on top of the pile. I opened it, felt around in it with my fingers, finally emptied it onto the floor. The keys were not in the purse. I stuffed everything — compact, lipstick, wallet, change, and bits of paper — back inside and put the purse next to the overnight bag.

Where could I look next? I went to the bedroom and quickly looked through the bureau drawers. Next, I looked in the bathroom, then in the kitchen again. The keys were not in the apartment. "It'll be OK, Melinda," I said. "I'm going to check the car. They're probably there."

The car was locked, so I scraped the frost from the window on the driver's side and peered in. The keys were not dangling from the ignition as I had imagined they might be. Then I looked over at the white Plymouth, and I realized it would simply have to do. We had no choice. I went into my apartment and came out again with my coat, my purse, and my car keys.

I made two trips from Melinda's place: one with her bag, purse, and the blanket, the other with Melinda. She clung to me and to the rail down the steps, and I held her tightly and talked without stopping, though I have no idea anymore what I said. The only thing I remember about the trip down the stairs is that Melinda could not stand up straight: she had to walk hunched over. And I could not keep my hands from shaking.

I tried to get Melinda to lie down in the backseat, but she wanted to sit in the front with me. I covered her with the blanket, anyway. It was a cold February morning, but I didn't dare wait for the engine to warm up. I inched the car down the steep, icy curve of road to the highway. It was empty and white. Because snowfall is infrequent and does not last long in that part of Virginia, in those days the state did not invest in snow-removal equipment. The snow was nature's problem. The hills were white, the sky gray-white, and the highway seemed to stretch before me forever, nineteen miles to the south edge of the base, then six more to the hospital. I tried to calculate the time, but my brain wouldn't concentrate on the numbers. I could only think that I needed help, and soon.

I pressed the gas pedal; on that desolate, deserted road it suddenly occurred to me that if I sped, went above the speed limit, a patrolman would surely come out of nowhere, and when he stopped me, I could tell him about Melinda. Then he would take her on to the base.

Melinda was bunched up beside me, holding the blanket to her chin, moaning a little every now and then, and crying softly. At one point, she sat up and said, panic in her voice, "I can feel the baby's head!"

"No, Melinda," I said, "you don't feel the head. Don't worry. There's no way you could be feeling the head." I was sure about this. I had read *Gone with the Wind* and *A Farewell to Arms*, and I remembered the woman in the Sudan who had walked all night in labor. I knew it took a long time to have a baby and that you had to lie down to give birth. After that Melinda stayed inside herself, and I suppose she was inside her pain, too, though I knew nothing about that then.

By this time it was clear that no highway patrolman was going to come to help me. I stopped thinking about help, and thought only of the miles ahead. When we finally entered the south gate of the base, I felt the scattered pieces of my mind coming back together again, settling in my body behind the wheel, seeing out the window again, and making sense of things.

The road was plowed and sanded, and near Mainside I met other cars at last. I did not stop — I was off the floating island of panic — and, besides, we were close now. So we drove on through Quantico Town to the Navy hospital on the other side. If there was an emergency entrance, I missed the signs for it. I drove into the

parking lot and stopped the car in the space closest to the
hospital's back doorway. There were a few cars in the lot,
but no people.

I went around the car to Melinda's side, opened the
door, and took the blanket off her. Her clothes were
soaked from where her waist would have normally been
down to the cuffs of her pants. Besides the splotches on
her dark pants, there was more wetness on her leather
shoes and on the rubber mat at her feet. I reached out to
her and, mute, she grabbed on to my coat sleeves. I pulled
her to the edge of the seat, as close to the door as I could
get her. Then I leaned inside and drew her arm across my
back over my shoulder so that I could drag her out of the
car.

When we were both steady on our feet, we began the
trip from the car to the door. Like the roads near Mainside, the asphalt pavement had been plowed and sanded,
but Melinda could still not stand up straight, never mind
walk under her own power, so I had to pull, drag, and
half-carry her over the gritty slush. Melinda had been
about my size before this baby got big in her belly. Now
she was much bigger. But I don't remember her being
heavy at all.

My goal — our goal, though Melinda was not making
any decisions at this point — was the double doors of the
back entrance of the hospital. Once inside, I knew that
the right person would step forward and my responsibility
would be over. I pushed the heavy doors open with my
hip, and we were inside a small, square waiting room.
Straight ahead was a high counter. Behind it, Navy medical personnel, corpsmen in white duck pants and middy
blouses with blue insignia on the sleeves, were doing paperwork.

Benches crowded with very young enlisted Marines in
green field utilities lined the wall to the far right and the
wall to our immediate right, too. To our immediate left

were the large, gray, metal doors of an elevator. The wall
to the left of the elevator ran into a long corridor. Every
man in the room looked at us, but no one moved. I pulled
Melinda closer to the high counter — my chest and face
barely rose above it. Melinda was by now so bent over I
imagine all they saw of her from behind the counter was
the top of her head.

"This woman," I said, trying to sound in control, "is
in labor and needs help." The corpsman nearest me on
the other side of the counter looked at me, then at Melinda. He was doing triage with his eyes, and we were
quickly and professionally judged walking wounded. He
threw an upturned thumb toward the elevator. "Third
floor," he said, glancing back down at the papers he was
shuffling. I stared stupidly at him. He looked up, saw that
I was still there, and said, not really unkindly, but with a
fine edge of exasperation in his voice, "Take her to the
third floor."

I resented his tone. I was beginning to get fed up myself.

Melinda was by now one big, tight, contracted muscle,
harder to propel, but I did get her to the elevator. After I
pushed the call button, before the silver doors hushed
shut, I looked out into the room. The men on the benches,
all in olive green, heads shaved, still sat motionless, their
hats balanced on their knees or hanging from loose grips.
They were staring at us. I glared back at those faces struggling to appear vacant, all those curious eyes trying to be
indifferent. Then I saw it, a thin trail of little, wet spots
from the door to the counter to the elevator. *That's something for you all to sit and look at,* I thought. *And it serves
you right.*

When the elevator doors opened onto the third-floor hallway, another counter faced us. Behind it stood a woman
in a white, board-stiff nurse's uniform with black and
gold trim on the cap. She was reading something on a

clipboard, holding her head back, her chin down, peering through a pair of glasses balanced on the end of her nose. She looked up at us when we approached her. "End of the hall," she said, jerking her head to her right.

"This woman's in labor," I cried out, "and we need help."

"You'll find OB if you just take her to the end of the hall," she said. She looked back down her nose at her clipboard. I didn't stop to argue. *What more?* I wondered, and I dragged Melinda as fast as I could down the hall.

Suddenly, from all sides, people were reaching for her and calling out to one another, rushing up and down and bringing things. I stood alone in the middle of all of this — confused but glad — until someone asked me, told me, to move out of the way. They had brought a gurney, and in a flash Melinda was on it and they were pushing it away. A nurse in green scrubs was cutting Melinda's clothes off her, taking small running steps beside the gurney and snipping at the wet, black pants with shiny, blunt-nosed scissors at the same time. They made a frantic, shushed, clipping sound.

Someone said to me, almost in passing, "If her husband's around and you know where to reach him, it might be a good thing if you got hold of him."

The road to Camp Barrett was not good. There were patches of black ice and strips of snow stained every once in a while with sand, someone's efforts to make it better. I followed the narrow pavement through the woods, up and down the low, gentle ridges. I drove fast, almost as fast as I had driven to the hospital. Thinking back, I realize that there was no reason to, except that I desperately wanted to get rid of the last bit of the responsibility that had settled uneasily into my life that morning.

The road was as quiet and deserted as the road to Mainside had been. Except for one car a long way behind me, I was alone on the road. The eight miles to the Basic

School was going slowly in spite of my trying to rush, but when I was almost there, less than one mile to go, in a place where the road dips for the last time, the car slid. In one moment it skidded to the right edge of the pavement. I pressed my foot hard against the brake pedal, and suddenly the trees by the side of the road were blurs in front of the windshield and the car was fishtailing to one side of the road, then to the other, and heading in the wrong direction.

I twisted the wheel, hand over hand, to the right, the left, the right again. Nothing I did made things better. The car spun on, the world outside flashed in front of me, white, gray, bits of green running together in wide, grainy stripes.

Then, just as suddenly as the spinning had begun, it stopped and I was sitting in the car on the snowy shoulder of the road, facing the wrong way. I rested my head on the steering wheel and tried to breathe. A stillness floated over everything — the hills, the trees, the car, and me. At first I could only hear the silence; then I heard the muffled slam of a car door.

When I looked up, through my windshield I saw a man in a tan shirt and dark green trousers running toward me, his necktie flapping against his chest. He opened my car door and stuck his head inside next to mine; I could feel his warm breath on my face. "I've been following you," he said. He was gasping and exhaling the words. "I knew something was going to happen. What the hell were you trying to prove?" He paused and added in a lower, gentler voice, "Are you all right?"

"Yes," I said. "I think so."

"Here," he said, and he held out his hand, "let me get you out of there." Taking my elbow, he guided me out of my car, and I sat in his while he drove mine off the shoulder and turned it around so that it faced the Basic School again.

His jacket hung on a hanger in the back of his car, and his cap was on the front seat; I saw that he was a Marine major. He took my message to Scott while I waited in his car, because when I tried to walk, I could not. My knees were shaking too hard. When he returned, he helped me into my car where I sat in the cold, afraid for a long time to start the motor. At last, I stopped trembling, and my heart stopped thudding and began to beat regularly again. I went on to Camp Barrett then, where the clerk in Heywood Hall, the administration building, told me Scott had already left. Slowly, I drove back to the hospital.

I didn't bother with the counter and the jaded corpsman at the entrance, but went right to the elevator, carrying Melinda's purse and overnight bag, straight up to the third floor, past the counter, to the end of the hall. A nurse took Melinda's things from me and told me Melinda was fine; the baby was a boy and he was fine, too, but no one except fathers and grandparents were allowed to visit in maternity. "You'll have to leave," she said.

I looked past the nurse's shoulder, and through an open doorway I saw Melinda. Forty-five minutes had passed since I had seen her last — on the gurney in the very hall I was standing in. Now she was sitting up in bed, propped against sparkling white pillows, wearing a clean, white hospital smock. Her face was pink and her hair was brushed. Scott, still in his field utilities, stood next to her, smiling down on the top of her head. Melinda was eating from a tray on a table that fit across her lap.

I don't know why, but they both looked toward the door then, and Scott smiled at me — more broadly, though less tenderly, than he had been smiling at his wife. Melinda smiled, too, and she waved her empty fork in the air. "Thanks for the ride, Marian," I heard her call out happily as the nurse gently pushed me toward the elevator.

War is in everyone's eyes, war is made
in the kitchen, in the bedroom, in the car at stoplights.

— Robert Mezey, "How Much Longer?"

Seventeen

I ATTENDED only one other just-for-wives
function besides the welcoming coffee where I had first
met Bonnie. Toward the end of February, four weeks before Basic School graduation, a few of us wives from
Companies D, E, and F of Basic Class 3-67, those of us
who could get away from our jobs for the morning, sat
scattered in the first two rows of the theater auditorium
in Little Hall. Mrs. Thorburn had found someone to re-
place me — I had decided to leave Quantico when Dave
graduated — and the new teacher, a good-natured, understanding woman named Marie had insisted on getting
to know the class. "Take whatever time you need to get
ready," she told me. "I'll take care of things in the classroom. I know you must have tons to do."

I was grateful. And one of the things I wanted to do
was to attend the "predeployment briefing." Standing in
front of us, in the middle of the front row, an officer,

someone I had never seen before, spoke to us about how to schedule a mover for our personal effects, how disbursement could be arranged, how we would be notified if our husband should be wounded or killed. This was, the officer announced, information that those of us who were "going to be left behind" would need.

We sat quietly, listening carefully, turning the pages of a little mimeographed, stapled brochure someone had handed out. On the cover was a stick figure of a woman with curly hair and a wide smile. The only thing the stick wore was an apron tied at the waist and ruffled at the bottom. The brochure artist had drawn a moving van in the background. Instead of headlights, the van had large eyes with long lashes, and its grille was a broadly smiling mouth with huge teeth.

The officer — I think he was a major — led us through pages listing government-approved moving companies and offering tips on packing and dealing with the movers. I remember a page with facts and figures about life insurance and medical options for those of us who would not be living on or near a base. There was even information about letters and packages to and from the combat zone.

A section about "R&R" — rest and recreation — offered names of the places married servicemen in Vietnam could travel to in order to meet their wives, and details about how long they could stay. As I sat in the auditorium and listened, R&R seemed only a vague promise light-years away, a distant possibility in a very unreal world. Dave would be coming home that very night, to our apartment. We would have supper and watch TV together. Sitting in the auditorium at Quantico, I found it impossible to imagine months of fearful waiting to see my husband, and then for only five short days. I barely glanced at the page on R&R.

But when we got to the last page, I began to pay attention, for here was a paragraph that contained the words *wounded* and *killed.* If our Marine was wounded, we would be notified by telegram; if he was killed, an officer, accompanied by a chaplain when possible, would come to our door, though not before six o'clock in the morning or after ten o'clock at night. Suddenly, nothing else in the little booklet, or in the room, or in the world, mattered.

I wasn't interested in the numbers or the regulations the major had discussed with us. I didn't care about damage claims against moving companies, or how much mail would or would not cost. R&R was too far away even to consider. The information about the telegram and the officer at the door was all I could think of. The words sat in purple print before my eyes, and the major's words hung in the air beside my head: "I hope none of you experiences any of this last part, ladies. But you should know what to expect if it does happen. Our country is engaged in warfare, and your husbands are warriors."

All at once, the war came to me like a seed on the wind, settling in the rich, newly turned soil of my fear.

March of 1967. One Sunday morning near the beginning of the month, I stood in the kitchen, at the small gas stove, with a metal spatula in my hand, lifting the edges of brown and bubbly eggs from the bacon grease I was frying them in. The eggs were for Dave and Kim Yaeger, an old friend of his from Tacoma. Kim was a former enlisted Marine who had reenlisted after going to college, getting married, and having two children. He was in Quantico to begin Officer Candidate School. While Dave showered, Kim was drinking black coffee at the kitchen table, watching me cook and talking to me.

"Do you think I'll get much bigger, Kim?" I asked. I lifted my loose sweater, one of Dave's civilian castoffs, and pointed with the spatula to my waist. I was wearing some old, tan pants that would no longer zip up. To close them, I had pushed a piece of green ribbon through the

waistband loops on each side of the opening and then tied
the ribbon over my stomach. A five-inch gap remained. I
covered that with Dave's brown sweater.

My question, simple as it was, seemed to surprise Kim.
His coffee cup was raised to his lips, but instead of drinking, he set the cup back in its saucer and stared at me.
The corners of his mouth struggled with their muscles for
a moment, then he said, sweetly, sympathetically: "I'm
afraid you're going to get a lot bigger, Marian. You'll be
huge."

I turned back to the stove. Much bigger? Was I going
to be big and ungainly and helpless, as Melinda had been?
No. I would not accept that. And yet I knew that Kim
was right. Suddenly, then and there, with Kim sitting at
the table, Dave in the shower, the sun streaming through
the window and onto the floor at my feet, I was too
frightened to move. I stood in front of the eggs, watching
the yolks turn hard and the whites on the edges burn.

Dave came into the kitchen, damp and barefoot, but-
toning his shirt. "What's wrong?" he said, looking at me
and then at Kim.

"Don't go," I said. "Please don't go and leave me like
this." Dave didn't say anything. He went to the open
door and looked through the screen. He was tucking his
shirttail into the back of his pants. His palms jabbed back-
wards into the waistband. "If you'd change your
MOS" — I was speaking to his back — "if you'd change
from the infantry, they'd send you to another school. Two
more months in the States. With your leave that'd be
enough to keep you home until the baby comes." I
stopped, because I had begun to cry.

Dave sat down across from Kim and poured a glass of
orange juice. "I'm not changing my MOS," he said quietly, not looking away from the glass in his hand. "I'm
going infantry. That's not going to change, Marian." He
looked at me. "I think a man with a rifle is the fairest

weapon there is, and a lot of the time it's the best, too. For me, a rifle platoon is where a Marine really belongs. Everything else is just support.''

Dave looked down at the glass in his hand again for a moment — then back up at me. "Most of all," he said, "I don't want to mess with fate. I'm leaving the first of May. That's my time to go, and I might as well get it over with.''

For a minute the only sound in the room was the popping of the grease in the frying pan. Then Kim scraped his chair back and rose to pour himself more coffee, and when he brushed past me on his way to the counter, he patted me on the shoulder. I don't know why, but just then I wanted to run to my room, to hide far back in the closet, in the dark. Instead, I dried my eyes on my sleeve, lifted the burned eggs into the garbage pail next to the stove, and cracked some fresh ones into the pan.

What I felt was something awful pressing on me — something I had sensed at Quantico the first time I passed through the main gates, but that until the predeployment briefing I had managed to push back. Whatever it was, it had no name, and until now it had not really found a place with me. But it found me in my own kitchen that sad morning, and there seemed no way I would ever escape it again.

On Friday, March 17, the 545 student officers of Dave's class made an amphibious assault on Red Beach at Camp Pendleton, Virginia. I took Dave to Camp Barrett and then drove through Quantico Town to the docks to wait for the buses carrying the student lieutenants and to watch them load onto the USS *Mountrail*. The ship left harbor and headed for Little Creek, where a small aggressor force of enlisted Marines waited for the boys to land.

They were gone three days. Bonnie called on Saturday morning, and Diane came over for a few hours on Saturday afternoon. We went shopping in Fredericksburg, but we didn't have much fun; we were a little lost, I think. Our husbands had spent nights away before, but this was different. They were on a ship out over the water. Unreachable. I felt very keenly that a part of my life was missing, and I didn't like it at all.

That evening, the apartment was bleak and silent. Melinda's mother had come to help her with the new baby and had ended up taking both the new baby and the new mother back to Arizona with her. Scott moved into the BOQ at Basic School, where attrition had left a spare bed. Above me, their apartment sat empty — and very silent: I missed the homey sounds of Melinda's sewing machine and record player, and the comforting creaks of the floorboards overhead.

But we are coming to the sacrifice.

— Edmund Blunden, "Vlamertinghe: Passing
the Château, July, 1917"

Eighteen

THE TORRENTIAL RAINS of March
took all the remaining dirty patches of snow from the
sides of the road pavement, from the fields, and even from
deep within the woods. The sun came out more and more
often and sat higher and higher in the sky. At recess with
the children, on the days when the wind did not blow, I
found sunny spots in the clearings around the schoolhouse where I stood with only a sweater over my shoulders for a coat and let the warmth fall over me. The earth
was thawing and soaking up the moisture. When I poked
at the damp, flattened layers of dead leaves with the toe
of my shoe, I could see that the soil below was wet, dark,
and rich.

The other teachers gave me a baby shower after school
one day in a corner of the empty basement lunchroom.
Another day, I brought my camera and took pictures of
my first-graders — it took three frames to get them all,

all those rows of little, smiling faces. I knew and loved each one, and now I had to tell them good-bye. We had had school pictures taken in January, and the class asked to keep my eight-by-ten-inch copy. Someone taped it to the side of the file cabinet. Mrs. Thorburn wrote to me months later that the picture stayed there until summer vacation, and that she often saw children talking to it. I missed my class for a long time.

We began to make real plans for the thirty-day leave, and our itinerary started to look like a pilgrimage. Dave wanted to visit friends and relatives — in Florida, Georgia, Washington State, and California. So I telephoned, wrote letters, and made arrangements and reservations.

I also reluctantly began to look ahead — knowing there was nothing else I could do — to the time after leave. Since we wives were to be left to make our own way, I, like the others, had to find a place to wait. I was armed with little except what I could remember of the officer's words that morning at Little Hall.

I decided to divide the thirteen months Dave would be gone between my parents in California and Dave's in Tacoma. My parents were eager to have me home; I understood that. I also understood that it was going to be a difficult year for Dave's parents, and that perhaps I and, later, the baby could be comforting. I knew that being in Dave's house near his family would help me. And Dave wanted me to have the baby in the hospital where he was born. For some reason, he was reassured by this plan.

It didn't help my state of mind that as graduation approached Dave became what I can only call childlike, though not in the worst meaning of that word. The change was subtle, but real, and I can see it even more clearly from the distance I have now. He wanted me to fix his favorite foods: cheeseburgers, spaghetti, baked potatoes, and steak. He polished the old rifles of his childhood and talked to me about hunting seasons of his past, about how he had liked to stalk deer with his uncles near Mount Saint Helens, and track chukars, a kind of partridge, over the hills of eastern Washington State, and how he would like to do that again, only he would be in Vietnam before the season opened.

He wanted a new car, too. It was clear the day we bought the old Plymouth that it could not make a cross-country trip. So we went to Fredericksburg, to the new-car dealer, and Dave told the rumpled, fat salesman that he wanted a new car, one he did not have to order and wait for. He wanted a car from the floor. The salesman had a practiced eye and he raked it over us quickly, smiling; then he said, "I've got just what you want." He started walking, with us behind him, toward the hangar-like garage that served as showroom and repair bay. In the middle of the confusion there, among other new cars, older cars, and mechanics in stained overalls operating noisy equipment — on the grease-spotted concrete floor — sat a sleek, brand-new, two-door, 1967 V-8 Camaro, painted the brightest red I had ever seen. Dave ran his hand over its hood, and he smoothed the door with his palm. He opened it and slid onto one of its black-leather bucket seats. Then he looked up at me, his hands gripping the steering wheel, and asked, "Can we get it?"

The salesman fingered a ring, selected one of the silver keys hanging from it, and reached in past Dave to the ignition. He switched it on, turned a knob on the tape deck, and Lorne Greene started to sing "See the U.S.A. in Your Chevrolet." We didn't drive the car home that day, but were assured by the Navy Federal Credit Union that financing would be approved in time for our trip across the country. I wondered at Dave's buying the car when he wasn't really going to get to enjoy it for a long time. I also wondered about his buying a car so unsuitable for a woman and a baby. But I did want him to have it, and when I heard a shaken Leah say that Sam had awakened her in the middle of the night and said, "Hold me . . . I'm scared," I said a little prayer of thanksgiving that all Dave had asked of me was that I cook his favorite foods and let him have a gleaming red Camaro.

At the time, buying the car was not personally satisfying for me, but it did make me happy to see how much Dave liked having it. Reveling in the car made it easier to put off what we were really thinking about, what we were both too frightened to acknowledge.

In time I came to treasure the Camaro for itself. For one thing, the highway patrol stopped us in it twice on leave, not so much because we were speeding — though we may well have been — as because it was a new-model sportscar, and a very bright red, too. Both patrol officers, one in Nebraska and one in California, spotted the Marine uniforms hanging in the backseat. Both times, Dave was asked the same question: "Are you on your way over?" And when he said, "Yes," he was given a pat on the back, a handshake, and the words "Good luck" — and sent on his way without a ticket.

Later I would remember those two patrolmen for their being the first to offer us any kind words of encouragement — and they were among the last for a very, very long time.

I came to love the car, too, because it was Dave's. Alone in Fresno and Tacoma, the towns in which I waited for him, I loved to look out the window and see the car parked in front of the house. Sometimes I would drive away to be by myself. I'd play the tape deck; "The Anniversary Waltz" was one of the songs on the tape that came with the car, the recording featuring Lorne Greene, and that was my favorite song. Car tapes weren't very common then, and for half of Dave's leave we had only that one, which we played over and over. "The Anniversary Waltz" became very important to me — and it still is. We hadn't even had an anniversary by the time Dave left for Vietnam.

It made me sad to play that tape and drive down the back roads of Fresno and Tacoma, but it was a satisfying, restful sadness, a gentle melancholy that made me feel somehow closer to Dave, riding in "his" car and playing the song we had listened to together, mile after mile across America.

The naked earth is warm with spring,
    And with green grass and bursting trees
Leans to the sun's gaze glorying,
    And quivers in the sunny breeze;
And life is colour, warmth and light,
    And a striving evermore for these;
And he is dead who will not fight;
    And who dies fighting has increase.

— Julian Grenfell, "Into Battle"

Nineteen

MARCH IN VIRGINIA brought spring with it: early dawns filled with light that stretched past suppertime. The top branches of the trees that lined the back roads and highways soon thickened with leaf buds. For the first time in my life, I noticed that the color of a tree's death is in its bud: red for the maples, yellow-green for the willows and the birches, light gold for the oaks. And along the roadsides and in the woods, each tree stood in a haze of color that foreshadowed its dying.

I was happy to see the spring, but sad, too. I was relieved and anxious at the same time. It seemed to me that my life, and Dave's, too, had come to the crossroad that the sign at the main gate at Quantico seemed to promise. I was ambivalent about everything. Besides not knowing how I felt about leaving Quantico, I was not sure how I felt about having a baby. I had certainly wanted a baby, and I was happy about being pregnant. At the same time, when I thought about being responsible for a real child, some little body placed in my care, I was worried. I did not like the unexpected visions I kept having of raising a child alone, and I pushed them off almost as soon as they came to me. Still, I had seen them. More insistent and more real was the morning sickness, a nausea that in my case came and went throughout the entire day and never completely went away as the cheerful doctors had told me it would. And I was growing larger and feeling more awkward and unattractive all the time.

Once, passing the long mirror in our hallway, I saw myself in one of my trousseau nightgowns; that night, I packed away all the filmy white and satiny black lingerie I had bought for my "honeymoon." The next day, I bought some large-sized flannel nightgowns at the PX. Practical, not too pretty, they were comfortable and they hid a lot. Dave and I went to Richmond, where I picked out some maternity clothes in a large department store; incredibly, there was no place to buy maternity clothes on base, or even any nearer to it than DC.

The clothes we brought back did not do much to make me feel better. The slacks were drab, plain, with stretch panels across the front and billowing tops in what I sup-pose someone thought were inconspicuous patterns. The dresses were tentlike and hung shapelessly from the shoulders. Only the ruffled bathing suit, pale blue and lavender-striped, had any spark of style to it, but I only had nerve to wear it once.

The same week we bought the Camaro, I hired the movers, Red Ball Moving Company, and scheduled them for three days before Dave's graduation from Basic School. The movers were big men in a big van that inched its way up the hill in first gear and quaked in the small parking lot while lurching to a stop. They packed almost everything we owned into fewer than twenty boxes. I kept out Dave's uniforms, clothes for both of us to travel in, our photo album, the camera, and some toiletries. I used a piece of a broken black crayon I had brought from school to write "Normal Clothes" on the boxes that held my nonmaternity things, and I set these aside, too, to take in the car with us. I would need these clothes in the fall. Everything else went onto the van, bound for storage in Fresno until Dave came back.

The movers were quick and careless men with sullen faces and thick arm muscles. After I pulled a six-pack of beer from the refrigerator and handed it to one of them, they did try to be friendlier. They were thorough, though, if nothing else. They even packed the morning newspaper, which I suppose I had left on the kitchen table. Months later, when I was unpacking these boxes, I had the strange experience of coming across that paper and having the headlines mean nothing; only the memories of leaving Quantico came to me.

When everything I had decided should be moved was packed, taped, labeled, and loaded, I gave the moving men what was left from under the sink, the soaps and the scouring pads, and those things in the cupboard I could not cook because the pots and pans were in the boxes on the truck — the cans of soup, the boxes of rice and spaghetti.

The van pulled away — a huge semi packed with other families' furniture and belongings, and jammed among these, our few boxes. The apartment seemed empty. It wasn't, of course; it had come furnished, and furnished we left it. But the closets and the dresser drawers were empty, and the white vase that had sat on the dresser top from the day we had moved in was gone. The organdy curtains hung at the windows, limp now from my repeated laundering. The worn, dark-patterned rug still covered the floor in the living room, and the white table was still in the kitchen, but the salt and pepper shakers

shaped like cobs of corn and the blue-and-white can of
Brasso were gone. The table was blank, like an erased black-
board that had had something important written on it.

We were gone, packed in a dozen and a half boxes
bound for storage. Life on hold.

I dreaded this leave and looked forward to it with the
same mixture of feelings I seemed to have about everything in those days. I wanted to have the time with
Dave — we had had so little time together since leaving
school in Washington State. I looked forward to spending
long days with my young husband, to being free of work
and responsibility, to having nothing to do but enjoy each
other. At the same time, I knew that at the end of the
thirty days, we would have to say good-bye — for a long,
long time. I knew this, but I shoved the knowledge of it
into a far corner of my mind, back into that place where
the young try to keep their knowing about sickness,
growing old, tragedy, and death.

By the end of March, all twenty-one weeks of Basic
School was over. Dave and his classmates had seen the
last of Camp Barrett. They would not even return to those
buildings and drill fields for graduation: that modest ceremony would be held on March 29 at Mainside — in Little
Hall, of course.

On the evening of the twenty-eighth, Dave and I
packed what the movers had not taken and put it into
the trunk and the backseat of the red Camaro. We drove
up Highway 1 for the last time, past the gas stations and
auto body places whose names I have now forgotten,
though then I knew them all by heart. We drove over
the small bridges that crossed the runs flowing high with
melted snow and spring rains, and on through the bud-
ding woods. We checked into a motel near the base. I
could not sleep that night, even as exhausted as I was

from packing, from instructing the movers, and from the dull heartache I had had since I said good-bye to my first-graders and the people I worked with at school.

The morning of the graduation, I was pale; dark purple shadows lay beneath my eyes, emphasized by the pale blue-and-white plaid of my cotton dress. Makeup didn't help. To make things worse, I had not packed the shoes I needed, and the black heels I did bring hurt my feet, which tended to swell easily then. The tossing and turning I had done all night made my hair hard to comb, and I awoke with a vague feeling of loss — a feeling that part of me was fading away, and there was nothing I could do about it. That morning I felt all wrong, in both body and soul.

Outside the motel window, the world was beautiful: seventy degrees and bright. In two days the Marines' white dress uniform of summer would be the order of the day, but for now — even as warm as it was in the morning and as hot as it would be by midday — it was dress blues for graduation. When I saw Dave slip on his blouse — saw him standing before me trim and tanned and solid, looking as though he could take on the world — I forgot for a moment my misgivings about myself and my fears about the future. After I pulled the large hook and eye of his high, tight collar together, he bent down and kissed me.

"Well, kid, this is it," he said. He took his white cover and white gloves from the low dresser, and we left for the base.

Graduation itself is a clouded image in my mind, a hurried confusion. In my memory there is a picture of the small auditorium, its pale gold and bright red curtains, and red cushioned seats. There is a roomful of blue-black shoulders and short-haired heads; few civilians, only a scattering of wives, are at this ceremony. I have a vague recollection of the class honorman striding across the stage to claim his prize, an engraved sword. But it's a faded picture. I cannot see his face.

I do remember vividly afterwards, on the lawn in front of the old, brick building, where we all gathered in a bunch at the edge of the parking lot. A light, cool breeze blew over us from across the water beyond Quantico Town. Lumpy clouds sat like white islands in the sky, which was broken along the horizon in the distance by yellow forsythia bushes and white dogwood trees lining the riverbank. It was a lovely, lilting day.

Libby and Ken were there, Jon and Bonnie, Sam and Leah, Diane and Matt. And, of course, Dennie. It was impossible to believe, but we were saying good-bye, a real good-bye. Not good-bye until tomorrow, or next week, or until the party or the ball, or even good-bye until after leave. Just good-bye.

Ken, Matt, and Dennie were off to Fort Sill in Oklahoma, for two months at artillery school. Jon was going to Newport, Rhode Island, for special legal training. Sam and Dave were in the infantry; there would be no more formal military training for them. They would make do with the basics they had learned at Camp Barrett. After the thirty-day leave, they were off to lead men in combat.

We stood in the warm, spring sun, the breeze stirring the hair and the dresses of the women and drying the beads of sweat on the necks and foreheads of the men, and we tried to go. We wives hugged each other, then we hugged each other's husbands, too. The men shook hands and grabbed one another by the shoulder. They slapped each other on the back and said, "See you around." "Stay out of trouble." "Good-bye, good-bye."

And that was it. Before the world saw another spring, three of the young men were dead, gone forever, and with them went a piece of the souls of those of us they left behind.

I have asked Dave how the boys in the platoon he was

assigned to at Quantico formed such close ties so quickly, and why they loved one another so much, and why he mourns so deeply, even now, those who died after he had known them only a few months. He can't tell me. But I think part of what bound them together, those boy-men, was the knowledge that they were about to go through the same crucial experience at the same time. I think that, before the fact, most of them were inspired and excited by the thought of it. Young men's rites of passage are nothing new, but this particular one, in those early days of our youth and of the war, was awesome and mysterious — and more: it was wonderful, perhaps even glorious.

There was nothing of those things in the enterprise for us wives, though. We would gain nothing from it; no glory, no self-knowledge. By the time we gathered for graduation, we knew there was a chance we might even lose.

What we did not know was how certain it was that we would lose. We did not know then that not one of our men would come back to us the man he had been. We learned that part later, each of us in her own time, each in her own sad way.

So we must say Goodbye, my darling,
And go, as lovers go, for ever;
Tonight remains, to pack and fix on labels
And make an end of lying down together.

— Alun Lewis, "Goodbye"

Twenty

THOUGH I HAD BEEN DREADING IT for months, April 30, 1967, seemed to come out of nowhere. Suddenly, it was simply there on the calendar. Dave's orders stated that he was to fly to Vietnam, via Okinawa, from Travis Air Force Base, northeast of San Francisco. With this in mind, we had ended his thirty-day leave in Fresno, where I'd taken him to Tidyman's Photography Studio to have his portrait taken, in his dress blues, standing with his sword upright on the floor in front of him and his hands resting on the hilt; and sitting, his left hand over his right arm, so that his gold wedding ring would show.

Sometime in the late morning of the thirtieth, my parents and Dave and I drove the 183 miles to San Francisco. We crossed the San Joaquin Valley over miles of land planted with grapevines and fig trees. The days of heat had already arrived, and the air was oppressive, thick and dusty.

San Francisco is well out of the valley, on a bay, and the air there was fresh and only slightly warm when we drove into the city. We had dinner on Fisherman's Wharf and then drove out, away from the coast, to a motel near the base. Dave's flight was not scheduled to leave until the evening of the next day, May 1, but his orders required him to check in twenty-four hours earlier. I was determined to see him off, and my father did not want me to drive back to Fresno alone, especially not at night, so there we were together: my father and mother, unhappy with Dave's role in the war, and Dave and I, frightened and sad, trying to hide our fear and sadness.

In our room that night, we made love, and afterward, lying side by side in bed holding hands in the dark, we tried to say the things we thought were important. "Please be careful," I remember saying more than once.

"Don't worry," Dave told me. "I'm more worried about you and the baby than I am about me. I can take care of myself. I'm just sorry I won't be here to take care of you." And he caressed the mound that was my stomach and his baby. I had promised myself he would not see me cry, and I kept that promise. But it was hard.

Morning came quickly, too quickly. I put on the same plaid dress I had worn at Dave's graduation the month before. Dave dressed in his summer tans, a uniform the Marines no longer have, but the summer class-A uniform of the day then. Tan trousers, tan blouse, tan tie, tan cover. He had been promoted to first lieutenant in February, so his bar was silver now.

He sat on the edge of the bed and went through his olive green seabag one more time. It held everything he was taking with him to war: olive green underwear, thick socks, combat boots, utilities.

We passed the morning at breakfast with my parents,

strained, awkward, somehow unfitting. My father was mostly silent, but I was touched to hear tenderness in his voice when he did speak. My mother was grim, and everything about her seemed reproachful: Dave and I had blundered. We were wrong.

As soon as we could, Dave and I went for a walk, alone. Holding hands — we could not let go — we walked around the flower beds and over the grass near the officers' club at Travis. I could hear the high whines of the planes as they took off and landed, and above me, in the blue sky, thin vapor trails crisscrossed beyond scattered clouds. The dusty-blue uniforms of the Air Force were everywhere around us, and among them, in lines on the huge, concrete runways or in small groups on the grounds, the summer tans of soldiers and Marines bound for Vietnam.

We went into the hushed, dark bar at the officers' club and sat in thickly upholstered swivel seats at a small, round table against one wall. Only two other people besides the bartender and the waiter were there. For the first time in months and months, Dave and I didn't seem to know what to say to each other. A good-bye waited in that dark, cool, quiet place, but we were determined not to recognize it, not to say its name out loud. This thing that Dave had to do was, after all, only an interruption in our "real" life together, the life we had had, more or less, until now, the one that would continue after the war.

So we sat in the dark and drank margaritas and agreed on names for the baby — Jeannie for a girl and Shane for a boy — and I worried about the clock on the wall: was it a correct clock, or set ahead like those in civilian bars? I felt a terrible tension, not foreboding exactly, but a nervousness, an anticipation that made me sit up straight and clench my fists. If Dave was upset or nervous, he did not show it. Perhaps he was excited. If that was so, he

did not show that, either. He was calm, and quiet. When
it was time to go, time to collect his seabag and go to the
departure gate, all he said was, "Well, hon, this is it. I
guess I'd better be going now."

We rose from the table, and Dave opened his wallet to
pay for our drinks. Just then an Air Force captain got up
from his chair and came over to our table. He put money
in the waiter's hand. "These are on me," he said. He
pressed Dave's shoulder and said, "Good luck." And then
he was gone.

In the corridor outside the bar, the newspaper rack had
been filled with the day's late edition. I looked at the front
page through the wire holder — at Elvis Presley and his
new bride, Elvis in a dark tux and Priscilla in white chif-
fon, cutting their wedding cake. I stopped in front of the
picture and looked for a long moment. What I saw
stunned me: my husband and thousands of young men
like him were leaving for war, many would not be coming
back, and the headline news was Elvis's wedding.

I remember almost every detail of that year, the year
Dave left for Vietnam. But I do not remember saying
good-bye to him. I watched him board the plane from
behind a barricade. As far as I could tell, I was the only
wife, the only civilian, there. The other men in the long,
tan line on the runway had left for Travis from airports,
train stations, and bus terminals across the United States.
Wives, parents, and friends had seen their men off sepa-
rately, had said good-bye alone. I was almost alone. A
Marine sergeant stood near me, his foot raised on a bar
of the barricade, his elbows resting on the top rail, a cigarette in his hand. "You seeing someone off?" he said.

"Yes," I answered. "My husband."

He stared in the direction of the 707 and the stream of
young men climbing up the portable steps and disappear-
ing, one by one, through its door. Then he turned his
head and looked beyond me and pointed with his ciga-

rette toward a large hangar across the field and another 707 taxiing into it.

"That's the way a lot of them come back," he said.

"Inside the hangar?" I asked.

"They don't want people to see."

I looked at the sergeant. He had rough skin, wrinkled and pitted, ruined by the sun and some long-ago case of acne that must have made his youth horrible; but his face was shaved so clean and close it had a kind of smooth beauty.

"What don't they want people to see?" I said, finally.

"Coffins. They don't want anyone to see them unloading all the coffins. Especially not them." He nodded toward the line of men on the runway and then dragged deeply on his cigarette.

I looked at the line, too. I couldn't see Dave anymore. The sun was going down, and the half-light, a not-quite-dusk, odd pink light, made it hard to see. Perhaps he was on the plane already. Anyway, I waited next to the sergeant until the plane itself was out of sight, off into that pink-red glow along the horizon.

"From the war in body bags. Then cleaned up and put into shiny coffins and sent on." The sergeant was talking as much to himself as he was to me. "A planeload of shiny coffins," he said. I moved away from the barricade and went to find my parents.

For years I wondered why the sergeant told me about the plane of coffins. I was obviously young, obviously pregnant, and I had told him I was seeing my husband off to war. I was hurt by what I thought at the time was the man's insensitivity, cruelty almost. I know now that like so many veterans of that war he was simply angry. He was just a Marine who wanted someone, *anyone*, in a world that did not seem to care, to care.

At home, very late that night, I went looking for the map of Vietnam my father had spread out on the kitchen

table for me to study the summer before. I found it folded
in a thick square in the bottom of the desk in the spare
bedroom my family used as an office. When I flew into
Sea-Tac, the Seattle-Tacoma airport, a week after Dave
left from Travis, the map was in my purse.

Because I had decided to have the baby in Tacoma, I
was going to live with Dave's parents for the first few
months of his tour overseas, then with my parents for the
remaining months. Unlike my parents, Dave's folks did
not seem to have a definite opinion of the United States'
involvement in Vietnam. I don't think they understood
it. But they were proud of Dave's service. They missed
him and worried about him, and so we had that in common. Together, we might be a small triangle of support.
And I needed support.

Dave's brother, Dennis, was a happy-go-lucky twenty-
year-old out of school for the summer and living at home.
His primary concerns, like those of a lot of boys his age in
every age, were parties and girls. I had a kind of emotional
schizophrenia the first week I lived in the house on Tyee
Drive in Tacoma. Dennis was in and out with friends,
laughing, calling girls on the phone. He drove a truck
then, and during his lunch breaks he parked his rig on
the small, dead-end street in front of the house and came
inside to watch "Let's Make a Deal" or "The Dating
Game" while his mother fixed his lunch. She fried his
hamburgers and worried that he would have a car accident coming home from one of his late-night parties and
kill himself or someone else. His father worried that Dennis was not taking his job seriously, that he might be fired.

And over all this was the shadow of worry for their
other son — not specific, not voiced, but always there.

Bonnie called from Newport, where Jon was finishing
school. They were thinking of me, and of Leah, too. Leah
and I were the first to be left. Was I OK? Did I need

anything? I assured her I was fine, that it all hadn't been as bad as I had thought it would be.

In fact, the leave-taking had been worse than I had imagined it would be in even my lowest moments. I was lost and frightened. But I didn't want Bonnie to know that. It was probably just me, anyway; I was in a strange city, living with near-strangers — even if they were my husband's parents. Bonnie and Diane would do fine with their families in their hometowns. Libby and Leah had grown up in the same towns as their husbands, so they had two families to lean on. The rest were going home to family and friends. That would make a difference. Soon after my baby was born, I would go home, too.

The first month of his absence
I was numb and sick,
And where he'd left his promise
Life did not turn or kick.
The seed, the seed of love was sick.

— Alun Lewis, "Song"

Twenty-One

DAVE'S PARENTS and I made Dave's old room into a nursery. It was my bedroom, too, while he was away, but I wanted it to look like a cheery room for a baby. So Dave's father hung new wallpaper, a white background with huge yellow roses splashed all over it. I made new white-and-yellow curtains, and I painted Dave's dark boyhood furniture white — his desk and bed and chest of drawers.

I taped my map of Vietnam to the inside of the closet door.

Shortly after I arrived in Tacoma, I settled into a pattern. I wrote to Dave at night after my bath before climbing into bed. It was easy to find things to write about at the end of the day — the day's events, if nothing else. Even tired, I could find more to say to him at night than I could in the morning. During the days, I got ready for the baby, and, also important to me, I wrote letters to my friends from Basic School whose Marine husbands were also bound for Vietnam.

Dave sent a postcard from Hawaii, where he had a twenty-minute layover. Then letters began to arrive, the first from Okinawa. He had run into Sam on a three-day layover, and they had played poker and drunk beer at the officers' club together one afternoon. He wrote his first letter from Vietnam on Saturday, dated "6 May, 1940 hours." He was at regimental headquarters, waiting to be moved to a battalion. "We're just sitting around," he wrote, "waiting to find out where we'll be going."

I took a black felt-tipped marker and circled Da Nang, for that was as near as I could figure Dave's location.

We lived under extraordinary circumstances in those days, but it seemed to me in the first weeks of Dave's tour of duty that except for the waiting and loneliness, the days would pass rather ordinarily after all. I began to feel lucky.

Dave had been gone almost three weeks when I learned suddenly that my life was not ordinary, and that I was not lucky. The twenty-second of May, 1967, was a Monday, and Dave's mother had gone next door to visit her mother. I was bringing the paint and brushes and thinner from the garage, ready to finish the woodwork in the nursery, the last of the painting. As I passed from the kitchen across the dining alcove I looked out the picture window of the living room. A tan car sat in the driveway and a tall Marine major in summer tans was coming up the walk to the front door.

I set the paint bucket and the can of thinner on the floor, dropped the brush beside it, and pulled the front door open before he had time to ring the bell. I could not speak. I stood in the doorway — the door wide open, the screen still latched — and stared.

"Does Mrs. William Novak live here?" the major said.

"I'm Mrs. Novak," I managed to say. My mouth was

very dry. "Is this about my husband? Is something wrong?" The world seemed frozen, and everything — movement, sound, thought — seemed to take a long, long time.

The major held some papers in his hand. He glanced down at the one on top, looked at me again, and said: "I'm here to see Mrs. William A. Novak, regarding her son, First Lieutenant William David Novak. Does Mrs. Novak reside at this address?" From behind me, a million miles away, her voice muffled, my mother-in-law, home from her mother's house through the back door, said: "I'm Mrs. Novak. Can I help you?"

"May I come in?" the major asked.

I struggled with the little metal latch and opened the screen door. The major removed his hat and stepped inside. Standing in the living room, his cover in one hand and the papers bunched in the other, he seemed puzzled. He looked at the papers again, and then he said, "My information states that First Lieutenant William D. Novak's next of kin is his mother, Mrs. William A. Novak of this address." Dave's mother was still standing near the back entrance to the living room. The major and I were by the front door. He held the paper out for me to see.

"I'm his wife," I said. I felt my face grow hot and I pulled my maternity smock by its hem. "Since August," I added. "Wait. I'll show you." And I went to my room, Dave's old room and now also the nursery, jerked my purse off the dresser by its strap, and walked quickly back to the living room. I pulled my orange-tan military ID from my wallet and handed it to the major. He looked at it and gave it back to me.

"Ladies," he said, "please sit down."

Obediently, we sat down on the couch as my mother-in-law, ever gracious, gave the major a small smile and gestured toward my father-in-law's big, green La-Z-Boy.

The major sat on its edge, his cover on his knee. "Your husband," he said glancing at me, "and your son," and he looked at my mother-in-law, "has been wounded in the right arm. This happened while he was on patrol south of Da Nang, and he has been evacuated to a field hospital at the First Medical Battalion at Da Nang."

Nobody said anything for a moment. Then the major added that we could write to Dave at the hospital at Da Nang for the next two weeks or so. The wound, he said, was not life-threatening. Dave was expected to return to his unit at the end of his hospitalization. The major was kind, earnest, and soft-spoken. The sunny living room was hushed, and Dave's mother and I sat quietly, our hands in our laps. His mother's face had drained of color — even her lips looked pale — and her hands were trembling in her lap. She looked as though she might cry.

I did not feel like crying. I wanted to shout, to run out the door into the street and tell the first person I saw that my husband was alive. Alive! For as many long minutes as had passed from the moment I saw the tan car in the driveway and the major on the walk in front of the house, until I heard his words "has been wounded," I thought my husband was dead. I thought I would never see him again, never talk to him again, that he would never see his baby. The loneliness, isolation, and sense of having been abandoned I felt in those moments made the loneliness I had felt before the major came to the door seem almost frivolous. I sank back into that old, familiar loneliness and with relief felt it, rolled around in it inside my mind. It was comfortable, the old loneliness. I missed Dave. But he was still on the earth. He was still somewhere. Such an ordinary, kind loneliness. It left me hope.

But when I sat down that night to write to Dave, I realized there was something new, too. I still had hope, yes, but I did not feel lucky anymore. I went to bed that night with hope, and I was grateful for it; but there was with it a tremendous sense of vulnerability. At any moment, another tan car could pull into the driveway.

Before I wrote my letter, I called Bonnie, who was still in Newport, to tell her that Dave had been wounded, that he was going to be all right. She asked for his hospital address. She wanted to write to him and to pass along the news and the address to the others. In my letter to Dave, I asked about his wound. Where was it on his arm? How did it happen? Was anyone else hurt?

On Tuesday, a letter arrived from Dave. It was written on Red Cross stationery — white, white paper with a small, blood-red cross in the center of the top of each sheet and on the flap of the envelope. The letter had been mailed Monday, the twenty-second, and in it Dave had written in pencil, in barely legible handwriting:

> Honey, I'm back off that operation I was talking about in my last letter. It was pretty hot out there. I had one case of heat stroke in my platoon and almost another one, too. Don't worry. I didn't even come close to it myself.
>
> I'm really enjoying my platoon. They are real professionals, although most of them are just youngsters, really. So far they've taken real good care of me. . . . I love you very much and miss you. . . .
>
> Dave
>
> P.S. I'll probably get a chance to write tomorrow.

Nothing about being wounded. The next day, I received another letter scrawled in pencil on the white paper with the red cross. "How do you like my new stationery?" Dave began. He went on to ask for a care package — small cans of juice and presweetened Kool-Aid envelopes. Then: "Nothing much new over here. The temperature is

100–105 degrees most of the time. It'll start to get what they call hot here about July." And that was it.

I was starting to get angry and frustrated. The major had been reassuring, but vague. I called the Pentagon and left a message in some office whose name I cannot remember. Whether in response to my call or to some military protocol I know nothing about, the next day a telegram came to the house. It repeated the few details I already knew and closed with these words: "His condition and prognosis are good. Your anxiety is realized and you are assured that he is receiving the best of care." It was signed "Wallace M. Greene, Jr., General USMC, Commandant of the Marine Corps." And it was addressed to Mr. and Mrs. William A. Novak. It seemed to me that the Marine Corps would never understand that First Lieutenant William D. Novak had a wife.

Eventually Dave managed to get out of the hospital before his arm was healed, by telling the doctors he would stay in the battalion area and not return to his platoon until his wound had mended. His worry over his "men" changed his mind, though, and from the battalion area he immediately hitchhiked back to his platoon. "In the field, you could trust my corpsmen like you would the best Harvard doctor at Massachusetts General," he told me later. "They took good care of me."

My letters had not gone to Da Nang but had been re-routed to Dave's unit, so he finally read my questions and wrote answers. The wound was a clean one in his upper arm — a rifle shot through his arm and into his side, leaving only a large bruise on his torso where a trajectory hole would have been except that the bullet had embedded in Dave's flak jacket. Even sweaty, dust-covered, and shirtless, the men in Dave's outfit wore these heavy protective vests. The enemy snipers were good. The bullet that struck Dave was headed straight to the heart. "It was just a flesh wound," Dave wrote, "and I received my first, and I hope last, Purple Heart."

Spring was in full bloom in Tacoma. Trees of white, pink, and purple blossomed on deep-green lawns and bulbs bloomed in neat, woodchip-covered beds. Sea breezes from Puget Sound cleared and cooled the afternoon air. Local colleges — the University of Washington, Tacoma Community College, the University of Puget Sound, Pacific Lutheran — were all letting out for the summer, and students filled the beaches, where they picnicked and played volleyball. They rode to the mountains in convertible cars with the tops down, the trunks filled with coolers of beer.

That summer, the newspapers and magazines began to focus on yet another set of young people. The "flower children" of Haight-Ashbury in San Francisco had caught the media's imagination. The spring of 1967 was about to give way to what is now called — perversely, to those of us who had men we loved in battle — the Summer of Love. It was a strange kind of love these young people preached, one I did not understand. It was an exclusive love, a love that did not include the young men in the armed services.

In fact, the Summer of Love bred disdain and hatred for a war that eventually centered on the young men who were fighting it and dying in it. The generation split, and the fissure was deep, so deep it is perhaps irreparable. In the end it was the shattering of our times.

In his letters, Dave was very careful to keep things from me. It was as though he thought that if he told me much, no matter how selective he might try to be about what he chose to say, he might slip and tell me something he really did not want me to know. Rereading these letters more than twenty years later, in light of all I know now, is a sweet, but very frustrating, experience. Dave tried to hide a lot. These letters, so longed for, so patiently awaited, and so wonderful to me then simply because they existed, are somewhat disappointing in retrospect. Time has changed them in this way.

They are short, and in them Dave writes almost exclusively of ordinary, everyday matters, things he thought we still had in common, I suppose: the thin and fragile framework of our life together, what very little there was left of it. He wrote about the car insurance — long passages of instructions in several letters. He wrote in every letter before R&R at least a line or two about our plans for it. After R&R, he wrote about coming home. He wrote about the heat in the summer. It did get hot — 120 degrees Fahrenheit in July. In the winter, he wrote about the damp chill. And the whole thirteen months of his tour, we played long, drawn-out games of ticktacktoe.

If Dave did write to me about the war itself, it was to tell me his general opinion of it, or to talk about his platoon and the other men he came to know in his unit. To a man, he seemed to think his platoon was wonderful, skilled and brave both. On June 8, when he had been "in country" only a few weeks, he wrote: "I'll tell you, this war is a dirty, filthy one. It's a hard one to fight, but my troops don't seem to get discouraged. I'm really proud of them."

I continued to hear from Libby and Bonnie and Diane. The miscarriages Diane had suffered, two at Quantico and one since then, haunted her, and as the months passed and we worried together about our men, I watched her grow increasingly dispirited and resigned. But she told me once, in one of her efforts to cheer herself up, "Maybe God'll think he owes me." And I knew what she meant. I played that kind of game, too. Sometimes I felt despairing because of it: how could I hope for Dave's safety and a healthy baby, too? It really did seem too much to ask for, to pray for, to hope for. I felt always that something terrible was going to happen, would have to happen, to me, as it already had happened to lovely, kind Diane before her husband had even left for the war zone.

It's hard for his child, and it's rough on his wife,
There might have been — sooner — a chance for his
life.
But it's *War!* . . .

— Edgar Wallace, "War"

Twenty-Two

FOR THE FIRST TIME in my life, I read the newspaper carefully — not just the comics and the first and second pages, but all of it except the sports page and the obituaries. And I watched the evening news every day, too, something I had not done before. In the spring of 1967, I began to watch Walter Cronkite, a warm, kind-looking man, every weeknight on CBS in the living room on Tyee Drive.

My father-in-law could not watch for long without becoming upset. He became angry when he read the newspapers, too. He would fold the paper together, quickly and messily, and slam it on the thick arm of his recliner. Then he would throw it onto the living-room floor and go to the backyard, where he sat alone for a long time, smoking and staring off down the sloping lawn into the alley below. Through the dining-room window, we could see the little, red glow of his cigarette in the dusk. Watching the news on TV seemed to be even worse for him than reading the paper. He simply could not bear it. After a few minutes of the broadcast, if the news was about Vietnam — and it usually was, in some way — he would leave the house and the yard altogether and walk over the ridge at the end of the street, toward the waters of the sound. He did not stay away long, and neither he nor my mother-in-law nor I ever mentioned his leaving.

Remembering now, I do not see how I could have read the newspaper and watched the news broadcasts, but I did. The papers and the networks covered the war thoroughly, if not always thoughtfully or sensitively.

Every night, I watched young Americans in combat gear struggling through jungle, trailing across rice paddies, lying in the dirt, living and dying in mud and danger — and fear. I saw them under fire, and I saw them wounded.

Sometime around the first of July, I saw in the news thousands of what the media were calling flower children, young people who had gathered for the Monterey Pop Festival in Monterey, California. It was, we were told over the airwaves, a celebration of love and peace. There was music, and there were drugs, and there was, we were told, uninhibited, "free" sex. Everything good came together at Monterey, or so it seemed, in a wonderful, wild spirit of joy, a stark counterpoint to the somber, deadly beat of the war going on halfway around the world.

This was before we knew the full extent of the harm drugs could, and eventually would, do, and this was before we learned that "free" sex could be as dangerous as war.

These awful feelings of vulnerability and being at the mercy of fate did not go away and only got worse as time went on. On July 5, 1967, Leah's husband, Sam, got separated from his unit during an ambush; he was found dead the next day. Bonnie called with this horrible news.

I was heartbroken for Leah. Our babies were both due at the end of the month. And I could not forget them, Leah and Sam, the night of the Marine Corps Birthday Ball, him standing close to her, his arm around her waist. They looked like twins, both dark-haired and mirroring each other's features. And I remembered Bonnie saying to me: "They never dance with anyone else. They're inseparable. I don't think they could survive without each other."

Added to my feeling of vulnerability now was an almost unbearable sadness — and a guilt, too, because somewhere in the dark bottom of my heart I was glad it was Sam and not Dave, and I felt that Sam's death somehow had moved the odds in favor of Dave's survival.

The world was out of control, and I had eleven months to go before Dave would be home. How would I hold on? How were any of us going to hold on? But we did. Time had stopped for Diane's babies, and for Sam and all the others who had died, and it began to seem that it would go on only if we willed it onward. The days moved forward slowly.

Gradually, the passing of time came to be marked for me by the mail. The mailbox took on a significance so strong I feel it even today, and I still feel a faint shiver of excitement and hope when I see the mail truck. The mail truck and the mailbox became the physical focal points of my existence, the time of the mailman's arrival the center of my day. I found it almost impossible to leave the house before the mailman had come. I could see the little red metal flag from the living-room window. I raised it every morning Monday through Saturday when I put my letter to Dave in the box, and I checked throughout the morning to see if the mailman had lowered it.

Sometimes I heard the truck and went out to meet the mailman. His name was also Sam, and he always asked about Dave, and if there was a letter from him, Sam smiled broadly and handed it to me. He was always apologetic when there was no letter, and he seemed personally disappointed if it had been several days since I had last heard.

Toward the end of July, about the time the baby was due, I became desperate for some direct communication with Dave. When he was wounded and could not communicate, I began to understand that not only thousands of miles separated us; time did as well. Letters took days — if the system was working well, that is, and often it was not. The men moved around, and the mail had to follow them. Or they were in the field and mail did not go out. I wondered how they would tell him when the baby was born. How long would it take for both of us to know a thing at the same time?

One hot afternoon — two days past the baby's due date but still no baby, and, even worse, four days since the last letter from Dave — I called the Red Cross. Dave had mentioned the Red Cross more than once in his letters. Its workers sent paper, soap, and other extras for the men to the field, provided comfort in the field hospitals, and were conduits of information between families at home and their men at war. I asked the young woman who answered the phone if it would be possible to call my husband in Vietnam. I had heard of women who spoke by phone to their husbands overseas. She explained that there were duty stations in the war zone with telephones or telephone radios, and that radio hams in the United States did volunteer their time, sometimes hour after hour of it, so that men could call home.

Sometimes, she went on, if a man happened to be near a radio telephone, the Red Cross could arrange a call; but otherwise a message had to be delivered through the units. After a minute or two of checking, she told me that Dave had no access to a telephone; a message would be delivered to him in the field if one needed to get to him.

"How long will that take?" I asked. "How long after our baby is born will it be before he knows?"

The young woman did not answer for a moment; then she said: "Seventeen hours. It takes seventeen hours to get information to the field, and seventeen hours to get information from the field."

I thanked her, hung up the phone, and sat for a few minutes at my mother-in-law's kitchen table thinking about what I now knew: that at that very moment my husband could be lying on the jungle floor nine thousand miles away, that he could be wounded, bleeding and in pain, or dead, and it would be seventeen hours before I would know. And the next moment would be the same. Whatever lay before us — the future we had counted on before Dave went to war, a marriage altered by his crippling, or my widowhood — seventeen hours would pass before I would even know. It was strange, too strange even to try to understand, but I dwelled on it and thought about it every day. Whatever I pretended was real — that I was a wife waiting, that there would be a life after the war, that a joke someone told was funny, that I was doing fine — the truth was that I really did not know.

I lived in a never-never land of seventeen hours — a time zone of not knowing, not knowing anything except that as long as the very moment I lived in passed and there was no call, no telegram, and no uniformed Marine at the door (at least between the hours of six in the morning and ten at night), then I could be fairly certain that seventeen hours before, my husband still lived and walked unhurt somewhere in that sad land whose name I had heard for the first time less than two years before.

Twenty-Three

FROM THE TIME I LEARNED I was pregnant in the fall of 1966 until we left Quantico the following spring, I had visited the base's obstetrics clinic five times — and had seen five different doctors. During my sixth month of pregnancy, during which we were on leave, I had not seen a doctor at all. But by the end of June, settled in Tacoma and expecting the baby sometime past the middle of July, I found what turned out to be the last obstetrician I would see before giving birth.

He was a big, gruff, unfriendly man, and I suppose if things had been only slightly different, if the baby had not been due so soon, or if I had felt somehow freer to cause trouble, I would have looked for another doctor. But things were not different, so I kept my thoughts to myself, and I kept my appointments.

They were supposed to be weekly until the baby was

born. Although I had to have only four or five appointments in all, I hated them. I was weighed, insulted over
my weight — this was before doctors decided a maximum
weight gain of fifteen pounds during pregnancy was un-
healthy — prodded and poked at, then left for some half-
ashamed, apologetic nurse to put together again as best
she could without offending the doctor, and sent home.
I left these appointments no wiser, no more informed,
certainly more insecure. I was not familiar with Lamaze
then; in fact, I had never even heard it mentioned. I
thought then that women should not be unpleasant patients, and since I was afraid that a show of anger might
leave me without an OB — and it was getting to be late
in the game — I tried to be nice to the doctor, and to
hope for the best.

I was very vulnerable, afraid and alone, and at this
man's mercy. I know now, in retrospect, how harmfully
his treatment affected me, but I tried not to think about
it then. I just wanted to hang on — and survive.

By July, I had finished turning Dave's old room into a
yellow-and-white nursery. I had washed and put away
all the baby clothes I had collected, those I had been given
and those I had bought. My mother-in-law had borrowed
a crib, and I had bought a white wicker bassinet and had
sewn a huge, obscenely fluffy lace-and-ribbon skirt for it
in yellow and white.

I was very excited about the baby by this time, but all
the same, I still worried constantly about Dave and the
baby both. Then, as the time for the baby drew nearer, I
began to concentrate my worry on myself. It began to
seem as though I were the weak center of that chaotic
world I had entered when the war in Vietnam came to
me so real, so violent. I knew that I was going to have to
live and function for Dave and for the baby. I did not

know if I could. I thought about Leah all the time and wondered how she managed — to get out of bed in the morning, to eat, to get tiny clothes ready for her baby.

At one in the morning, July 24, 1967, I woke up with a light but steady aching in my stomach. Nothing else, just the cramps. I got out of bed and walked around the bedroom hoping the pain would go away. It didn't, and I didn't tell anyone about it, either. Dave's parents and his brother, Dennis, had jobs to go to, and even though the baby was well due by the doctors' estimations, I was not sure what was happening. I showered, washing my hair, too, and got dressed.

By ten o'clock that morning, the aching had settled into regular contractions three to five minutes apart. I had been told about these and what they meant, so I called a neighbor to drive me to the hospital. She helped me fill out the admission papers, but she could not stay with me; she had left her own baby with friends. Strangers took me in a wheelchair to a labor ward, where I was told to undress and put on a short gown. Then I was shaved and given an uncomfortable, unnecessary enema. At last, exhausted, scared, and in pain, I climbed into a high hospital bed and waited.

I waited a long time, it seems now, in a small room of white and steel and glaring light. Down the hall, in other cubicles I guessed were like mine, I could hear women moaning, and every once in a while one screamed. Nurses and doctors scurried up and down outside my open door. My doctor did not come, though, and when I asked one of the nurses who came to take my blood pressure and check on me when he would be coming, she told me he was out of town, on vacation, and they were trying to reach him.

At noon, my mother-in-law came to the hospital and stood just inside the door of my room for a moment. She did not stay. "I couldn't stand to see you like that," she told me later. A young intern came to my room often, all afternoon and through the evening. And during the very worst of it, in the night, he sat on the edge of the bed with me and held my hand.

When I went to delivery at eight o'clock the next morning, he was still holding my hand. In delivery, he wiped my forehead and talked to me. He was and is nameless, but I remember his face and what he said and did, and I will never forget him. I had a baby girl, and she was named Jeannie.

Back in my room, a lifeless, square ward that I shared with three other women, I found a bouquet of yellow roses. The card was one of Dave's military calling cards: his name engraved in black ink across the middle and the words "Lieutenant, United States Marine Corps" on the bottom right. On the back he had written "To my darling Marian, With all my love, Dave." Before he left, he had given the card to his mother and asked her to order the flowers for me when the baby was born.

Even in a ward of other new mothers, I was lonely, especially when the fathers came to visit. I wanted to hold my baby all the time, but we were only allowed to do this for a few minutes every few hours. So the morning after Jeannie was born, I went back to the house on Tyee Drive, where I could be with my baby girl, her father's black-haired daughter. Two days later, Leah had a baby girl, too.

Just how or when the Red Cross learned that a baby girl named Jeannie, eight pounds and four ounces, had been born, and that her father was in Vietnam and needed to be told, I don't know. But they did tell him, though it took longer than the seventeen hours I had counted on. In a short note dated July 28 — July 27 in the United

States — Dave wrote: "I just learned I am the very proud father of a little girl. . . ." It had taken more than two days for the news to get to him.

It bothered me that it had taken so long. Dave had led me to believe, in the days just before Jeannie's birth, that he was near a radio, in close contact with the battalion headquarters. This comforted me. In fact, all the letters he had written toward the end of July had been calm little pieces about the boring nature of his new job — he was XO of the company. "I don't do much, mostly paperwork," he had written. "Don't go to the field anymore, which should make you happy. The company is guarding an old bridge south of Da Nang, an old French structure we need now to keep our supplies moving north. Don't worry, it's safe."

The truth, which I finally learned more than a decade later, was that the company had gotten a new commander, a career captain who had been severely wounded several months before. He had just been returned to duty, and as it turned out, he had come back too soon and was not physically ready for field operations. The battalion commander, I suppose trying to buy time for the captain, took Dave from his platoon, made him XO — second in command of the company — and sent him to the field in charge of the company. That's where he was when Jeannie was born: supervising the patrolling of rice paddies by day and the setting of ambushes by night.

But I did not know that then. The letters I carried in my purse to the hospital, the most recent four or five, were reassuring lies. Dave had painted pictures for my mind of him in a bunker near an old, French-built bridge, waiting by a radio for the call from the Red Cross.

The plan to have Dave lead the company as XO was abandoned when the regimental command removed the wounded commander and replaced him with a captain

able to go to the field. As XO, Dave still went on operations in the field, but he no longer had ultimate responsibility. I think he must have missed it. I can only guess,
because he did not write to me about any of this. Instead,
he continued to create for me images of his safety and
even of a certain contentment. "I'm in a secure area," he
wrote on August 10. "We're still at the bridge." Three
weeks later, while Dave was elsewhere with the company
headquarters, the "secure" bridge was overrun. When
Dave got there with a relief squad, he found that eight
Marines had been wounded and two killed — one of
them Dave's former corpsman George Gallagher, a small,
sandy-haired kid from Vermont who liked to make people laugh. His was the only death in Vietnam Dave ever
wrote about, and then only one line: "One of my corpsmen died at the bridge."

I made Dave a small, olive green pillow, small enough, I
thought, to be carried in a pack to the field. In his letters,
Dave had complained more than once about sleeping on
the hard ground. On the top right-hand corner of the
pillow, I embroidered an eagle in gold, and I made a small
pillowcase, too. This was my present to Dave for our first
wedding anniversary.

On the day of our anniversary, August 12, Dave's
brother took me out to dinner. Just as when Dave's
mother sent the yellow roses to the hospital when Jeannie
was born, Dennis was following Dave's instructions, written down before he left.

I felt ready for a social life — eager to go out, especially
after those horrible, restraining last months of pregnancy.
I had lost most of the weight I had gained during pregnancy, my stomach was flat again, and I had a new dress.
Dave had asked Dennis to buy me a corsage, too, which
he did. It was made up of yellow roses, like the bouquet
I'd gotten from Dave when Jeannie was born.

Dennis drove me downtown, down steep hillsides to the wharves, where he knew of a good place to eat. The evening was warm and clear, and beyond the docks the water was black with white edges where it lapped against the pilings. Outside the car, the air smelled of fish and seaweed.

The restaurant had a small band and a dance floor. After we ordered, Dennis asked me to dance; the band played a few fast numbers, and it was good to feel young again. Then the music changed, and the dance floor was transformed. Slow dancing on the darkened floor. Couples all around us in one another's arms, Dennis holding me — not tightly, a friendly embrace — and lighthearted talk about a girl he was interested in. I knew then, on that crowded dance floor dancing with my brother-in-law on my first wedding anniversary, what it was like to be really alone. It wasn't like having Dave and Bob in the same room but not talking to me; it wasn't like having Dave gone into the woods overnight; it was like having my body in one place and what made me myself in another, separated from it — and having no one know that I was stretched out so far in the universe.

I talked too much, I laughed too often, and I danced every dance, because I wanted Dennis to write to Dave that his anniversary gift for me had been a success. But I really just wanted to go home, to sit quietly in the rocking chair in my room and hold my baby and sing "The Kerry Dance" to her, and later, when I had put her, asleep, in her crib, to write a letter to my husband. I did not belong among the normal people of home front America 1967. In the pleasant restaurant, with the soft hissing of the bay and the darkened skies against the plate glass windows making the dance floor small and peaceful — its own world — I did not belong.

Defeated, I told Dennis I was tired and it was time to go home. He dropped me off at the top of the driveway and drove off to join his friends. After all, it was Saturday night, there were parties all over town, and it was much too early for the evening to end.

In July Dave had begun to write especially upbeat letters. One explained: "I've made a good friend here, an artillery officer named Skip Stephenson. It's nice to have someone to kid around with."

Dave had come to love every man in his platoon, but as platoon commander he had been responsible for them, and I do not think that he ever allowed himself to forget this for even a moment the whole time he was with them. With Skip, another young lieutenant attached to the company, Dave was able to loosen the knot of responsibility a little; he could relax and be himself, young, even unsure.

I was sorry for Dave when he wrote in late August that Skip had been transferred. I can see now that Skip's leaving was just one more little piece in the pattern of loss that eventually became the great design of Dave's life in Vietnam. As men at war do, Dave formed deep friendships very quickly then. And as happens in time of war, these friendships were lost, through natural rotation, medical evacuation, or unnatural death. I can only imagine the pain of these constant losses. And I can only guess at what deep, peculiarly human need drove my husband and the others like him to continue loving one another in the face of the almost certain knowledge that no friendship stood any real chance at a long life.

After Skip left the company, Dave never mentioned him again.

And my bed was like a grave
And his ghost was lying there.
And my heart was sick with care.

— Alun Lewis, "Song"

Twenty-Four

MEANWHILE, we waiting wives clung to
patterns. When their husbands left for Vietnam — within
weeks after Sam and Dave had gone over — Bonnie,
Libby, Leah, and Diane had all gone home. And like them
I went home, too, flying to Fresno with Jeannie in early
September. We were not weak women — time would
prove that — but separated from our husbands and from
one another, there was really no other place for us to go.
Our husbands had no stateside base where we could live
together, support one another, and be supported by a
system. We had been cut loose to manage as best we
could, left to find our own comfort and resources. So
we looked for comfort and refuge where we thought we
could safely and honorably find it. We went home.

Our college friends not connected to the military were
going on with lives that had little to do with ours. They
went to work, came home, watched the news, ate supper,

and went to bed — without much idea of the gut-wrench-
ing fear the war inspired in those of us who had loved
ones in it. Some Americans protested the war, some ig-
nored it, some worried in an abstract way about it, some
were so upset by the constant replaying of war scenes on
the news, they turned their TVs off in disgust. But I think
you had to have someone there to feel real home-front
terror. I felt it, and it seemed all the more terrible to me
because those of us waiting suffered it behind closed
doors, on the life-as-usual streets of Hometown, USA.

In the familiar living rooms of our recent girlhoods,
reading our letters from Vietnam and watching the
nightly news, we wives found ourselves immersed in the
world of war and some of its accompanying horror. It had
been a distant war only a few months ago at Quantico,
but now our men had gone to join it, and so it gathered
force every day, moved closer, until a land thousands of
miles away, a land of jungles and rice paddies we would
never see, became as loathsome to us as if it had been in
some more direct way our own awful fate.

The days had dragged by so painfully, each one marked
off with a black *X* in the small pocket diary I always
carried, that it seemed impossible that fall had arrived.
The summer, a whole season, was gone — and with it,
Sam. Yet all around me the world went on as usual. As
odd as it seems, I felt as though I were the only person
who knew how much had really changed, the only person who knew that nothing would ever be the same
again. I watched life go on as though I were looking
through plate glass showcases in a living museum.

I looked for comfort in another pattern, too. Every fall
I could remember had meant the beginning of a school
year for me, and the fall of 1967 was no different in at
least that one respect. I planned to enroll at Fresno State
College.

Bonnie, Libby, and Diane had taken their own apart-

ments in their respective hometowns, but Leah and I both
decided to live with our families. We had small babies,
and, speaking for myself, I welcomed the help my parents
offered so I could go to school. My father wanted to arrange his teaching schedule so he could watch Jeannie
while I was in class, and since my parents lived only a
few blocks from the campus, the commute would be easy.

The short walk to campus was a pleasant one through
the middle-class tract houses of my parents' neighborhood. Fresno is a flat town with a core of old buildings
and houses and parks with wide, thick-trunked trees.
Newer subdivisions spread out into what used to be fig
orchards and vineyards beyond this center. My parents
lived in one of the developments to the northeast of the
city, a subdivision only five or six years old at the time,
whose trees were spindly, and whose shrubs struggled to
establish themselves in spite of the heat.

The campus was new, too, and nothing could have
been more different from the massive brick buildings surrounded by ancient and huge firs and oaks at Washington
State than the stark, modern buildings of Fresno State
and the flat, bare lawns in front of them.

Because Fresno was home, I expected that I would find
solace there — help with the heavy, awkward burdens I
had picked up since I had last lived there in the summer
of 1966. After all, it had been just a little over a year, not
quite thirteen months, since my wedding day.

What I hoped for, in the bottom of my heart, was not
perfect understanding or sympathy. My parents tried, in
their way. They were as opposed to the war as ever, and
not shy about saying so, but when the mail came with a
letter from Dave in it, my father stopped whatever he was
doing and came to ask what I had heard. My mother
had started to send him packages of fruit and candy and
whatever else he expressed a desire or need for.

I not only hoped for a truce at home, I hoped that the modern buildings and the wide lawns of the small state campus in Fresno would offer me a more interesting, friendlier place to wait than the indifferent, almost out-of-touch neighborhood and the life-as-usual social gatherings in Tacoma. Fresno State was still a quiet campus then, a peaceful campus, especially if you compared it to campuses like Berkeley. Every once in a while, someone would post an antiwar sign of some kind; and the peace symbol, formerly the anti–nuclear bomb symbol, appeared here and there, too. There were small, sporadic rallies, ripples from the larger waves being made on the larger campuses in the nation. But the violent, aggressive disruptions that in time became part of the peace movement had not yet come to the valley.

The first week of school — registration and settling into the routine — gave me hope. My father and I managed to coordinate our schedules so that he could baby-sit Jeannie. She was his first grandchild, and they adored each other, so I felt good about leaving her with him. The time they spent together seemed good for both of them; I had never seen my father so happy. And I know now that Dave's stock skyrocketed when my parents had to admit that Dave was partly responsible for the perfect creature that was their granddaughter.

It was wonderful to me that on campus I looked like just another graduate student. I dressed like the others, was about the same age as the others; some were married like me, and some even had children. I ran into people from my classes in the bookstore that first week, and we talked about the professors and the prices of the textbooks — everyday things.

I was very happy then. The sad summer in Tacoma, I thought, had only been the unhappy result of terrible coincidences: Sam's death, Dave's wounding, the heat, and my pregnancy. No wonder, I told myself, that I had felt so isolated then. I had become a mother, was afraid of being widowed, and was grieving — all at the same time. I became convinced that the summer had been unusual, just a freakish monster of a summer.

Until that summer, my life had been full of friendships and pleasant work and school relationships, easily made and long-lasting. It would continue that way now. And the waiting would be so much easier. I was home, at school, in the heart of my old life.

After class one day toward the beginning of the second week of classes, I sat with two other women from my history class at a small table on the outside terrace of the student union. The weather was gently warm; the sun that had scorched the campus the day before was tempered now by a faint breeze, one of the first signs that fall was coming in the San Joaquin Valley. The three of us had just gone over some class notes and were drinking coffee and talking about general things, when one of the women, the older one in the picture in my memory — though now I know she was very young — said, "And what about your husband? What does he do?" Putting my cup down, I said, "He's in the Marines. In Vietnam."

The woman said simply, "Why?"

"Excuse me?" I said.

"Why? Why is he in Vietnam?"

"Because he's a Marine, and that's where they sent him."

"And can you tell me why anyone would want to be a Marine?" she said. "I will never understand if I live to be a very old lady why anyone would want to do that." She lowered her eyes, arranged her face into a tight mask of disgust, and raised her cup to her lips. I couldn't think of a thing to say that would answer her.

After that I sat by myself, away from the student union, usually on the rim of the fountain near the campus bookstore. If I had to stay on campus late, I packed a lunch and ate it as I sat on the lawn or on a bench by the tennis courts. By October it seemed the country would explode in one place or another, so heated had antiwar feelings become. The march on the Pentagon was looming straight ahead, and everybody, it seemed to me — everybody but me — was headed in that direction, if only in heart and mind.

The war was getting worse, too. Over the summer, the number of Marine casualties in Vietnam had exceeded the total number of Marines killed in the entire Korean War. Since July, we had been seeing news clips of the fierce fighting of the Marines at Con Thien. I grew more tense at school and at home both.

And there was no one to talk to.

Even though I was so much like the other graduate students in so many ways, especially the married women with children, our thoughts and feelings ran in different directions. It wasn't just the so-called rightness or wrongness of the war in Vietnam; it was the circumstances of our lives. They had lives grounded in the here and now, and they were tied realistically, or so they thought then, to a future. They were living, sure of what they were and where they were going. They had staked out their claims for life. A degree on this corner. A job on that corner. I was only marking time in a no-man's-land, certain of nothing. That was an important difference between me and the others. Not all the difference, but it was enough difference to really matter.

Nothing but hearing from my Quantico friends connected me to the reality that was my life. Like most young people, I loved to listen to popular music on the radio, but there were no songs in 1967 that applied to me, no love songs for war brides that year. For the first time since my first preteen crush, there was no background music to my emotions. No war songs fit. The poetic and elegiac

"Where Have All the Flowers Gone" didn't have the hope, melancholy as it may seem, of WW II's "I'll Be Seeing You"; and I needed hope.

It was truly a make-do home front for families during the Vietnam War. In that spirit, I mentally adapted songs, listening to those parts that seemed to me somehow to fit. I liked the theme from *The Umbrellas of Cherbourg*, the part that said: "If it takes forever I will wait for you, For a thousand summers I will wait for you." And I had an old Sinatra 45-rpm record of "Softly, As I Leave You" that I played over and over. But my favorite was "I Say a Little Prayer":

> *The moment I wake up,*
> *Before I put on my makeup,*
> *I say a little prayer for you.*
> *While combing my hair now*
> *And wond'ring what dress to wear now*
> *I say a little prayer for you. . . .*
> *To live without you would only*
> *Mean heartbreak for me.*

Whenever I heard that song on the radio, I sang along, though I knew the song was about a woman separated from her lover by feelings, not by water and war and seventeen hours — or more — of black, meaningless time.

My morale was lifted in the middle of all this unexpectedly, and by a stranger. One day toward the end of September, a letter arrived for me postmarked Washington, DC. The name on the return label was "Kitty Bradley." The letter was dated September 13, 1967, and it said:

Dear Mrs. Novak,

General Bradley and I returned last week from Vietnam where we had the pleasure of meeting your husband.

I know that a letter will not fill the void of your husband's absence, but I thought it might help you to know that when my husband and I met Lieutenant Novak on August 22nd he looked fine and seemed cheerful and proud of the teamwork he and his unit share.

I want you to know what a privilege it was for General Bradley and me to visit with your husband. He wanted me to tell you that he loves you and Jeannie and he'll see you soon.

We also want you to know how much we hope that your husband and all the boys over there come home to us safe and soon.

Sincerely,
Kitty Bradley
Mrs. Omar Bradley

Mrs. Bradley was a stranger to me, but she knew what to say to a war wife. Her letter is still a shining page in my album of mementos from those dark days.

Twenty-Five

BOB AABY had been in Vietnam since the
first of June. By the first of September, he and Dave had
managed to get together for a few hours somewhere south
of Da Nang. "It was great seeing him again," Dave wrote,
". . . the best thing that's happened over here so far. We
talked on into the night."

September dragged on hot and dry in Fresno. Because
the vineyards were ready for harvest, they were no longer
irrigated, and the earth dried and cracked like ancient
crockery. In Vietnam, the rains had started. It was, according to Dave, raining every afternoon for about two
hours — horrible, drenching, dispiriting rains. The men
trudged about in the mud with the water streaming over
the edge of their helmets, or huddled under their ponchos
in futile attempts to stay even remotely dry. "The monsoons," Dave wrote, "will come in October or November.

The men say that's really wet. As far as I'm concerned, this is wet and gloomy enough."

Bonnie, Libby, Diane, and I laughed on the phone about the constant complaining we heard about the weather in our husbands' letters home. Ken particularly hated the rains. Libby said he complained all the time about wet feet, and he wanted more socks. He had written to her that if you had dry socks, you could at least feel a little dry yourself. Dave never mentioned needing socks, but I sent some anyway. If Ken needed them, I figured Dave must, too.

Melinda and Scott were still in California, where Scott had been assigned to a unit not yet called to Vietnam. Melinda wrote and called and comforted me with her every word, written and spoken. She dreaded Scott's leaving, but did not dwell on it much. Scott wrote me twice. He mailed the letters from his base office, and he asked me to answer him there. He wrote that he was worried about Dave, that he did not like the waiting to "go over," that he was thinking about asking for a transfer to one of the outfits already "in country." But mostly his letters were about Melinda. Would I be sure to write to her and make sure she was OK when he did go?

"Of course," I answered. "But don't worry — she'll be fine."

The mail, the telephone, and my daughter were now the central features of my existence. Jeannie was only two months old, but she added to my life in ways I never thought possible. She was her father's legacy, yes, with his dark eyes and hair. But she was herself, too, from the moment I first held her. Whatever else I would ever be, wife or widow, I was her mother, and she needed me to be that, competently and wholeheartedly.

I did not completely give up trying to make a social life, though. It seemed too much to ask of myself that I rely solely on letters, phone calls, and a baby for human companionship. That's why, when a friendly female voice called me on the phone one day, my heart gave a little leap of excitement. "Your college chapter of Chi Omega sent me your phone number," the voice said. "They thought you might want to get involved." The Fresno chapter of the alumnae club of my old sorority had found me.

I had never been a "good" member of the sorority. It wasn't only that I didn't like the rules; I thought some of the principles and practices were elitist and unfair. It troubled me to see girls hurt over rush, the method used for selecting members. By my senior year I had begun to go my own way, and though I don't think I ever embarrassed the house, I know that several times I came close to it. And I had made a vow that I would never, ever be active in the sorority after graduation. The "alums" seemed sometimes to be the worst of all, snotty and dictatorial.

But now, in Fresno, looking for something to belong to, I reconsidered. And I remembered with some nostalgia the friends I had made in the Chi O house, the sing-alongs, the long games of bridge in the smoking room. It was probably worth at least going to an alumnae meeting, I told myself. It might be nice to meet the local sisterhood.

The meeting I was invited to was held on a Tuesday night in mid-September, at seven in the evening. The address was in Fig Garden, the most exclusive section of Fresno in 1967. In fact, the house I parked in front of looked a lot like the mansions on fraternity row at WSU: large, made of brick, with a picture-perfect front lawn. But this was a private home. I had had some trouble finding the street — I was not familiar with the area — so when the hostess led me into the brightly lit living room full of pale-blue-velvet-and-brocade-upholstered French furniture, a large group of women, fifteen or twenty of them, was already there. They were mostly middle-aged women, sitting on the chairs and sofas, balancing coffee cups in their hands. Standing in the doorway, I was glad to spot three or four who looked younger than the rest, and one, a plump blond with a pageboy haircut, who, I guessed, was probably even near my own age. The hostess was a tiny, fine-boned woman with a very tanned and lined face that crinkled all over when she smiled. She held her arm around my waist — I felt like a giant next to her — and introduced me, "a sister from Chapter Beta Beta." Someone shifted on the sofa to make room for me, and I crossed the room, into the smiling faces, and slipped into the empty space. The meeting, which I had clearly interrupted, resumed.

Looking at me and still smiling all in crinkles, our hostess explained: "We were just in the middle of planning the next meeting — a barbecue for our husbands. We try to include the men every once in a while. You know, make a social time of it. Have fun. We hope you'll come and bring Mr. Novak."

I sat quietly through the preparations. No one asked me whether I was coming and bringing Mr. Novak. I held my breath hoping no one would. Who could tell how people felt about why he could not come? I had learned very well on the campus at Fresno State what to tell and what not to tell. I waited for the evening to end so that I could leave.

It was a long evening. I hated having to sit and listen to plans being made for ordering steaks, borrowing a badminton set, locating a horseshoe game, and at the same time remembering Dave's letters about the rain and the gloom and the loneliness. I hated being afraid someone would say something cruel about my husband, or about what he was doing, or simply about what he was. I had not only learned that it was dangerous to tell about Dave, I had learned that it hurt to hear him attacked. It hurt badly.

After the meeting of the Chi Omega Alumnae, Fresno Chapter — the first and last one I went to — the other wives from the Basic School platoon became more and more important to me. I tried to forget about finding a place in the outside world and depended only on those other wives. How comforting it was, how peaceful, not to have to explain, not to have to hide anything.

I depended on Bonnie in particular, for she was the one who made sure we all stayed in touch with one another. She even told me once that I should "be sure to write to Sam's mother; she likes to hear from his friends." She not only knew where all of us wives were and what we were doing, she seemed to know more than any of us what was happening to the men — where they were, and what assignments they had been given. Jon was a legal officer working with a good communication network, and he was able to keep track of our friends from the old platoon. Whatever he told Bonnie, she passed on.

That fall Bonnie, Libby, and I continued the exchange of phone calls and letters that had begun in the summer, only now they took on a pattern of patient regularity. I don't remember too much of what was in Bonnie's and Libby's letters — we shared important information in our phone calls. Only a very few of the letters have survived, but I do remember that all were chatty letters, girl talk, friendly connections.

Phone calls were a different matter altogether. Bonnie's calm, reassuring voice through the wire could make me feel everything was going to be fine. "Jon saw Dave last week," she told me in one call, "and he says he never saw a finer example of Marine manhood, or a dirtier one, either!" And we both laughed. Libby's singing accent brought her close through the miles. "Honey," she'd say, "I was just sitting here thinking about you, and I couldn't do another thing until I called." And I would think, *If we can just hang on, we'll be all right. I know we will.*

Diane and I talked on the phone only one time, when Dave was wounded; but we wrote regularly. Her letters, comforting to me as well as to her, were, predictably, almost always about her plans for the future. She wrote about furniture for the home she planned for Matt and her — "I'm going to buy Karastan rugs for my house," one of her letters began — and about the family she wanted so much: "I have to find a career that will allow me more time on the weekends so I can spend it with Matt and the children we'll have. Maybe library science is the solution."

Now and then, I heard from Leah, though not regularly. After Sam died, our connection seemed to die, too. Bonnie continued to keep in touch with her, though, and she kept me informed about Leah's life, about how she was doing, and about the baby. So there was among us all a steady passing back and forth of reassurance, hope, understanding, and, in the end, love.

Those minutes on the phone with these women, those words shared on flowered and brightly colored stationery with my companions in isolation, turned out to be some of the sweetest moments I had that fall and winter; now they remain some of my sweetest memories. The voices of those other wives over the telephone wires and their words in ink on paper were the only real homes I had while Dave was away.

Perhaps I don't speak for the others, the other wives who waited, when I say we were almost unbearably lonely, and that we were always frightened, afraid of what might happen to our men. But I think I speak for most of us. The connections between us helped; I clung to them. But sometimes they brought bad news. The cost of comfort was the price of shared grief.

About the third week of September — it must have been the twenty-third or the twenty-fourth — Bonnie

called. She was not crying. Bonnie never cried, that I
knew of, but her voice that day was thick and sad. She
called to tell me that Dennie Donald Peterson — sweet,
quiet Dennie — had been killed in combat on September
6 in a place called Quang Tin. A few days later, one of
Dave's letters, this one dated September 21, brought me
the same terrible news. "Dennie was killed over here,"
he wrote. "He was a hero, and they're putting him up for
a medal."

Dennie received the Navy Cross. In the spirit of what
he was, a Marine, he earned it most appropriately — for,
among other actions, saving the lives of his fellow Marines. Even now when I read his citation, I remember the
slight, shy boy who always — so much like Dave —
seemed to be in the background. I wish I had talked to
him more, had known him better.

> "For extraordinary heroism," the citation reads,
> while serving as Artillery Forward Observer with the
> Second Battalion, Eleventh Marines and attached to
> Company I, Third Battalion, Fifth Marines, First Marine
> Division (Reinforced), in Quang Tin Province, Republic of
> Vietnam. On 6 September 1967, during Operation SWIFT,
> the advance of Company I was halted by devastating au-
> tomatic weapons fire from a massed, entrenched North
> Vietnamese Army force. Fearlessly exposing himself to en-
> emy fire, Second Lieutenant Peterson moved over the fire-
> swept terrain to a position from which he could bring
> supporting arms to bear on the determined enemy force.
> Courageously, he moved from one position to another to
> gain a better vantage point to adjust his fires. Fearing for
> the life of his radio operator, he took the radio, put it on
> his back, and moved into contested ground beyond the
> company perimeter to a position where he could better
> observe and continue to direct and adjust artillery. His
> prompt and accurate fires immediately inflicted heavy cas-

ualties on the enemy. Although he was drawing fire from
at least five enemy automatic weapons and was painfully
wounded, he remained in his unfavorable position for
two hours adjusting artillery. After darkness fell and the
enemy was soundly repulsed, he crawled back to his own
lines, and despite his own wounds and the heavy volume
of fire, assisted another wounded Marine into the pe-
rimeter. After being treated and with temporary discon-
tinuation of artillery fires, Second Lieutenant Peterson
organized groups of Marines and led them through the
enemy lines on three occasions recovering casualties and
carrying them to protected areas in the company area.
Although he was wounded on four separate occasions, he
disregarded his painful wounds and continued to direct
and coordinate fire and aid wounded Marines at great
personal risk. While being treated for his wounds, he was
hit by a burst of automatic weapons fire and mortally
wounded.

His "calm courage," the citation continues, his "in-
trepid fighting spirit and dynamic leadership," inspired
"all who observed him."

They still inspire me. Dennie was a hero, is still one of
my personal heroes. All of us who knew him at Quantico
were affected by his death — perhaps most of all Ken,
who vowed, when he heard about Dennie's death, "to
make someone pay, if it's the last thing I do."

Dennie had been in Vietnam only five weeks when he
was killed. When I heard he was dead, it had been almost
one year since I had first met him at the Marine Corps
Birthday Ball. Meanwhile, at Quantico another class of
fresh lieutenants was gearing up to begin the Basic
School.

In Fresno, life went on, of course. By the end of September, I had adjusted to school, adjusted to the idea that
I would simply go to classes, study, and be alone, both

on the campus and in the town, too. I wish now I had put
an ad in the *Fresno Bee*: "Wanted: Other military wives to
talk to." There must have been others like me in a town
of 150,000. I couldn't have been the only one — though
that's what it felt like.

But if there were other waiting wives, as surely there
were, they were not obvious. Like me, they must have
decided to keep to themselves. In Vietnam, Dave's unit
moved — from the area around Da Nang to Quang Tri
Province — and the really bad rains, the long-dreaded
monsoons, had finally come. "It rains all the time," Dave
wrote. "We can't sleep because of the rain, we can't eat
hot meals because of the rain, it's even hard to write
letters because of the rain. But we're supposed to get a
tent soon."

Our needs had been reduced to the basics: for me, the
courage to keep on going; for Dave, a tent. Our wants —
besides the obvious one of Dave's safety — were also
simple: someone to talk to for me, a platoon for him.
What a strange world it was becoming.

On the thirteenth of October, a Friday, Dave wrote that
he had decided he wanted to stay in a foxhole all day,
even one filled with mud. By the fifteenth, he was resigned to never having a platoon again. "But I'll never
get over missing mine," he wrote. Finally, on the seven-
teenth, good news: "We have a tent now — got it from
some doggies [Army infantrymen] for a fifth of whiskey.
Thank God — it rains all day and all night now."

In Fresno, bright, sunny fall days were interrupted only
rarely by misty drizzles. But once, I woke in the night to
the sound of a soft rain falling, dripping off the thick
leaves of the ivy that climbed by my bedroom window. I
was warm and dry and comfortable in a clean bed, and
Jeannie slept safely in her crib a few feet away. I awoke
and heard the rain, and I thought of Sam and Dennie,
who were now dead, and of Dave and the others over

there and all they lacked, and my chest ached so painfully I thought I knew what it must be like to have your heart break — not from loneliness, not even from loss, but from the feeling that some sort of horrible injustice was being commited, that things somehow were not fair.

And, strangely — it surprised me then — I did not blame the NVA or the Viet Cong; those were not my enemies. My enemies sat next to me in the classrooms at Fresno State; they passed me in the aisles of the stores downtown; perhaps they were even asleep in the houses of my own neighborhood. For the first time since Dave left, I cried.

But oh! the drag and dullness of my Self;
The turning seasons wither in my head;
All this slowness, all this hardness,
The nearness that is waiting in my bed.

— Alun Lewis, "Song"

Twenty-Six

I STILL DON'T KNOW for sure what the initials "R&R" stand for. I have been told that they stand for "rest and recreation." I have also read that they stand for "rest and recuperation," "rest and relaxation," even "Romeo and Romeo." Whatever they are intended to represent, R&R is an astonishing thing — a brief furlough from the war zone. During the time of the Vietnam War, R&R itself was not a new concept, but as far as I know, the widespread, militarily approved practice of men at war meeting their wives and girlfriends on their leaves was new to the United States military in this strange conflict. Other things were different in this war, too. The men, for example, as a rule did not go to Vietnam in units, as they had done in past wars. They boarded commercial airlines as individuals to fly to the war in air-conditioned comfort, and if they were lucky enough to come home alive and in fairly good shape, they flew home again, as individuals, on the same kind of commercial flight they had flown on to get to Vietnam.

I found it odd also that the Marines not only arrived in Vietnam "alone," they often hitchhiked on passing motor transports, still weaponless, to get to their units. They stayed thirteen months, then often hitchhiked back to Da Nang to catch a flight home.

And then sometime about halfway through this tour of duty, these men were flown, courtesy of the United States government, to the Pacific paradise of their choice — such places as Hawaii, Bangkok, and Singapore. Most of the married men chose to meet their wives in Hawaii. Though Dave wrote once about the possibility of spending his leave in Australia, we settled on Hawaii in the end. I think the idea of being "home" in the USA — even as far away as that bit of home was from anything Dave was familiar with — was too appealing for him to resist.

We would have five days for R&R, and by the first of October, Dave's letters had become little more than lists of plans for things to do and lists of things to bring. He would not know until about two weeks beforehand when his leave would be, but I was determined to be more than ready, whenever it was going to be.

I talked to my professors at school, and we planned the extra work I would do to make up for the week of classes I would miss. I wrote away to Hawaii for travel brochures, hotel prices, and information from rental-car agencies, and I passed this information on to Dave. At the end of almost three weeks of letter exchanges, we managed to agree on a hotel. A lot of the hotels offered special rates to servicemen on R&R, and one of these was a bright, tall hotel on Waikiki overlooking the Kahanamoku Beach Lagoon. It was called the Ilikai.

In the pictures in its brochure, the Ilikai gleamed white above creamy sands, by sparkling, blue water, under a sunny, cloudless sky. It was one of the more expensive hotels, but we chose it anyway. We had never had a real honeymoon. We might never get the chance again. We would now. Dave's airplane ticket was paid for by the military. Mine wasn't. This was not a problem. The airlines offered wives a special round-trip fare of $165 from the West Coast. And Dave's monthly allowance, including combat pay ($65) and living allowance ($168), was $607. Our regular deductions were minor: the government took $40 a month for Dave's food (officers paid for their own rations in the field), $2 for life insurance, $6 for a savings bond, and $15 for FICA. Our only bills above normal living expenses were the car payments and insurance, my books and tuition, and Dave's cigars — ordered from Tampa, Florida, mailed to Vietnam, and billed to me. We managed well.

Still, I saved carefully for the trip — for the hotel, the food, and, of course, the entertainment. I used to wonder how enlisted men, privates and corporals, managed an R&R on their salaries. I know now that for from $3 to $7 per night per person, depending on rank, servicemen and their families could stay at Kilauea Military Camp on the island of Hawaii, where meals and tours were included in the daily rate. Or for $2 a night, couples could stay in rooms at the R&R Center. Even so, the cost of the airfare must have made financing R&R difficult, if not impossible, for most wives of enlisted men. Because we could manage it, though, we decided on a break-the-bank holiday.

As always, the paradoxes of the time played their familiar roles. In the evenings, I wrote to Dave, pored over the sunny Hawaiian brochures, and watched the war on the news. I sat on the floor close to the TV so I could see the faces of the men as the camera zoomed in for its close-ups. Perhaps one would be ours; I was always hopeful one of the men interviewed would be. I was always afraid I would recognize one of the wounded. They did not show the dead Americans unless they were zipped up in body bags. But sometimes the camera followed the jagged path of the litter bearers rushing their burden to a waiting chopper. I stared hard at the dirty, anguished faces, relieved not to see anyone I knew. But it hurt to know that someone else watching TV that night probably would.

During October of 1967, while I planned a Hawaiian holiday, while more and more students joined the demonstrations, the strikes, and the marches at home, the casualty lists from the fields of combat in Vietnam grew longer. In Washington, DC, on Saturday, October 21, Jerry Rubin, Abbie Hoffman, and David Dellinger, leaders of what came to be called the New Left, spoke to thousands of students — more than thirty-five thousand, in fact.

Someone read a message of solidarity from North Vietnam. Young men burned their draft cards; young women put flowers in the rifle barrels of the National Guardsmen patrolling the crowds. Both men and women spat on, taunted, and kicked the soldiers in the front lines. The antiwar, antisoldier feeling spawned on the Washington Mall that Saturday afternoon spread even as far as the small campus at Fresno State College. Calm, comfortable, familiar academe, to which I had looked for a place to "hide," became more and more an alien environment. "Polite" but nevertheless hurtful comments were gradually replaced by openly confrontational and rude remarks. "Baby killer" became another name for a Vietnam veteran.

The truce at home with my mother and father made life there slightly more comfortable. But I had known for some time that my parents thought Dave was a fool, and though they did not say so anymore, I also knew they thought he might be an immoral fool, at that. In contrast to the aggression I felt at school and the lack of support for Dave I felt at home, the bland, disinterested world of

Tacoma, which I had found so wanting only a few weeks before, now seemed attractive and benign. I decided to return to it at the end of the semester. I was tired and heartsick, and I only wanted someplace to wait quietly.

Despite the kind and unkind advice, the orders and threats from my various doctors, I had gained about forty pounds during my pregnancy. This was thought to be a considerable weight gain then, too big by far. Because of all the dire warnings about the consequences of the extra pounds, I was relieved that I was able to lose them easily. In the weeks following Jeannie's birth, they simply dropped off. Within six weeks, they were all gone. But my muscle tone was not at all what I remembered it had been, and since I wanted to look good — even wonderful, if possible — for R&R, I decided to join an evening exercise class. I found one advertised on a bulletin board at the supermarket, called the number on the index card, and signed up.

The class was held in the instructor's converted garage. The room was a bare and bleak place whose studs still showed, but it was clean, and a matlike carpet covered the middle of the cement floor. We were about a half-dozen or so women in stretch pants and loose tops, a small group for the double-garage: two spry grandmothers, a couple of middle-aged matrons, and two of us young women. Behind us, against the back wall, a portable electric heater buzzed and glowed off and on.

We lined up in front of the closed garage doors facing our very shapely, very enthusiastic leader. I don't remember her name, or much about her, except that she wore very bright red lipstick and a short, blond hairstyle. And I remember the muscles in her thighs. I wasn't sure I wanted muscles like those. We went through our paces; in that pre-aerobic-exercise era, I think they were just simple calisthenics — sit-ups, push-ups, jumping jacks. I know I had been able to do everything effortlessly the year before, and it dismayed me that I was now so weak. At the end of about thirty minutes, we ran slowly in place for a few minutes, and then we were told to walk around the room and "cool down." We were given small paper cups of orange juice.

I sat down with mine in a steel chair next to the other girl in the group. She was dressed sort of like a harlequin doll, all in white and black. Her pants were black, her sweatshirt white. Her shoes were black, her socks were white. Her hair was black, shiny, and short. It fit her head like a bathing cap. Her pale face looked almost empty except for her dark eyebrows. Her name was Karen, and she told me she was a secretary in a law office in downtown Fresno. I saw that she wore a gold wedding band welded to a gold-and-diamond engagement ring, and she was out alone. Good, I thought. She has a nonthreatened, nonpossessive husband. And she was out at night. Even better. That meant she was probably independent, unafraid.

Best of all, Karen was not a student, probably had not even gone to college, and so was not likely to be involved in antiwar activity — or even to care about the war. I saw all of this as very hopeful, and in a split second my imagination had designed our friendship: we would meet at exercise class, talk afterward about general things. Maybe on a Sunday afternoon we would go to a movie, or on a Saturday morning take a walk together, stopping at some café along the way for a cup of coffee.

"How many calories in the juice, do you think?"

"Excuse me?" I said. Then I saw the paper cup Karen had lifted toward me. "Oh," I said, laughing. "I don't think many. Not bad ones, anyway. No fat."

"Good," she said.

We talked about the class for a few minutes, about how we wanted to look in bathing suits the next summer. Very small talk, but still it was nice. And I was thrilled when she said, after a while, "Is there any chance I could hitch a ride home with you? I don't live far — in fact, I walked here."

Out in front of our instructor's house, standing in the dark on the gravel driveway, Karen pointed toward Dave's Camaro parked under a streetlight in the road. "Is that yours?" she asked.

"Yes, I said. "I mean, it's in my name, too, but I guess it's really my husband's. At least it's his pride and joy."

"That insignia," she said, stopping on her way to the passenger side to stare at the small, round decal on the back window. "It's the Marine Corps'. Does that mean your husband's a Marine?"

My mouth went dry, but I took a deep breath, swallowed, and said, "Yes." I hoped she wouldn't be mean, that she would just say she had decided to walk after all.

My husband's a Marine, too," she said. "He's over there now, and I can't tell you how much I've wanted someone to talk to." She looked at me across the top of the car roof. "Someone who would understand what I'm going through."

I began to breathe normally again, and I smiled. "How about a cup of zero-calorie coffee before I take you home?" I said quietly. It was hard not to shout for joy, I was so happy. Another Marine wife!

We drove down Blackstone Avenue toward Shaw, an intersection near her house and mine, too, where I knew there was a restaurant with a coffee shop. Blackstone was busy and bright, not just from all the headlights, but from very powerful overhead streetlights, too. The traffic was slow for such a busy street, because of the stoplights at almost every block, and because the teenagers liked to rove up and down it in their cars looking at one another. Cruising, they called it. I'd done it myself only a few years before.

"When is your husband due back?" I asked.

Karen had taken a pack of cigarettes from her purse and was lighting one. "Soon," she said. She rolled her window down and exhaled toward it. Then she added, "He's coming home in February."

"You've been on R&R, then," I said.

"Yes," Karen said, "I have."

"Boy, do I ever have a list of things to ask you. For one thing, what do you say to someone you haven't seen in months and who's been through what the guys over there have?" We were stuck at another light, and Karen was looking at me.

"I never thought about it," she said. She was quiet for a moment. "The truth is," she said finally, "I just wanted to get through it. R&R, I mean. Just get through the five days without hurting Kit — that's my husband — without hurting him." The car moved on through the traffic. The music and calling out from the other cars made it hard to hear.

"Hurting him?" I said. I thought I hadn't heard right.

"Look," Karen said. "I've got to tell you something." She stubbed her cigarette out in the car's ashtray. "You must know how it is. I know you must. It's so lonely, and I never asked for this."

We were pulling into the parking lot of the restaurant. The place was called Bob's Big Boy, I think. Out front there was a huge plaster statue of a freckled, fat boy wearing checkered overalls and holding a hamburger. I wasn't saying anything, but Karen didn't seem to notice. She didn't seem to need anything but what she had told me she needed — someone to talk to. Or, to be more precise, someone to listen.

"Kit left for Vietnam one year to the day after we got married, on our first wedding anniversary. That was in January. In February I got a valentine from someone at work, a guy I'd joked around with before I married Kit,

but no one serious. It was a cute valentine, not romantic — a funny card, really. But after that we had coffee a
few times, and then lunch. Somehow things got serious.
And I wasn't lonely anymore. Just guilty."

We had pulled into a space in the parking lot next to
the cement base of the giant fat boy, and I sat there with
my hands on the steering wheel, watching people getting
in and out of cars and going in and out of the glass doors
of the restaurant. I didn't like listening, and I wasn't glad
anymore that I had found another wife.

"I know it sounds horrible," Karen said. "But I can
stand the guilt. I can go on with that. But the loneliness
made life impossible. Sometimes I couldn't even leave my
bedroom. I'd lie on my bed and hold Kit's picture and
cry. I thought sometimes I would die from the loneliness.
Then Stan came along, and I'm not lonely anymore." She
looked at me. "But even so I need someone to share it
all with, someone who understands."

I knew without thinking about it that I wasn't the one.
I don't know even now why that was so. Maybe instinc-
tively I was afraid of Karen's weakness, or maybe I was
angry. Maybe I hurt for Kit. Whatever it was, it came to
me without warning and without my wanting it to, and
it made me cruel. I started the car's engine again, and
turned the headlights back on. "Look, Karen," I said, "I
just remembered my baby'll be waking up for her ten-
o'clock bottle pretty soon, and my parents have to get up
early for work in the morning. I'd better not take time for
coffee after all." I backed the car out of the crowded row.

I remember that a dark look crossed her face, and she
stopped smiling. I was sorry, because I knew I had hurt
her. "Sure," she said. Then, more quietly and in a different voice, "I'll bet having a baby helps." And we changed
the subject to Jeannie.

I dropped Karen off in front of her mother's house, at
the end of a long drive that was the only opening I could

see in a tall, dense bank of shrubbery lining the sidewalk. She opened the door on her side, but before she got out, she said, "See you next week?"

I said I would.

But I didn't go back to the exercise class. The last time I saw Karen she was walking toward her mother's house, up the long driveway. Her white sweatshirt was all I could see of her in the dark. I have never been able to forget her, or her husband, and I have wondered ever since what happened to them both.

It was sweet to rest, forget oneself,
unchain the body from reality
as from dusty armour,
bed voluptuously. . . .

— Ernst Stadler, "Decampment"

Twenty-Seven

THE EXACT DATES of Dave's R&R turned out to be, according to his orders, "11 Nov 1967 to 17 Nov 1967." His flight from Vietnam was due in Hawaii sometime in the afternoon of November 11. He was supposed to be back at the Honolulu International Airport at 7:30 AM on November 17. We would have five days and six nights together.

I made the reservations we had discussed in our letters — at the Ilikai Hotel, for the nights of November 10 through 18. Our room rate was $18 a night. I also wrote to Budget Rent-a-Car and reserved a Datsun sports car. I made my plane reservations with United Airlines. When I went to apply for the reduced fare, I was given a brochure that admonished that the special rates applied "only to the wives of military personnel in Viet Nam on R&R leave to Hawaii."

I received two copies of Dave's orders — "Permissive

Travel Orders for Out-of-Country R&R" — one copy to give to the airlines when I purchased my ticket, the other to be "retained in [my] possession": "During actual travel, the traveler must have this form and ID card in her possession." No one ever asked me for the form, or even to look at it, but I kept it. I still have it.

Another piece of paper I still have is my "list of things to take on R&R." Under the heading "Dave," I find written: "cowboy boots, pair pants, two shirts, 3 pairs socks, 3 underwear, shaving lotion." The list under "Me" is longer. There are ten items here — nightgowns, curlers, nylons, perfume among them. Jeannie's list includes twenty items — among them, dresses, diapers, wrapping blankets, bottles, baby powder, and diaper liners (this was all before disposable diapers became the norm).

Dave and I had discussed in our letters whether or not I should bring the baby to Hawaii. In a letter written October 23, he told me, "I'll have a hard enough time going back after seeing you — seeing her would make it impossible." It was a difficult decision either way. Dave and I had been married only two months before I became pregnant, and he had left for Vietnam before the baby was born. We had had very little time together, alone, to get to know and enjoy each other. We needed that kind of time, just the two of us. Every marriage needs it. And Dave, I knew, would also have special needs now, needs neither he nor I could articulate, but which we were somehow aware of. He would need peace, and affection, and quiet care.

I knew these things, and I knew also that a baby would interfere and interrupt and make everything harder than it would be otherwise. But looking beyond the moment as thoughtfully and as realistically as I could, I saw the possibility of a lost chance. A precious lost opportunity. The time in Hawaii might be the only time Dave would ever see his baby, hold her, know her. For him — and for her, too — it might be all there would be. Sam and his baby had not even had that much.

So at last, in spite of Dave's initial uncertainty, I decided to bring Jeannie with me. I wrote to the hotel, asking for a crib for the room and a list of reliable baby-sitters.

The US government and the Hawaii Visitors Bureau worked together in those days of R&Rs to make things convenient and pleasant for both the men and their wives. For one thing, they set up an R&R Center in Honolulu, and they provided transportation between the airport, the center, and many of the hotels; they also ran the guest house, and they provided information, advice, and practical help. The center sent Dave a gold card with the red silhouette of an ancient Hawaiian warrior king on it and, in black printing, the words "Aloha R&R Hawaii." On the back of the card were the dates and hours of his arrival and departure.

I spent November 10, 1967, the Marine Corps' birthday, my second as a Marine wife, in the hotel room on Waikiki Beach. The room was beautiful — on the seventh floor and overlooking the water. It was big, airy, and furnished with gold-brocade drapes, beige carpeting, and a light-wood bed and dresser. I unpacked, laying Dave's shirts and underwear in the drawers with my folded cotton blouses and the collection of silk and satin sleepwear I had brought. I hung my sundresses and his slacks side by side in the closet. I put my perfumes, lipstick, and my brush and comb on the dresser. A hotel worker delivered a crib to the room and set it up in a secluded alcove by the door, and I put Jeannie in it with her favorite toys, a stuffed dog I had bought for her and a cloth doll Dave had sent from Vietnam when she was born.

The wall facing the bed was mostly glass doors; they led out to a small balcony — a lanai, the manager told me when I checked in. After I put Jeannie to bed that evening, I ordered a sandwich and a glass of milk from room service. When they arrived, I took them outside to the lanai. I watched darkness fall, a beautiful sunset that I imagined would soon fall on Vietnam, too, and I hoped — in my usual small-prayer way — that Dave was safe. I toasted the Corps with the glass of milk.

It was impossible to sleep, of course, I tossed and turned, and actually looked forward to Jeannie's waking up for her two-o'clock bottle; I craved the company. When dawn came, I was exhausted, but excited and nervous. I prepared for the worst of the waiting.

Since the men had to be processed at the R&R Center, we wives did not meet our husbands at the airport. And Dave had told me, in no uncertain terms and in more than one letter, not to meet him at the center, where most of the wives waited for their husbands. I suppose he did not trust his emotions, or maybe he was not sure of mine. He was, and is, a man who cherishes privacy.

I resented being told to wait in the hotel room: precious minutes when I could be with him would be lost while he traveled from the center to the Ilikai. But I did as he asked. I had thought of R&R from the beginning as more for Dave than for me. I waited in the room and fixed my hair and makeup and fussed over my clothes and over Jeannie until both of us were frazzled. I paced the room and stepped in and out of the glass doors.

Dave had written that he thought he would get to the hotel room "sometime after noon." His plane was due in at twelve. Neither of us could even guess how long it would take for him to be brought to the R&R Center, processed, then taken on to the hotel. So I worried and paced and tormented myself with thoughts of great and tragic ironies: a fatal rocket at Da Nang, an airplane crash over the eastern Pacific, a fiery bus accident on an island road.

And then, at about one-thirty, there was a soft knock on the door. I opened it and there Dave stood in the hallway, his garrison hat in one hand, a small ditty bag in the other. Though it was November, he was wearing summer tans. A sharp, musty, foreign odor drifted forward from where he stood.

"May I come in?" he said.

Inside the room, Dave tossed his hat on the bed, dropped his bag on the floor, and put his arms around me and kissed me. Nothing since has made me as happy as the feel of Dave's arms around me and Dave's face against mine that day in Hawaii. Then he turned to Jeannie's crib, where she lay on her back, wide-eyed, staring at the stranger with her mother.

Dave looked at me. "Is that the kid?" he said.

For a moment I thought Jeannie would cry. But suddenly her face opened in a smile, and she started waving her tiny arms and legs. Dave smiled back, and that was that.

Jeannie was tired. I gave her her pacifier and turned her on her tummy and patted her back. Dave hung over her crib with me. We both felt a little awkward, I think — so much had happened to us. It took the baby only a minute or two to fall fast asleep, and then Dave straightened up and headed for the bathroom. I followed him to the door and saw him unbuttoning his blouse with one hand and turning the water on in the bathtub, full force, at the same time with the other. I saw the bullet scars on his upper arm, just above the two thin scars I had made when I scratched him on his forearm. His scars were stark white against his sun-darkened skin.

He grinned at me. "I'm going to take a long, hot bath," he said. "I've been thinking about this for months." We both laughed, and I picked up his clothes from the floor as he dropped them. They held the foul odor I smelled at the door, thick with must and mildew and a sharp sourness I have never been able to identify. I remember it and have smelled it since, in the corner of the basement where his seabag now hangs from a rafter. It is the only smell of the war I know.

I put Dave's uniform in a plastic bag and placed it outside the door with a tag made out for the hotel laundry. Dave did soak in the tub, for almost an hour. I went to the lobby and bought him some cigars, and soon the bathroom was a fog of steam and cigar smoke, damp and warm. I sat on the toilet lid and we talked, small talk. How were my parents? His parents? His brother? What had I heard from Bonnie and Libby? How were Leah and her baby?

It seemed then, in those first minutes we had together in that steamy bathroom, that all I had ever wanted or ever would want was within my reach. Jeannie was asleep in her crib just outside the door. Dave was happy, relaxed, and, most important to me, safe — smoking his cigar, soaking in a hot tub, and talking to me about ordinary, everyday things. The topics could not have held any real interest to him — what must have been in his mind then? — but the subjects were our common ground. He came to where I was to meet me. I did not find our talk interesting, either. I only wanted to look at Dave, to touch him, to have him in the same room with me. I only cared that for five days and six nights I would know where he was, that he was alive.

I admire the young people we were then. We had come to R&R with very little left in common except a love that had not been very well nurtured, but instead strained beyond imagination, and a small daughter whose birth and being Dave knew little about. Our relationship, our marriage, our small family — all had been defined and maintained through the mail. What Dave and I knew about each other — about the world of each other — when we met in Hawaii in November of 1967 was the total of those things we had chosen to tell on paper. I had not wanted to worry Dave about my troubles: how much

I worried about him, how fearful I had been about child-birth, how horrible I found my loneliness and isolation.

In the same spirit, but with so much more at stake, Dave had done everything he could to spare me the reali-ties of his world. So when at last we came together on R&R, we came as strangers, to meet someone we no longer really knew, who no longer knew us. Still, we honored our commitment, as generously and as gra-ciously as we could. We had nothing but faith and hope, and they made us more than we were, I think.

The rental-car company had delivered a small, gray Datsun to the hotel, and as soon as Jeannie was fed and changed and Dave was dressed in the clothes I had brought for him, we climbed into the car and drove off into the countryside. The weather, the sky, the water, the trees, the flowers — everything was as the posters and brochures had promised.

Dave loved having the baby with us. When we stopped to walk along a beach or in a park, he carried her cradled in his arms, taking his eyes from her face only long enough to see where he was going.

We were all three very tired that first night. But only Jeannie slept. Dave and I had 132 hours to be together, and sleep seemed such a waste of time. We held each other in the dark and talked softly. Dave had protected me from the war when he wrote, and holding me in bed that night he protected me when he spoke. We clung to each other, to feel flesh and bone, something real next to us where for months there had been only emptiness outlined in fear. Dave was real at last, but when we talked, what we kept from each other was the truth; our words skimmed over the surface of our life, ghostlike and hollow. But we talked on into the night, for the sheer pleasure of hearing each other's voice.

Toward morning, we made love. I know we both ex-pected a scene of pent-up passion, perhaps even looked forward to one. But instead it was a sweet, tender communion. We were both shy at first, uncomfortable with our intimacy, though that is strange to admit. My breasts were different from pregnancy, and I had episiotomy scars. Dave was thinner and his muscles had hardened; his skin was rough and he had infections, open sores, on his legs. And there were the new scars on his arm, the bullet scars.

Perhaps more significant than the physical changes were the emotional and psychological ones, though we did not acknowledge those then. I was a mother now. Dave must have felt the new tilt of the axis of my world. As for him, he had had the responsibility for men's lives. I had seen a boy off to war, and he had come back to me a warrior.

Youth is resilient, and it did not take us long to become joyful lovers again. It was embarrassing but not surprising when, the next morning, I could not find the black bikini panties to the short nightgown I had worn the night before. I looked under the bed, through the bedclothes, behind the nightstands. No luck. "Forget them," Dave said. "You don't need them, you know," and he laughed.

But my face burned at the thought of the chambermaid finding them, especially since they had to be someplace very unusual to be so thoroughly lost in that one room. So while Jeannie gurgled and laughed at us from the blanket where we had put her to play on the floor, we tore the bed apart, lifting the mattress off to one side, looking under the springs, taking the pillowcases off the pillows. We never found the panties, and if the maid did, she was too polite to let us know.

We went everywhere during those five days and six nights. In the daytime we took Jeannie with us — to Punchbowl Cemetery, where the poinsettias bloomed red and wild over the edges of the crater; to Pearl Harbor, where we did our Christmas shopping at the PX; to the USS *Arizona* war memorial, the Iolani Palace, Diamond Head, and Koko Beach.

At night the hotel sent us a baby-sitter — an elegant champagne blond in her midfifties, who wore beige and white evening dresses and large pieces of jewelry to her jobs in our room; she spent the evenings there writing letters and listening to classical music on her portable radio while Jeannie slept. Dave and I went to dinner and dancing, at the Beau Rivage Restaurant, the Canoe House, the Beef 'n Grog. During those outings, we talked a lot, but not about the war. Never about the war. One night, we went to see Don Ho. We drank sweet, good-tasting rum drinks from ceramic pineapples and real coco-nuts and watched the show. A woman sang "Soon It's Gonna Rain" and "It Must Be Him," and Don Ho told jokes and sang and played with his band.

We walked on the beach in front of the hotel that night, late, under a beautiful, blue-black heaven full of glowing stars. Dave said: "It's just like I thought. I don't want to go back, especially since I've seen the baby."

Sometimes during those five days, Dave grew quiet while drinking a Coke or smoking a cigar on the lanai, or when we went for a walk. There was nothing for me to do then but fall silent, too, and wait for him to find the resources from within to carry on. And he always did, though I cannot see how. The body can leave the war zone, but the mind doesn't abandon its post so easily. Most of Dave was still in Vietnam.

The father and husband in him tried to be all they could be for Jeannie and me. But the warrior in Dave, the strongest part of who he was in those days, was anxious and sad. The notions about adventure and glory had dis-appeared, evaporated into the ammonia-filled air of ex-ploded mines, into the dust of mortar rounds hitting their mark. What was left were the worry and the feelings of responsibility he got from his job, and the fear from the knowledge — the certain knowledge — of what waited for him back in the war zone.

The second leaving was far more painful than the first: it was, in fact, traumatic, and I am not over it yet.

At the Honolulu airport, at seven-thirty on the morning of November 17, a Friday, we were all — Jeannie, Dave, and I — waiting to leave Hawaii. At first I had thought it would be good to stay on at the Ilikai a day or so after Dave left. I had planned to leave Sunday morning, the nineteenth, which would have allowed me two days to enjoy the sun and the beaches with Jeannie. But I could not bear even the thought of being in the hotel room without my husband, so I changed my plans. My flight to California would leave less than an hour after Dave's to Da Nang. Dave checked in, and then the three of us sat in the waiting room of the airport — Jeannie in her little plastic carrier, Dave and I holding hands.

It was a civilized scene on the surface, but madness underneath. My stomach churned, and I thought I was going to be sick. I remember being dizzy, too. Against all that is sane, Dave was flying back to Vietnam, and I was going to see him off — again. It took everything I had to do it. I stood with Jeannie in my arms, still in her carrier. I stood behind a chain-link fence and saw the long, tan line of brave young men file onto the Pan American jetliner. I made myself watch each one step onto the portable stairs, and I tried to see each face. I asked God to bless each man, because I knew for certain that some were dead men, and perhaps among these, Dave.

Jeannie and I left Hawaii flying out over the Pacific; the ocean and the sky were many shades of blue in the brightness of the morning sun. I left a different person from the girl who had come to meet her husband. Going back, I was aware of a deep and unsettling fright that I attributed then to the flight, though I had never before been afraid in a plane.

On the ground again, I began to feel this fear often. My fear of flying became a nervousness about driving a car, an apprehension about riding in elevators and crossing busy streets. The list grew. The fear stayed the same: formless, nameless, overwhelming at times. And — oddly — its real cause went unrecognized for many years; I now know it was the fear of death, though not specifically Dave's death anymore. I had seen death in the face of each of those men climbing aboard that Pan American flight, and later, it seemed, I saw it everywhere.

Before Dave left for the war, I had seen death either as an abstraction — something that would happen in my life, but much later — or as an aberration, the result of unexpected, unusual accidents in other people's lives. Now, suddenly, death seemed the norm, the only reality I could count on in my world.

And in despair I bowed my head;
"There is no peace on earth," I said;
 "For hate is strong,
 And mocks the song
Of peace on earth, good-will to men!"

— Henry Wadsworth Longfellow,
"Christmas Bells"

Twenty-Eight

WHEN DAVE RETURNED to Vietnam from R&R, he was out of the field for good, at least technically speaking. Enlisted men often spent their entire tours in what could be considered, in that war without any real fronts, the front lines, but officers usually rotated to the rear after six months or so. The reason for this, supposedly, was to give every officer a chance to lead men, an experience necessary for promotion. I think there was also a need to relieve these men from the psychological weariness that responsibility in the field brought with it.

In effect, the practice took experienced men out of the field, where they were needed, and in this way perhaps cost officers' lives and the lives of some of their men, too. The death rate for servicemen in Vietnam was 2 percent. For the young officers from Dave's platoon at Quantico, it was more than 11 percent, and most of these were killed during their first few weeks in the field. You got

smart fast, and it seems to me that it would have been a
wise thing to have kept experienced officers in the field
as long as possible and to have found some practical way
to relieve the stress of the responsibility. It's no wonder
that Dave learned quickly to rely on his "salty" sergeant
for advice and support.

Out of the field now and promoted in the last days of
October to captain, Dave was at regimental headquarters,
where he was a staff officer. More precisely, he was legal
officer, psychological-warfare officer, and civil-action officer all at once — one of those charged to win the hearts
and minds of the people. "We are planning and building
wells for the villages," he wrote. "After almost five
months in the field, doing combat or having to be prepared for it, it's strange to worry about procuring cement
for wells." His life, he thought, was getting "boring."

It didn't seem to me he should be bored. But I understood. Dave was an infantryman at heart, and he found
it frustrating to be a staff officer; he would miss his platoon to the end of his tour in Vietnam. But as disappointed as he was to be in the rear, he set to work in his
new position. His first job was legal in nature. One of
the men in the battalion wanted to adopt a six-year-old
Vietnamese boy whose parents had been killed, and as
legal officer Dave was doing what he could to help the
adoption along. "The officials are so slow," he complained in one of his first letters from this new location.

The letters Dave wrote at headquarters were longer
than the ones he had written when he was in the field.
Many of these longer letters were written during night
watches. The quiet darkness with only moderate tension — direct contact with the enemy was rare at regimental headquarters — seemed to make him philosophical. "We're trying so hard," he wrote, "but they keep our
hands so tied. Oh, well, we can only do our best." And

in another letter, he spoke about the Vietnamese, those he was to help, or so he had thought.

> I've met some fine Vietnamese but the average one isn't worth a damn to us in this war. I can't blame them. They've been fighting or in the middle of fighting for the last 25 years or so. It's no wonder that a lot of them are indifferent as to who wins. All they care about is their little piece of land. Can't blame them for that. But I hate to see kids getting killed over here, losing legs, etc. The U.S. should either go balls to the wall or get the hell out. This pussy-footing around is a bunch of bullshit. So much for the war.

Philosophical, sadly resigned, and discouraged — but the letters did not deepen my worry. In those long-ago days, the state of my husband's mind and soul did not seem significant. He was out of the field and therefore unlikely to be wounded or killed. The odds I would have him home again, alive, looked good to me. That was all I cared about.

In spite of his discouragement at being assigned to the pacification program, Dave and his S-5 men worked hard to do what they could. One thing that Dave was really looking forward to was a series of Christmas parties they had planned for the children. "We need 3,000 presents at least," he wrote about mid-December. In the end they managed to "scrape together" more than 5,000, and on Christmas Eve one of the men dressed up in a make-do Santa Claus suit: baggy, bright red pants and blouse trimmed with white sheeting, a red ski cap on his head, cotton wool stuck to his face.

"The children loved it," Dave wrote. "They mobbed us for the presents and laughed and jabbered and followed us around wherever we went. Only one sour note the whole day — somewhere along the line one of the little bastards picked my pocket. I'd like to get my hands on that one.''

The letter from Vietnam dated December 25 began: ''Well, today is Christmas. Big deal.''

It *was* a big deal in Tacoma, where, looking for comfort and joy in connections, I went to celebrate. Dave's aunts and uncles, cousins numbering in the dozens, trooped through the house all day, bringing food and presents, admiring Jeannie, staying for the big Christmas dinner — adults at the dining-room table, children spread throughout the living room at card tables. Or they came by later in the day for a buffet of leftovers: turkey, Jell-O salads, favorite desserts. The house smelled like baking turkey mixed with the fir smell of the Christmas tree; stray pieces of torn wrapping paper and bits of ribbon littered the floor; and carols on the turned-down stereo filled the rare spots of silence.

People came in bringing the cold with them, and when they hugged me, they said, ''Next year Dave will be here, too!''

Christmas in Tacoma that year truly took on all the revelry of an ancient pagan celebration — a time to forget troubles, to laugh, to break the soul's long winter, at least for a while. We went to church, and mealtime prayers never forgot to mention that we were celebrating Christ's birth, but the emphasis was on a more immediate hope and celebration than those looked forward to in heaven.

A lot of the time, though, I was only partly in the room where all the celebrating was going on. Some part of me was with Dave. Maybe the others felt that way, too, for by Christmas, the family had two men in Vietnam. Dave's cousin Buzz had shipped over in September. But the noise of people talking, and of Bing Crosby and the Mormon Tabernacle Choir singing from records on the stereo, brought me back to the room when my thoughts drifted to the war; I was glad to be in the middle of all the bustle.

Jeannie was five months old to the day, and, full of joy, she added greatly to my happiness on Christmas Day of 1967. When I put her to bed that night, I had to admit that even in my bad times there were things that made life good.

Libby and Bonnie and Diane were spending the holidays with their relatives, as I was. I do not know what Leah did, or where she was. Just before Christmas, she had severed all contact with the wives from the platoon. I suppose this was her way of coping. She had told Bonnie she hoped we understood, and I tried to, but her efforts to make Sam's loss more bearable for herself in this way made his loss that much harder for the rest of us to bear. "It hurts so to lose the men," Bonnie told me, "and now we have to lose one another, too."

I missed Sam, and now I missed Leah; as fragile as our tie had been, it had been comforting to know it was there, somewhere. And now it was gone, and none of us would ever know the connection of the baby, Sam's baby.

I stayed in Tacoma for New Year's. December 31, 1967, fell on a Sunday, and Bonnie called in the afternoon to wish me a happy new year and to talk a little — "to touch base," we used to say about these calls. Jon had planned a February R&R, a romantic Valentine's R&R — wine, roses, the whole thing. But they had been put off the February list, and Bonnie felt cheated. She was more than the usual "New-Year's-alone" depressed. She had a right to be. I had seen Dave, and Libby and Ken had had their R&R leave only a week ago; they had spent Christmas together. Bonnie was worried she was never going to see Jon again. She thought that their being put off the list was a bad sign. "Something's going to happen," she said. "I just know it."

"Don't be silly," I said. "This year is going to be *our* year. You'll see." But the words felt weak and unreal. I had come to rely on Bonnie's strength and spirit, and when I didn't hear them in her voice, I felt them ebb in me.

After I rocked Jeannie to sleep that night, I put on jeans and a sweatshirt, said happy new year to my mother- and father-in-law, and drove across town to a party at the home of friends from my college days. Their house was near water, on a lake, and I drove through a sparse stand of birches to their house.

In my purse I carried Dave's most recent letter, the one telling about his plans for the children's Christmas parties. I always carried his most recent letter or two, but I was especially glad to have that one. If anyone asked, as they did sometimes, in the most casual of voices, "So, what do you hear from Dave?" I would have an acceptable, easy-to-hear answer: "He's organizing parties for the children."

I knew people who did not want to hear about Dave's loneliness, the rotten food, the rain, and the misery. I knew that our friends were familiar with the horrors of Vietnam. They had television sets. They read the papers and the news magazines. And I was sure that they did not want Dave's version of the details — not the sad, mundane ones I got from him, anyway.

There were other things I had to think about, too. Even among my old friends, it was often hard to guess a person's real feelings about Vietnam, for by December of 1967, the war had become a real issue even for some in the suburbs. I never met anyone in the neighborhood or at a party as openly hostile and combative as my fellow students at college in Fresno, but it was increasingly hard to find anyone who did not have a political-moral response, and these responses increasingly indicated some kind of condemnation of the American soldier.

I tried to be accommodating and sensitive to the dilemma my old friends — many formerly indifferent and unaware, but now newly politicized — found themselves in. They were still my friends — and Dave's — but they didn't want to talk about his life as a Marine on personal, human terms. They did not want to think about him as a man who was doing what he thought was his duty, a man who was doing what he thought was right.

There were, of course, others who still chose to ignore completely that there was a war being fought that involved American boys. As long as they didn't have to be involved directly themselves, they didn't care. But among the young — those who might be called to serve or their friends and loved ones — the war was decidedly a growing issue. People didn't want to be reminded too pointedly that boys they knew were fighting and dying in the name of the country they lived in so freely. It would be hard for them to go about their day-to-day lives — working, coming home to supper, playing golf and going to parties on the weekends — if they had to do those things against the specific knowledge of what life was like for the men, their friends perhaps, in the war zone. Much better not to know.

I played along. When Sam and Dennie died, I did not tell any of my old college friends. I was living in Fresno when I learned that Dennie had been killed, and I did not even tell my parents. I know I was quieter around the house, and perhaps they wondered, but they never asked.

At school, I sat in the lecture hall and played what I began then to call "memorial games." While the professor talked in the front of the room about the natural resources in the Ruhr Valley of Germany, I tried to remember as much about Dennie and Sam and the others as I could. That Sam liked the same kind of Pendleton shirts Dave

did. Dennie's beautiful, shy smile. How Ken's eyebrows
wrinkled when he talked. How Jon liked to compete, no
matter what the game or stakes.

My list, as I try now to replay the game with memories
more than two decades old, is short. In those days, in the
lecture hall on warm September and October afternoons,
the lists were very long. The details slip away from me
now, buried in my mind. But I still remember the men
as they were when they were boys at Quantico; I can
remember what they looked like then, and some of the
things they did.

On New Year's Eve of 1967, inside the house by the lake,
a split-level 1960s modern house, the lights were turned
low. It was almost eleven, and the party had been going
on for two or three hours by the time I arrived. I recognized a few people upstairs, where the living room and
the dining room were both full. Music thundered from a
black stereo at the top of the stairs, the Rolling Stones
screaming a song. Someone had placed an alarm clock,
the kind with silver bells, on the tall fireplace mantel. "Set
to go off at five minutes to midnight," someone passing
by told me.

I quickly looked around the room. I did not know any
of the couples well enough to join their conversations.
The party had hit its stride, and people were relaxed and
intimate in the dark corners of the room. I pushed my
way into the kitchen and grabbed a beer off a shelf in the
refrigerator. Then I worked my way downstairs, to the
rec room, where a TV was rebroadcasting the celebration
from Times Square for the West Coast. The great, illumi-
nated ball was about to drop.

A group was clustered around the wet bar in the corner
of the big room and someone was calling out the ingredi-
ents of a Singapore Sling while the host — a bit drunk,

and a ham even when he was sober — was making a big, soggy production of mixing a punch bowl of the drink.

I found a bottle opener for my beer on the counter by the wet bar and saw, when I turned back to the room, that Kim Yaeger was sitting alone on the sofa in front of the TV, watching the celebration in Times Square. I sat down beside him.

I had not seen him since March, when he had sat in my kitchen in Virginia and broken the news to me about now big a pregnant woman actually gets. He smiled at me when I sat down and said: "What's up with you, kid? And what do you hear from your old man?" Then, without waiting for me to say anything, he added quietly, "Seriously, Marian, how's Dave?"

I pried the cap off the beer and handed the bottle to Kim. "He hates it, Kim. He hates the war, the country, and the food and the rain. Sometimes he even hates the people he's supposed to be fighting for. He's fed up."

Kim took the beer from me. "That's the grunts for you," he said. He raised the bottle to his mouth, threw his head back, and swallowed. Then he wiped his mouth with the back of his hand, dried the lip of the bottle with the band of his sweatshirt, and handed the beer back to me. Kim was lanky, long-legged, blond, and boyish. His image hardly matched his role of husband in an eight-year marriage and father of two small children. And his dream, about to come true, of being a Marine fighter pilot in Vietnam did not fit at all.

"Pilots," Kim was saying, "well, Marian, pilots leave a clean bed and a well-set table, go do their dirty jobs, and come back to a clean bed and a well-set table. Dave's just tired of C-rats and foxholes." He reached for my beer. "Don't worry about him. Nothing's wrong that a hot meal and a hot bath won't fix. He's out of the field now, so it'll be pretty quiet for him from now on out. That leaves time and energy for complaining. Don't take it seriously." He patted my arm. Kim was sympathetic and truthful, and I felt better.

We finished the beer together, the ball fell to the bottom in Times Square, and Guy Lombardo's orchestra played "Auld Lang Syne." On the television, people sang and danced and hugged one another and welcomed the New Year. It was 1968.

I left Kim on the couch with his wife, a friendly woman named Sue who tried to make me stay. (She had come to find Kim when the warning alarm had gone off upstairs.) But it was a time for two. In the corner, by the bar, couples were embracing and toasting each other. The lights had been turned off completely, and the room was lit only by the flashing glow of the TV. I went upstairs, where I found another TV on in the living room and the same real-life scene I had left downstairs: couples everywhere, in all kinds of embraces. Someone pulled at me from a doorway. For a moment I let myself be drawn toward his face, but then I saw I did not know him and broke free.

In the master bedroom, I found my jacket and my purse where I had left them on the bed, and, unnoticed, I left the party through a door in the rec room that led into the garage. I left without saying good-bye to my hosts.

The moon was out and it hit the lake water like the beam of a giant flashlight. When I exhaled, I could see my breath; it was cold and frosty out, but the lake looked the way a lake does on a summer night under a full moon — quiet and dark and inviting. It looked like summer, except it was cold and the dark silhouettes of the thin birches were leafless. They would be full and thick by the time Dave got back.

It was the new year, another year. Dave had five months left of his tour, five more months we both had to get through. But Kim was right. Dave was out of the field;

I had to keep that in mind. Jon and Bob were relatively safe, too, at the base at Phu Bai, where Jon was a legal officer and Bob was in charge of an artillery battery. Ken, it seemed, was better off than anybody. He had recently moved to a very large base, at a place called Khe Sanh, isolated from the action, where they had an officers' club with showers and cold beer; someone told me they had movies, too.

Inside the car, I turned on the radio. Vikki Carr was singing, *Oh, dear Lord, it must be him or I shall die* . . . In Vietnam, it was the new year, too, and it had been for nine hours already.

Through weary [years of] separation; through fearful
expectancies of unknown fate; through the bitterness
of the sorrow which might so easily have been joy . . .
through all these agonies you [wives] fail not, and
never will fail.

— John Ruskin, "War,"
from *The Crown of Wild Olive*

Twenty-Nine

I WENT BACK to Fresno to finish the semester at college there. R&R was over; Christmas was
over; 1968 had arrived. The milestones of time took on
new meaning as they began to mark new events for me.
The Fourth of July marked the anniversary of Sam's
death. September, previously the time of the changing
leaves and the beginning of school, was now the time
Dennie died. The meaning of everything had changed,
was still changing, and I knew somehow that even Kim
Yaeger could not know for sure that the worst was over.
I had become used to expecting the worst.

No letters came from Dave during the first two weeks
of January. These were my final weeks of school, and I
took my final examinations sick at heart, and physically
ill, too, with the strep throat I had carried back from
Hawaii and had been unable to shake, even with antibi-
otics.

At the end of three weeks — weeks of packing, studying, and battling physical illness and the emptying heartsickness I always had when letters did not come — I was ready to leave Fresno. My parents would miss Jeannie — she was their first grandchild. They loved her, and they would miss having her so readily in their lives. But there was no place for me in Fresno, not even in my parents' home.

I stored most of our belongings in a warehouse in Fresno and drove the Camaro to Tacoma, arriving there toward the end of January. The first letter from Dave in two weeks was waiting for me, dated January 1. In it he told me the regiment was moving. "No one knows for sure where," he wrote. "You may read about it in the papers before I can tell you in a letter." Then, as an afterthought: "Today is New Year's, and it's quiet — just another work day, though someone has a bottle of Johnny Walker that we'll break open sometime later on."

The next day, I waited at the top of the drive for the mail truck. "I knew you were coming back," Sam said. And he handed me a small stack of letters from Dave.

While I had been in Fresno packing and taking exams and worrying about Dave, Dave had been taking part in the pacification of Quang Tri. His S-5 unit and the regimental surgeon managed to build a two-unit shower for a hamlet. And it worked, too. "The doctor," Dave wrote, "says most of the people's health problems come from not washing. Hope the shower pays off."

Dave and the other men in S-5 also built a laundry for a young Vietnamese woman who wanted to own and operate one. She was pleased to have her new business and gave Dave a beautiful, ebony scrapbook, lacquered and inlaid with mother-of-pearl in a flower design of large peonies and chrysanthemums. He put the pictures I sent of Jeannie in it.

Some of the Marines had entered a local pagoda, uninvited, and the Buddhist priest was angry. Dave went to talk to him about the incident, to apologize and find out what could be done to make things better between the old gentleman and the Marines. "We spoke in French," Dave wrote. "I only know a few phrases, and I say them rather badly. He thought it was pretty funny." The Buddhist priest and Dave became friends, and Dave went to the pagoda more than once after that first visit for tea and as much conversation as Dave's limited French allowed. He must have wanted to talk to the priest very badly.

The Marines in the S-5 unit also began a small industry for some jobless villagers in the area around Quang Tri. The S-5 provided supplies and machinery and showed the villagers how to make school desks, for which there was a demand in spite of the long, long war the country had been engaged in.

"Now we're trying to raise $1000 from the troops to buy uniforms for all the schoolchildren in Quang Tri," Dave wrote me. "I think we're going to do it, too."

They did.

Letters from Dave appeared in the silver-gray mailbox on Tyee Drive regularly again, and I settled into life in Tacoma. I woke to foggy, misty, rainy mornings that often never brightened the entire day; instead, they simply turned into damp, clouded, grayish afternoons. But life was peaceful.

I bought material, attached patterns, and cut out pieces for clothes I wanted to sew for when Dave would be coming back. I set up the portable sewing machine on a card table in the back room — Dennis's old room — and while Jeannie napped down the short hall, I stitched pieces of material together and daydreamed about how I would look wearing the things I was making when Dave and I were together again.

I was working on a pink sundress, a dress of blue cotton, and a pastel, flowered robe cut from a light, silky fabric. I saw myself in the robe having breakfast with Dave and Jeannie in a sunny kitchen somewhere. My kitchen, though. Our kitchen. And through the windows there was, when I imagined this scene, always a garden full of flowers and a yard with swings.

In a letter I received near the end of January, Dave told me that he had moved again — this time to a place called Camp Evans, twenty-five miles north of Phu Bai, twenty miles south of Quang Tri. "Hue, the old capital city of Vietnam, is only about 15 miles south of here & I hope to get down to see it," he wrote. "It's the cultural center of VN and has some beautiful and interesting places." I had taped my map of Vietnam back inside the closet door of my bedroom in Tacoma. I opened the door now and marked the move with a black felt-tipped pen. Black lines ran up and down the map from south of Da Nang to Dong Ha, near the DMZ — the "demilitarized zone" — and I couldn't make sense of any of it.

Dennie, Sam, and thousands like them, American and Vietnamese, killed in the fighting, and thousands more wounded, all in the same country. There had been terrible fighting in the same places Dave had been with the Marines of the S-5, providing school uniforms, showers, laundries, and machines to make desks for children. No, it didn't make sense.

In the same envelope with the letter telling me about the move to Camp Evans, Dave had enclosed a small, plastic Buddhist medal on a thin, gold cord. This, he said, was a good-bye gift from the Buddhist priest he used to visit. "It's to ensure my good fortune," he wrote. There was also a picture of a large, French-colonial building with a steeple and a cross on the top — the Quang Tri Catholic church; the picture was a farewell present from the local Catholic priest, a cheerful Vietnamese who used to offer Dave small glasses of sherry imported from France. "Believe it or not," Dave said in his letter, "they were honestly sorry to see us go. I think they liked us."

January 26, 1967 — to Phu Bai this time. And although Dave was disappointed to find that Bob's battery had left the area, he was happy to see Jon there. "We got caught up on each other and the rest of the gang," Dave wrote. "What do you hear?"

I was hearing a lot from Bonnie. "It's for sure this time," she had written to me. "Our R&R is set for March 6 through the 13." Her school board had been reluctant to give her the time off to meet her husband in Hawaii on his R&R leave, but she had insisted. They had finally relented, after she agreed to leave detailed lesson plans and pay for her own substitute. She was nervous and excited, of course. "I'm holding my breath and keeping my fingers crossed. I can't really believe it's actually going to happen!" she wrote.

I envied her excitement, and I hoped she would have a wonderful time with Jon — that fear would not get its grip on her as it had on me. I said nothing in my responses to her about what had happened to me on the flight home from Hawaii. I only wanted to encourage her happiness. We had so little of it, so little good to look forward to. Our days had become days of dread; of waiting, hoping against hope; of grieving; of an odd, horrible, yet strangely necessary guilt because the grieving was not for our own. But I wanted to warn her at the same time. I had not managed as well after R&R as I had before.

Libby was not doing well, either. She had hated the idea of Ken's going to war so very much. I feel silly writing that. Bonnie, Diane, and I did not like the idea of our men going, either, and we were often afraid they might not come back. Bonnie had the same nightmare again and again; in it Ken and Dave got off the plane at Travis

without Jon. And I used to see — as in a daydream and at
the most unexpected moments — replays of a nightmare I
had after Sam died: a silver coffin with Dave inside being
lowered into the earth, sliding from two ropes. If I was
in the car going someplace and I spotted an official-
looking tan car, I turned to follow it until I was sure it
was not turning toward my home. Or with my nightgown
wet from sweat, I would wake up frightened because I
had dreamed a tan car driven by a Marine major had
pulled into the driveway.

But Libby had fought Ken every inch of the way, from
his joining the Marines in the first place, to his leaving
for Vietnam. At Quantico, where I can remember crying
only once — on the morning Dave told me he would not
be with me when our baby was born — Libby had, she
said in one of our phone calls, cried almost every day:
alone after work, before Ken got back from the base, she
sat down at her old, oak kitchen table, buried her head
in her arms, and wept. "And I cried on the weekends,
too," she told me, "when he'd gone to the field, or to the
basketball court for a game of pickup with the guys. I
couldn't stand it when the door closed behind him. Every
time he went out the door of that apartment, it was like
it was for the last time. I don't know why, but it was, and
it just about killed me."

Bonnie, Diane, and I worried about Libby. We had no
help to offer, though — nothing we could think of to say
that would make things better for her. Platitudes never
occurred to us. We were all far beyond platitudes. So we
just listened when she called, and we answered her rare
letters with as much compassion and wisdom as twenty-
three-year-old war brides have.

I have seen a green country, useful to the race,
Knocked silly with guns and mines, its villages vanished.

> — Edmund Blunden, "Report on
> Experience"

Thirty

I READ IT in the papers and saw it on TV
before Dave's letter reached me. "The VC and the NVA
are raising hell," he wrote in a letter dated January 31.
"I think it's their last-ditch effort. We've been lucky at
Phu Bai, only rockets and mortar rounds. Saw Jon again
last night. He's moving to Dong Ha. Hope he'll be OK
there. This is Tet."

I also knew before he wrote it to me that he had moved
on to Hue, where some of the worst fighting was. I turned
on the television news the first thing in the morning, and
I watched it the last thing at night; and I stayed tuned to
the news on the car radio when I drove anywhere. Tet.
Something big and awful. Dave's father brought the paper
inside in the evening and, against his pattern, he read it
silently. He was still silent when he put it down, silent
through the 6:00 news and supper.

His mother was silent, too, but hers was not the grim,

deadly silence stamped on Dave's father's gray face. She had put her trust and faith in a loving God, and He would not let her down. Sam and Dennie had meant nothing to her, only names. What she cared about still lived, in the house on Tyee Drive, and somewhere in a place called Vietnam. God was being good to her and would continue to be good to her, partly because she was passing this great test of faith. She moved calmly about the house, about her business, cooking meals, doing laundry, ordering and packing Tupperware for her customers. She only glanced at the headlines in the newspapers, and she listened to the news on the TV as though she were casually eavesdropping on a conversation that didn't interest her very much.

What went on in her heart and her head in the middle of the night, I don't know. She never talked to me about her fears. If I brought mine up — that I was worried about Dave and our friends — she prayed. For me.

On television, the battles raged on. I watched closely, looking carefully at the faces of the soldiers. Each young man belonged to someone who cared. They belonged to one another, if to no one else. I had learned that from Dave's letters. In those days I felt that I was made up of strings — loose and frayed and weak — and that somewhere inside of me, a hand was holding all those strings together, all in a bunch. And the hand was not my hand. I didn't know whose hand it was that was holding my life together. And I didn't know how much longer it was going to hold on.

Dave wrote two letters to me on the day he left Phu Bai for Hue. One was written on the morning of February 8. It is a typical letter from that time, about the weather and the food; and it is full of questions about things at home.

The second letter is short — a note, really. It is like the short letters he had written to me earlier in his tour when he had the platoon and they were about to go out on a patrol, on ambush, or some other field operation. It was one of those letters that had a good-bye in it. "You're a good wife and I love you and Jeannie very much," he wrote. In Phu Bai, they had heard about Hue.

Dave had seen Hue for the first time in late January when he had gone there with the regimental surgeon to get serum to inoculate the villagers in Quang Tri. In fact, he had been there the day before Tet. He wrote to me after that visit about the beauty of the city, about the Vietnamese culture, and the history the city represented: in the Citadel, the old palaces, the Imperial Palace, and the Palace of Perfect Peace.

The gardens were beautiful, Dave wrote, and the Perfume River — which separates the city, the old part from the new — was wide and gentle. Hue was not a military city, and it had not been a military target. So, before January 31, 1968, it was a peaceful oasis in a war-torn country.

Buddhists in Vietnam told a myth in which Hue City is a lotus flower growing in the mud. The myth proved to be true until Tet of 1968. The American military appreciated what the old imperial capital meant to the Vietnamese, and tried at first to save the old buildings of the city when the Tet offensive began. Instead of using air bombardment during the first few days of battle, the fighting was hand-to-hand and house-to-house.

Even when a person understands the reasons for it, it's still confusing and hard to think of young men, tired, dirty, and scared, fighting day after day like that in rubbled and torn streets to save stone and mortar. We are a strange, complicated species.

The First Marines fought in the battle of Hue, and because Dave was by then attached to Headquarters Company, First Marines, he was sent there from Phu Bai to do whatever Colonel Stanley S. Hughes, the regimental commander and the man in charge of the Marines in Hue, wanted done. As usual, in Hue, Dave wrote almost nothing about what he was doing or what was going on around him. He was eating C rations and could not bathe; those two bits of information were almost all he provided in the few letters I received from that fated city.

February was a dismal month in Hue and in Tacoma, too. What little communication I had with Dave was sporadic and unreliable. The mail was less regular than usual; either it was not coming out of Hue or Dave was not writing. For some reason, letters stopped arriving about the middle of the month and didn't begin arriving again until the beginning of March. Meanwhile, television broadcasts and the newspapers were full of accounts of the fighting.

So I was more shocked than surprised when the phone rang in the kitchen on Tyee Drive on Valentine's Day in 1968 and a radio operator — I think he said he was in Texas — spoke to me. "I have your husband on a MARS radio," he said. "From Vietnam."

I sat down, the phone pressed to my ear, and tried to breathe normally. On the line, Dave's voice seemed as far away as it was. There was a lot of static and we had to say "over" when we wanted the other person to talk. "Are you all right? Over."

Then Dave's voice crackling on the line: "Yes, I'm safe. In a MACV compound. Don't worry — would I be calling you if I weren't safe? Over." I couldn't argue with his logic, but when he spoke I thought I heard thundering in the background — sounds like armies make. Still, the silence in the room after he hung up was not welcome.

I had been receiving letters from Bob at the rate of about one a month since his arrival in Vietnam in June. His letters were funny and upbeat, illustrated with clippings from the "Peanuts" cartoon strip. "My CO is begging me to extend," he wrote, "but my reply is always the same." And taped below this sentence was a "Peanuts" panel showing Snoopy lying on his doghouse thinking, "How gauche!" At the bottom of the page, Bob had taped another panel, this one of Snoopy wearing his leather flying helmet and goggles, sitting on top of his bullet-riddled doghouse. The words in the bubble above his head were "I should have stayed in Paris. . . ."

Although in his letters Bob was not graphic in his descriptions of the war, he was more telling than Dave. The tone of Dave's letters was neutral and colorless; Bob's was tinted from the palette of war: "I really feel like I'm getting something done — we've had 72 confirmed kills in the last four days. And 'beaucoup' probables. . . .

"[These Marines] are the finest I've worked with. And they shoot their asses off." Still, after telling me about mortar-and-rocket attacks against his battery position, Bob cautioned me: "Don't mention any of this to my mom. She tends to get worked up over this kind of news. As far as she's concerned, I'm in a secure post, in Da Nang embarking troops and ships."

On his birthday, February 20, Dave wrote: "I don't feel twenty-five — I feel about fifty. This is a short letter because I don't have anything to write since I don't have letters from you to tell me what's going on." Years later I learned how very different the truth was. There was a lot he could have written about what he did and saw in Hue.

In Tacoma, Jeannie started to say words and began to take steps holding on to things, such as a chair or the coffee table. In Hue, the First Marines fought on. The civilian population was suffering terribly. Five thousand of them had been rounded up by the NVA and the Viet Cong and killed, their bodies covered over in shallow mass graves, most of which were not discovered until months later. For the men, women, and children of Hue who had not been killed, living was very hard. There was no food. They had had to leave their homes, and finding a place to stay was difficult, particularly finding a relatively safe place. The hospital had been bombed, and the wounded were everywhere, most of them without medical help.

Colonel Hughes told Dave to "help the people." That was all, and his words were typical of this quiet, gentle man. Every order he gave Dave was as simple and direct. I did not hear until much later what help Dave managed to give, or how he managed to give it. The hospital was opened, though, lights obtained for the operating room, rice given to those without food, and protected shelters made of the university buildings.

Dave did complain in his letters about being tired — not physically so much, but emotionally and psychologically. "I'm awful tired of C-rats," he wrote. "And we're not getting any mail. I'm so sick and tired of this damn country." But for all that, he was lucky and he knew it: he was on the south side of the river; the fighting was by then confined to the north side.

On February 26, Dave wrote that he hadn't had a chance to shower since the eighth of February, but he was hoping to get one soon. "No mail for a long time," he said. So much depended on pen and paper.

The nightly news came to be too much for America, all those fresh-from-the-front moving pictures of young boys in US uniforms, running through the destroyed streets of places such as Saigon and Hue, being shot at, lying wounded. Until Tet of 1968, militant antiwar feelings seemed to belong mostly to pockets of students and a small army of activists. But the eruption of this enemy offensive, an unexpected offensive during which the enemy managed to attack everywhere at once in South Vietnam, turned a lot of minds to action. The TV played over and over the attack within the very walls of the US Embassy in Saigon, one of the first places hit in the dawning hours of the offensive.

Jon was in Dong Ha, and Bonnie was frightened, as all of us waiting at home were; but our attention focused more and more on Libby. The base at Khe Sanh where we had thought Ken was so lucky to be was surrounded by NVA, perhaps more than two divisions — more than twenty thousand enemy soldiers — and the six thousand Marines there were in danger of being overrun. The news reports were full of the siege at Khe Sanh.

Bonnie held her breath, waiting for delayed R&R, when Jon could escape to safety for a few brief days. They were to meet in Hawaii on March 5, and the break could not have come at a better time for them. It was a late R&R, well past the midpoint of Jon's tour, but they were almost to it; afterward, they would have only five months or so left.

Ken and Libby had had an "early" R&R in December, after less than six months of Ken's required thirteen. Now Libby had only the final homecoming to look forward to, months away, in August.

Bonnie was more than ever nervously excited. She began to have trouble sleeping. "I lie in the dark waiting for a Marine to come to the door with the news that Jon has been wounded, or killed," she told me.

"I've heard they won't come after ten at night or before six in the morning," I said. After that, she did sleep again, but only between the hours of 10:00 PM and 6:00 AM.

As Tet wore on, Bonnie and I were scared and nervous, but Libby seemed almost paralyzed with fear. She was still working, but in her phone calls — she rarely wrote, and even then only a few lines — she seemed distracted. I worried a lot about her.

"I don't think I can stand it any longer," she told me. This was around the first of March, and Khe Sanh was having the worst of it. Almost every thought I had of the men seemed to be in the form of a prayer in those days.

Dave had left Hue by this time and was back at Phu Bai, where, he happily wrote, he had taken a shower, his first in almost four weeks. He had come to appreciate fully the support areas of the military — those who supplied the troops, those who evacuated the wounded, and those who provided air support — about which he said, "It's beautiful — like your mother pulling a soft, warm blanket over you in the cold dark." And he added, "I'll be here for the time being. Don't worry."

But like Bonnie and Libby, I was worrying, and the worry was beginning to show on me, too. I had strange physical symptoms for a twenty-three-year-old woman: heart palpitations, chest pains, weight loss. I had no appetite, only a churning in my stomach when I tried to eat. My in-laws were worried about me, so I went to see their family doctor.

"Is there something going on in your life to cause you extra strain?" he asked.

I looked at him and blinked. Was he serious? He knew Dave's family and Dave himself, and he must have known where Dave was; he must have known what was going on in Vietnam. But since he asked the question, I decided he did not feel having a husband at war was a cause for special concern, and I wrote him off. I would not explain what should have been clear.

"No," I said. "I think I'm just high-strung."

The doctor nodded and, pen in hand, bent over the small, white pad on his desk. In a few minutes, I left his office with a prescription for tranquilizers in my purse. I was upset with myself and embarrassed that I had come so close to admitting weakness, that I had almost talked about my worries and loneliness to an outsider.

In the wind that blows
The veils of widows
All float on one side

And the mingled tears
Of a thousand sorrows
In one stream glide.

— René Arcos, "The Dead"

Then she mourned, and the women wailed in answer.

— Homer, *Iliad*

Thirty-One

ON THURSDAY, MARCH 28, at about
five-thirty in the evening Pacific Standard Time, Bonnie
called. She had written a very excited letter about her
R&R, and I had not had time to answer it yet; now here
she was on the phone, even more excited than in her
letter. What more could she have to say to me, and in
such a happy voice?

"Guess what?" she said. "You'll never believe it, but
Ken is on the news tonight. I just saw him. We're an hour
ahead of you, but if you'll tune in CBS for the evening
news you'll see him — and, Marian, he looks so good!"

I moved the living-room rocker as close to the television as I could and, holding Jeannie on my lap, I watched
a CBS newsman talk to Ken at Khe Sanh. Ken and the
reporter wore helmets and flak jackets, and Ken was explaining how he made his decisions to call in artillery. He
did look good. We had been hearing of the awfulness and

the terror, bad enough in reality, but in our imaginations a living death: noise, guns, artillery, choppers — and that bleak, bleak landscape, cratered, desolate, all red dust and barren dirt. But Ken looked beautiful.

As soon as the interview was over, I put Jeannie in my mother-in-law's arms and went to call Libby. She had not seen Ken on television, having stayed late at work and missed the evening news. But friends in Louisiana had seen the interview and called her, and she was disappointed and upset. "This is too much," she said.

I hung up — still elated because I had seen Ken, but at the same time sorry and frustrated for Libby — and I started to help my mother-in-law with the supper dishes.

Later, when I was getting ready for bed, the phone rang again; this time it was a happy, breathless Libby. "I called the local station," she said in her·gentle Louisiana lilt. "They told me to come on down and they'd show me the piece in a screening room. And I saw him! I saw him, and didn't he look wonderful?" she said.

"Yes," I said. "He looked wonderful, Libby."

"It's been so awful, hasn't it? But I think I'm going to make it now. Now that I've seen him, I think for sure I can make it."

Two days later, Saturday, in the late afternoon: it had been drizzling all day, and I had gone to my room to sew the pastel flowered robe I'd been working on, off and on, since January. It was almost finished. I was covering buttons with the fabric of the robe, as the pattern suggested. Jeannie was in the kitchen with her grandparents. Most of my life was on hold — it had seemed that way forever now; but parts of it were still moving forward, and we were making progress. Time *was* passing.

Then my mother-in-law tapped on the half-opened door, leaned her silver-haired head into the room, and said, "Bonnie's on the phone."

Holding a button in one hand and a piece of the silky material in the other, I looked at her. Her tone had put a question in my mind and I asked it out loud: "Bonnie? Why?"

"Yes, Bonnie. She told me her name." And I knew from her voice that my mother-in-law had heard something in Bonnie's.

In the kitchen, I put the receiver to my ear and said, "Bonnie?"

All she said to me was: "It's Ken. He's gone."

"But we just saw him," I said. "We just saw him two days ago, and he was fine." Then I understood. Barely managing to get the words out, I asked, "How's Libby?"

"She's not good, not good at all. I just talked to her. She'll be at her folks' place tomorrow. She's sedated now, not making much sense. But you can probably talk to her tomorrow."

When I wrote to Dave that night, it was a different letter from the one I had planned earlier in the day. Seven of his letters had gotten through that week, a record of sorts. One had taken only three days — another record. Not since he had mailed letters from the hospital at Da Nang had a letter come so quickly from his hand to mine. I'd received Bonnie's exuberant, funny letter about Jon and R&R, and Jeannie had started to talk; more than old hat "mama," she had said "dok" for "dog" and "no-no." It had been a good week, as weeks of that war went on my personal home front.

Until that second phone call from Bonnie.

On Sunday evening, March 31, President Lyndon Johnson went on national television and radio to tell the American people: "I shall not seek, and I will not accept, the nomination of my party for another term as your President." I did not see or hear the broadcast. I understand that young people my age all over America celebrated, shouting in the streets, congratulating one another. The so-called war president was not going to run for office again. The peace candidate Eugene McCarthy had done well in the New Hampshire presidential primary and was on the verge of defeating Johnson at the polls in Wisconsin.

I did not care. Ken was dead.

His CO wrote Libby a letter, as COs traditionally do, and she sent me a copy.

> Ken was an artillery forward observer . . . and on 30 March 1968 [his] company was assigned a mission clearing and destroying an enemy trench and bunker complex a few hundred meters outside of the Khe Sanh perimeter. The company was enroute to its objective when . . . it came under a heavy enemy mortar attack. One of these mortar rounds struck a few feet from Ken and killed him instantly.

On April 4, 1968, as he stood on the balcony of a motel, Martin Luther King, Jr., was killed by a sniper in Memphis, Tennessee, and the cities of America blew up in fire and violence. The television news turned its wide, unblinking eye to the rubble-strewn streets of America.

Dr. King was buried in Atlanta on April 9. Thousands of mourners attended, many of them dignitaries, famous men and women. The nation watched the funeral and read about it for days afterward. A great civil-rights leader had been killed, and the nation not only rioted, it regretted and it grieved. Three days later, on April 12, under the sunless, gray sky of Good Friday, a young Marine was buried in Lafayette, Louisiana. It was, the local paper reported, a calm, dignified service, a full military service, attended by friends and family.

The death of one lone Marine was not, of course, national news — not when so many were dying every day in the same sad place, not when the nation had had its fill of the deaths of soldiers and was focusing on problems here at home. But it should be noted here, for my own record, that Ken Ouelette went to Vietnam because he wanted to help, and he died there doing his job.

The letter I mailed to Dave on the evening of March 30, 1968, telling him about Ken's death, took eleven days to reach him. And his reply to that letter did not arrive in the mailbox on Tyee Drive until ten days after that. So until the twentieth of April, I continued to receive letters from Dave that talked about "the World" — the world back home — as though it were still more or less in one piece, a reconstructed world made out of fragments left when Dennie and Sam died, but still recognizable.

In the letters that kept coming to me after I knew Ken was dead, Dave wrote about Libby and Ken as though they still had a life together ahead of them. I read these letters with heartbroken impatience. On April 16, I opened one in which my husband lightheartedly scolded me for talking to Libby so long on the phone. "I'm glad you two got a good visit in, but for so long!? There goes your spending money for the next month."

Finally, Dave's letter came telling me at last that he knew. "I feel so sorry for Libby . . . I liked Ken so much."

Libby did not sever ties, as Leah had done, but she was altered so much she was no longer Libby. Bonnie, Diane, and I were not wise enough, or mature enough, to help her in the ways that she needed to be helped. We still loved her and we kept in touch, but the issues of her life were changed, and we no longer shared the same concerns in the same ways. The rest of us lived for our husbands to come home to us. Libby had to learn to survive without hers. We were helpless to ease her pain. Her grief was awesome and terrible, and it constantly reminded us of our own possible fate.

She told me years later that she dreamed about Ken's

death at night, and she thought about it most of the day, every day: she felt it in the rare minutes she wasn't thinking about it. When they sent his things home to her in a box, his letters from her, and his clothes, stained by his sweat and the red mud of Khe Sanh, she smelled it, too. She sealed the box and put it away, out of her sight, behind other boxes in the back of her closet. But she told me she never forgot about it, not really, and she could never forget the smell.

It hurt me to imagine Libby's pain, to know that when she closed her eyes at night, tired from work, or her mind spinning from a busy day shopping or going to a matinee with her girlfriends, without warning, from nowhere, out of the manic, near-dream thoughts of the mall or the theater, the box of Ken's things would jump into her mind; she would see again the olive green cloth caked with red dirt, and marked with the salt-lined stains that had once been Ken's sweat.

I know that whenever she smelled that smell again, even in her imagination, it was more real to her than Vietnam, or Ken, or death. It was the sad, bitter smell of her loss.

Libby retreated into her grief, and though I cannot speak for Bonnie, I know that Diane and I did not try to stop her. "I'm sorry," Diane wrote to me, "but I just can't bring myself to call her. It's too painful. Maybe that's cowardly, but I can't help it." As for me, I listened when she cried, as Bonnie had taught me how to do during those evenings at Waller Hall back in the days of Quantico — before I really understood what Libby was crying about. But I could not think what more to do.

In letters to Dave, I worried about Libby. Because he could not hear her voice on the phone, he did not understand the completeness of her sorrow, the depth and width of her sense of loss. "I feel terrible for Libby, too," he wrote, "but I wish you wouldn't worry about her so much. I'm sure she'll be OK. She'll find somebody else, and I'll bet you she does get married again."

I had told him I was not so sure. But I think that Dave, like the other men, thought of a wife's youth as a kind of insurance policy, and that in an odd way he comforted himself with the thought that if it should come to his death, his widow would remarry. But it seemed to me then that Libby would have no other.

And she hasn't. Libby — bright, delicate, still pretty — remains Ken's widow. She had Ken until his death, and since then has had his memory. That has been enough for her, a monument to widowhood.

The rest of us were all afraid that Ken's fate would be our husband's, that Libby's would be ours. After all, what right did we have to expect more luck, or better treatment at God's hands? Deaths, big and little, seemed all around us. Sam, Dennie, now Ken. And all the nameless ones, too. Our hope, our courage, our spirit died a little every day. When the man you love is at war, life becomes a minefield, and you are forever — even in your dreams — walking point.

The flowers left thick at nightfall in the wood
This Eastertide call into mind the men
Now far from home, who, with their sweethearts,
  should
Have gathered them and will do never again.

— Edward Thomas, "In Memoriam"

Thirty-Two

REACTING TO KEN'S DEATH in his
own way, Dave tried harder than ever to protect me from
what was happening in our lives. This was impossible, of
course: the news of it was in the papers and on the television every day. But he didn't know then the extent of the
news coverage. No war had ever been covered like the
Vietnam War. I had only the clue of some red mud smears
and burn marks on the envelopes of his letters to tell me
that he was not "safe at Phu Bai," as he wrote me on the
first of April. He was actually on Operation Pegasus then,
with the First Marines, moving toward Khe Sanh to relieve that beleaguered, bombarded base.

It sickened me to learn that that was Dave's destination.
The very name Khe Sanh had come to be associated with
the worst tragedy of war, the death of a man we loved.
It did not help that in spite of Dave's attempts to write
more frequently and more reassuringly, April was the

worst month of all for mail. Letters came to Tacoma in small batches, days apart. And Dave got his letters that way, too. "Number them," he wrote, "so I can make heads or tails of the news." Shelling at Khe Sanh made the mail planes very irregular.

Well after Easter had passed, Dave remembered to mention it to me. "Happy Easter and all that rot," he wrote. He was tired, discouraged, saddened, not only by Ken's death, but by all the death, hardship, and destruction he had seen. "All I think about anymore is getting home," he added.

When he learned that I knew about the movements of his unit, he cautioned me not to "pay too much attention to the news about Khe Sanh or Phu Bai. I've seen what they report . . . they have a real art for distorting things — I guess that's what sells newspapers."

After Tet, ours was a war-weary army in Vietnam, a dispirited army. Because news flowed both ways, our men knew by then, the spring of 1968, that it was a dispirited, war-weary nation that waited at home. Earlier in the year, Ken had written that his men were worried about their families because of what he called "the conditions" in the United States. "They know why they're here and they're doing a wonderful job," he said, "but they're anxious about home."

Ours was a nation that wanted relief — relief from the threat of the draft, relief from the horrors of the nightly news. The light at the end of the tunnel. Peace. Withdrawal.

I prepared for Dave's homecoming. I couldn't bear to mention it to Libby; after Ken died I never mentioned Dave's coming home in my letters to her, and I tried to avoid talking about it to her on the phone. I couldn't forget that she would never know the blessed coming back of a man who had gone to war. They had brought her a silver coffin.

But she brought up Dave's return herself, and she was generous and loving. "Give him a kiss and a hug for me," she said.

I had not made it all the way yet, either, and as I planned for a life with Dave after the war, I crossed my fingers, I knocked on wood, I prayed. And I allowed myself one last, morbid act before I lost myself in a rush of preparation for Dave's homecoming. I planned his funeral.

I had witnessed Libby's pain long distance, but still I had seen how helpless it seemed to make her. She had been fortunate to have family and friends and Marines around her who knew what to do. Both she and Ken had grown up in Lafayette, in the same neighborhood, and had attended the same church. They had been married in that church, and Ken was buried from it. But I was a stranger in Tacoma. I shared little history with Dave there, and I was terrified that I would not be able to bury him well, if it should come to that. I also hoped that I could confuse the fates by showing them that I was prepared for the best — and the worst, too.

I knew I wanted a cemetery with perpetual care. I did not intend to live in Tacoma without Dave, and I would want his grave cared for after his parents were gone. So in late April, I drove to two of the large cemeteries in Tacoma that advertised this service, and I looked at some of the available plots. I found two or three that I liked, one especially — a large, grassy spot next to a chain-link fence that separated the cemetery from a row of weeds and a busy blacktop highway. This part of the cemetery was shaded by huge evergreen trees, and it looked like a clearing in the woods. I though Dave would like it.

I called the local Marine recruiter and asked how I

might arrange for a Marine honor guard. The matter-of-fact sergeant on duty gave me a Seattle phone number, which I slipped into the secret compartment of my billfold with the paper on which I had written the name of a funeral home and a list of prayers and songs I liked. When that was done, I felt better in a hollow way. Only then did I allow myself to plan for a coming home.

Dave grew thoughtful and philosophical in his last letters from Vietnam. I sensed in them his gradual pulling away from his own war: "Perhaps we shouldn't be here — that's JFK's doing — it would probably be better if we had just given military aid. The South won't fight as long as we're here to do it for them, and why should they? But we are here, and we should fight to win. . . . I hope we don't give in to the Communists."

On television, I watched antiwar protestors waving NVA flags: my countrymen, my husband's countrymen, carrying the flag of his enemies, and demonstrating not for an America at peace, but for an America defeated.

Love! you love me — your eyes
Have looked through death at mine.
You have tempted a grave too much.

— Isaac Rosenberg,
"Girl to Soldier on Leave"

Thirty-Three

A LETTER WRITTEN MAY 4 reached me
May 11, and in it Dave wrote: "I got my orders, and
they're real good — Naval Amphibious Warfare School
at Norfolk, Virginia, where I'll be an instructor. There's a
big base at Norfolk, so we won't be lonely."

The movers had to be told to take our few boxes of
household possessions to Norfolk; the car had to be
tuned, the tires checked. I got Dave's uniforms out and
sent them to the cleaner's.

I planned and unplanned a dozen times what Jeannie
and I were going to wear to meet Dave at the airport. I
finally chose a red, white, yellow, and navy blue striped
linen sheath with a navy blue linen coat. I bought Jeannie
a light blue cowgirl dress, fringes and all, and tiny blue
sneakers. She was only ten months old, but she was walking everywhere.

Dave's mother helped me with the packing, and we cleaned the house from top to bottom. We baked cookies and brownies and put them in the freezer, and we packed the cupboards and the refrigerator with Cokes and potato chips, hamburger and steaks. Dave's father put a fresh coat of bright barn red paint on the house, and his brother Dennis took the Camaro in for an overhaul.

I finished my sewing. The last bit of it was the robe I had been working on the day Bonnie called to tell me that Ken had been killed. I finally finished it, and I packed it away without ever wearing it. I could not bring myself to put it on or to give it away.

And so another sunny, bright, full-of-blossoms May passed in Tacoma under that brilliant blue sky you see only in the Northwest, in the spring.

On May 22, 1968, I wrote my last letter to Dave. It is one of the few letters of mine that were saved. "This is the last letter I'm going to write to you in Vietnam," I told him.

I'm happy about that, but a little sad at the same time — because until I see you again this is my last contact with you. . . .

I've been hearing from Bob about Da Nang . . . that the shelling is very bad there. I know that's where you're going next. Please be careful. . . .

Dave, I love you. . . . In a matter of days all this hell will be behind us.

Dave's last letter from Vietnam reached me on May 28. "I'm glad to get out of that hell hole called Khe Sanh," he wrote. "I weigh 170 pounds now [down from 190] — haven't weighed that since high school. That's from eating nothing but C-rats for the last four months. I'll be right behind this letter, hon."

Dave left Vietnam on May 29, 1968. He arrived outside

San Francisco, at Travis Air Force Base, on May 30, Memorial Day. From Travis, he took a bus to San Francisco International Airport, where he was to catch a flight to Seattle. He had been advised, for his own safety and to avoid unnecessary trouble, to change into civilian clothes before he left Travis. But he stubbornly decided to wear his long-stored, musty summer tans, the same tan uniform he had worn the day I saw him off to the war. He had had the uniform cleaned and pressed during his layover in Okinawa.

Once again the phone rang in the kitchen on Tyee Drive, and once again it was a call for me that changed the world. Dave was calling from a pay phone outside the airport bar in San Francisco. "I'm on mainland soil," he said. His lovely voice rang out happy and excited. "It's strange. They told me I might get attacked or spit on or something if I wore my uniform. But none of that is happening. People just ignore me. They move aside when they see me, and they look the other way. I feel like I have a disease, something horrible and catching. Even the bartender in San Francisco wouldn't look me in the eye when he took my money."

I hung up the phone, went to my room, and untaped the map of Vietnam that for the past thirteen months had been my record of Dave's war. I folded it carefully along its original creases and dropped it into the wastebasket beside the desk where I had sat so many evenings to write so many, many letters — letters mailed to that faraway place whose name I never wanted to hear again as long as I lived.

When his daughter Jeannie and I drove to the airport early on the evening of May 30, 1968, to welcome my husband home, I was going to meet a man who was in many more ways than I thought possible a stranger to me.

We had been married twenty-one-and-a-half months, but he had been gone for the last thirteen of those — longer than the time we had been together as husband and wife. I had lived with my husband less than nine months before he left for Vietnam. Besides that, he was coming back to a little girl he had seen only once, for a few days when she was three and a half months old.

Dave's parents followed in their car. I had decided that Dave and I would spend the evening with his mother and father and Jeannie, but after that we would send the baby home with his parents and go off on our own, to be alone.

"We're going to get Daddy," I said to Jeannie. She smiled, squirmed in her car seat, and said, "Dada," but she did not know what or who I meant.

I was not sure if I did, either. I was happy and excited — and very frightened. The man I had met for R&R in Hawaii was not the boy I had seen off to the war. How much had the next six months in that awful place done to him? Who was he to me, after all? And who was I to him? Certainly not the girl he'd left behind. What besides that terrible war and all of its hard lessons did we have in common now?

The airport was crowded with summer travelers, relaxed and bronzed people in sunglasses and colorful cottons, milling around the wide walkways and sitting in the waiting areas. Jeannie ran away from me, and I had to press through the crowds to catch her. Her grandfather held her while we stood — Dave's mother, father, and I, with Jeannie in her grandfather's arms — at the plate glass window and watched the big, silver plane land in the pink twilight.

Long before he finally found me in the crowd, I saw Dave, a darkly tanned man in a wrinkled, light-brown uniform coming down the steel stairs among a stream of ordinary civilians. The only soldier. I watched his eyes search the crowd with a serious and dark gaze. Old eyes. Lines across his forehead. But when he saw me, he smiled a wide and happy smile that erased worry and age from his face. A smile that made me laugh and run toward him, choosing him with each step, with each beat of my heart, all over again.

. . . in my heart
no one's cross is missing

My heart is
the most tormented country of all

— Giuseppe Ungaretti,
"San Martino del Carso"

Epilogue

IT'S IMPOSSIBLE for me to say what Dave's homecoming meant to him. He must have felt several kinds of relief and happiness: for being alive, for being home, for being with his family again. My own joy had one source. Dave was safe. But this joy was not pure. Once again there was the old ambivalence back in our lives — this time, our happiness over Dave's being alive crossed by our guilt over the deaths of others; our wanting to have a normal life all the while carrying with us experiences and memories that make that kind of life impossible; our trying to forget the unforgettable. But we didn't admit to any of that, not for years. In the meantime, we gathered ourselves together as best we could and left for our new duty station at Little Creek in Norfolk, Virginia.

At Little Creek, I settled back into military life. Compared to life among civilians during my war vigil, it was a safe and peaceful life. And I loved it. Because we still did not talk about the war in any meaningful way — this seemed to be a tacit rule on base among our military friends, as well as in our own home — Dave didn't talk about what he had experienced in Vietnam, and I did not try to tell him how it had been in what he called "the World." I had seen all the war news, of course, but he knew very little about America's home-front war, the war that erupted after he left for Vietnam.

For Dave, the transition was from one kind of life distant from the home front to another — both military. He looked forward to civilian life again, a life without orders given or orders received.

When I think about Little Creek and Norfolk, about the men and their wives who were my friends there, what astonishes me is how old and knowing we seem in my memory compared to that young and naive group at Quantico. Yet only thirteen months separated us.

I know the reason, of course; I know why this gulf existed between what we had been and what we now were. But still, it astonishes me. And in spite of the distance between our past and present selves, for the most part we survived with enough integrity to go on surviving. We've learned since of the exceptions, and looking back, I can see they were among us even then. One Marine combat officer we knew became unstable shortly after his return from Vietnam; among other strange behavior, he began stealing small items from the PX — things his wife found stacked under their dresser and on their back closet shelves. He was discharged from the Corps. The diagnosis: mental illness.

It's easy to see now that the officer suffered from shell shock, or, as it's called now, post-traumatic stress disorder. But no such thing was recognized in those days. No connection between the war and his behavior was ever suggested. It never occurred to us.

Though we did not want to talk about what we had

been through — wives or husbands — and though we did not recognize even in our own minds the power and effect of our experiences, we shared enough aspects of these to create a safe and understanding place to exist. I wanted to stay in the Marine Corps as long as the Corps would let us.

Dave had other plans. He wanted to go back to school for his PhD in mathematics. Back to college life.

I was pregnant again by the time he told me this. I stood big-bellied and terrified in the living room of our pleasant, project apartment in Norfolk as he read me his letter of acceptance to the doctoral program at WSU.

I could not imagine why he wanted to go back to school — not then. But how clear his reason is to me now. How sharp and precise retrospect makes it. He would have two children, very little money, all of the complications and responsibilities of providing for a family while going to school. But Dave wanted to try to take up where he had left off. He wanted to go back and rejoin the life he had left behind. Astoundingly, we thought it was possible.

For the next twelve years, through graduate school and into careers as college teachers, we managed to live this illusion. Or we thought we were managing. I know now there were hints along the way that we were not, even before we left Norfolk. One night, shocked, I heard Dave yell "Incoming!" and watched him dive under the bed when a fire engine, siren wailing, passed our apartment.

A few months later, back in Pullman to begin graduate school, Dave finally went hunting for chukars, something he had wanted to do since before leaving for Vietnam. He dressed in a set of his jungle utilities and he carried one of his boyhood shotguns. He left the house in the cool of the fall morning, excited and happy, and with a happiness and excitement of my own I watched the red Camaro roll down the street. We were finding our lives again.

I had waited in a timeless land of seventeen hours for Dave to return to me from the war. Now I could celebrate the return of ordinary days, with ordinary hours and minutes. In my relief and happiness, I forgot that grief and memory and the things we suffer have a kind of time of their own to be reckoned with.

When Dave came home from hunting that September day in 1969, it was dark. His face and hands and clothes were covered with dirt, and he was exhausted. Wordlessly, he put his shotgun away on the top shelf of our bedroom closet, and he sat on the bed and began tugging at the laces of his boots. Something was wrong, something more than an unsuccessful hunt.

"What happened?" I asked.

He stopped pulling at his boots and looked at me. "I winged a chukar," he said. "First thing this morning. It fell wounded into some bushes, and I found its track, its blood, but I couldn't find it. I tracked it all day, but I couldn't find it. I wanted to put it out of its misery."

I did not know what to say, how to respond to the sorrow and regret in Dave's voice, so I said nothing. That was the last time Dave hunted chukars.

And there were the dreams. One of the dreams Dave had over and over was one in which he found himself in a graves-registration tent, brought there to identify the bodies of his men. He cried out in his sleep during these nightmares, and I soon learned to wake him, gently, almost as soon as they started.

Bob was living in Washington State, too, and we visited him several times over the years. He had come back from his tour of duty a quieter man. In spite of the open tone of his letters from Vietnam, I never heard him mention the war once he was home. When we got together, we talked about our college days and looked at scrapbooks of pictures taken while the boys were living at White Trash. Bob married twice, and though neither marriage lasted, one did give him the lasting gift of a son he named John David.

Dave was surprised when Bob also left the Marine Corps. "I always thought he'd make a career of it," Dave told me. "He was so gung ho."

For the wives, too, the war had its legacy. We visited Jon and Bonnie in Denver in 1974. Bonnie was no longer the poised, assured, strong woman I and the others had depended on during those lonely months we waited. She poured herself one drink after another all day from a gallon jug of whiskey she kept under her sink. And in the evening, she stood in the middle of the pretty kitchen of her lovely new home and cried out to me, "I hate what's become of us!" I didn't know what she meant then.

For the most part, and for a long time, Dave and I managed to live with our past, though there was always the memory of our sorrows. When the young men I had known were killed in the war, I grieved for them and for their parents and wives. But I grieved for me, too. I had lost personally, and it hurt. Friends walking by my side over very rough terrain were suddenly gone, dead, and their leaving threw shadows of sadness and loneliness for a long time.

The war and then the years that followed brought changes in my relationships with the wives. I was happy to hear that Leah had remarried. It was wonderful news, too, when Diane finally had the baby she had wanted so much, and when another came close behind the first. Soon our correspondence was reduced to Christmas letters, but we both understood.

Harder, much harder, was Libby. I could not face writing to her about the births of my children, about Dave, even about myself — the housewife and mother parts that were so much of my life in those first years after the war. I am ashamed beyond words that I shut her out in this way. But that is what happened. I let a perverted survivor's guilt twist our relationship, and in the end contact with her became sporadic and uncomfortable. I cannot explain how I was able to leave her so alone when I loved her so much.

I eventually lost touch altogether with Melinda, but not through intentional or unintentional neglect. She and Scott spent the seventies moving around after jobs, just as Dave and I did, and when, after one of our moves, I sat down to write to her and send her my new address, I found I had lost hers. But in her last letters to me she was happy, and the baby born at Quantico that cold February morning had grown into a big, handsome boy.

Loss and the sorrow it brings did not stop with the deaths of husbands, and it seemed the war would never end when Bonnie called to tell me that Jon had left her — dropped out, as they say, and moved to another state. "I was so terrified something would happen to him in Vietnam," she said. "And in the end, it did." A few years before, a flood in their basement had destroyed Jon's ribbon-tied letters from Vietnam, letters Bonnie had so eagerly received and so carefully saved. "But," she told me, "at least I still had the man who wrote them. Now he's gone, too, just like the letters."

Only two pictures and one letter she had written to Jon in Vietnam were salvaged, and Bonnie sent them to me with a note: "They're all I have left from our time in the Marine Corps. You may have them now."

And so our lives changed. Over the years, my grief changed, too — though it did not weaken, as I thought it would, but instead grew stronger. I think this is because as I grew older, the men, boys in my memory, changed and became like younger brothers to me — much loved and much missed younger brothers.

This was in the seventies. Our children — Dave and I have four daughters — were growing up, and we were busy with them and with our careers; I earned my MA, and Dave earned his PhD during those years. To family, friends, and neighbors we were doing well. But whenever I thought of all that had gone out of our lives during the war, I felt sad and guilty. It was painful to remember, but I tried hard not to forget. I couldn't forget.

On the other hand, Dave wanted very much to put his memories somewhere deep and forgotten, and on the surface he seemed to be doing a fine job of it. In search of better teaching jobs and better opportunities for us and our children, we moved — from Pullman to Omaha, then from Omaha to the Boston area. We stayed in academe.

We grew used to the attitude of academia toward the Vietnam War, and in particular its attitude toward the Vietnam veteran. Many of the students and professors in college and university graduate programs in the late sixties and early seventies were active in the antiwar movement. In fact, graduate schools provided refuges from the draft for many males during that time, and the schools we studied and taught at were no exceptions. We never told our colleagues about Dave's service; I don't think any of our new friends and neighbors knew that Dave was a combat veteran. But Dave did include this information on his résumé, and even as accustomed as we were to campus attitudes regarding the military, it surprised us when the chairman from the Boston school where Dave had applied for a teaching job phoned Dave's chairman in Omaha to state openly a concern about Dave's having been a Marine.

"You can't tell," the Omaha chairman said. "He doesn't look like one."

The Boston chairman was reassured, and Dave got the job. We felt our life was at last in place. We bought a roomy Victorian house in a pleasant village north of Boston, our daughters settled into neighborhood schools, and I studied for my own PhD. We seemed to be living at least a recognizable version of the dream I had had of marriage when I was a college girl in the Chi Omega sorority house.

Then, in the last weeks of 1980, our tight, controlled, managed world started to fall apart. Dave's nightmares invaded our sleep more and more regularly — at least two or three times a week. The slightest "reminder" triggered one: a news program about the war, a letter or phone call from Jon, an advertisement on TV for a war movie, a picture in a magazine. He started to drink heavily and was even picked up once for drunk driving. Over and over, I asked *why*. "Why do you have to drink until you're drunk?"

"I can forget that way," he told me.

In late November, right after Thanksgiving, Dave left the house in the afternoon and by nightfall had still not returned — something he had never done before without calling first to let me know. I waited for him, and when he finally appeared at two in the morning, I was so frantic I could hardly speak. I had spent the hours certain he was lying somewhere injured — or even dead. His drunken explanation made no sense to me then, and it sounded more like a weak excuse than a reason. "I was looking for a Marine to talk to," he said.

Bad turned worse. Dave lost twenty pounds and grew a beard; he had boils on his legs from his thighs to his ankles, the same leg infection he had come to Hawaii with on R&R so many years before. He had a constant look of anger, bitterness, and confusion in his eyes.

And four days after Christmas, he disappeared. He left a note on the white enamel work table in the kitchen: "I don't know what's wrong with me. I love you, but I'm leaving. I'm no good to anybody this way."

He reappeared, living in a five-dollar-a-night rooming house for transients in a small town an hour west of our house. Though he spent most of his time with the family in our Victorian house in the village, he kept the room at

the rooming house for months. He was living a nightmare: awake in the middle of his life in a dark woods,
looking for a comfort I could not give him, helpless to
help me understand.

"I can't offer you anything," he said to me once. "I'm
all used up."

And then they brought the hostages home from Iran.
There were yellow ribbons and signs everywhere. The
country was celebrating because the fifty-two hostages
had survived — though all the time they were in captivity
they had been sheltered, fed, and not shot at. That was a
happy time for the country and for the hostages and their
families. Still, it was a hard time for us.

Dave watched the special coverage of their homecoming on television in our living room. He watched in his
easy chair at first, with his hands gripping the arms like
someone strapped to an electric chair. After a while, he
began to pass his hand over his eyes again and again as
he watched.

There they were, the president, the joyful crowds, all
hailing the victorious former hostages — every one of
them a hero for having survived 444 days of captivity. No
cause. No right or wrong. They had simply survived, and
the nation was grateful.

Dave got up from his chair and left the house. It was
dark when he finally returned. As I knew he would be,
he was drunk. But the next day, sober, he pounded the
steering wheel with his fists as we sat in our car in the
parking lot of a restaurant and said: "I need help. Please
get me some help." He was crying. I had never seen him
cry before.

I had heard of a veterans' center in Manchester, New
Hampshire. These outreach centers are everywhere now,
even in many small towns. But there was only the one
in the area then, and we drove over an hour to get to it,
only to find it closed for the night.

I called friends for advice about psychiatrists and psychologists. I phoned a specialist someone had recommended as being particularly good at treating men. "What's your husband's problem?" the doctor asked me.

"I think he needs to talk about the war," I said. But once therapy began, the subject was never brought up, not by the doctor, and not by Dave.

But I did not give up. I had become the toughest fighter of all; I was not fighting for freedom, but for survival — my survival as wife and the survival of my family. Sometime in the middle of all this, I picked up a book about the Vietnam War: Philip Caputo's *A Rumor of War*, his memoir about being a Marine lieutenant in Vietnam. At last I had an image — vague and distant, but nevertheless an image — of the land Dave had walked over for those thirteen months lost to me. At last I had a sense of his real wounds. I was grateful for the knowledge about what Vietnam looked and smelled and felt like, most grateful to be told a little of what being there as a warrior did to a young man. I wrote my thanks to the author.

Philip Caputo visited us in the spring of 1981. He came to interview us for an article he was writing about the difficulties soldiers returning from Vietnam had faced. "Do you think your husband will talk to me?" he had asked over the phone.

"I don't know," I said. "He usually won't talk about the war, but I will."

But Dave did talk. He talked to the writer-Marine, and for Dave that was the beginning of the end of the silent but searing hell he had somehow plunged into sometime in the late sixties, someplace between the United States and Vietnam.

Dave and I answered questions and talked to Caputo all day the day of his visit; we talked in the car on the way from Boston, where we went to pick him up; we talked over lunch in our dining room; then we talked on the sidewalks of our village, Georgetown, where we walked after a spring rain. Finally, we talked in our living room. It got late, and I left the men sitting across from each other, still talking. But instead of climbing the stairs to my bedroom, I sat on the bottom tread, just outside the living-room door, and listened.

Some of their talk was jargon, the kind men who have been to war in Vietnam use — about red and green tracers, M79 men, U-shaped sweeps, FOs, Hueys, medevacs, and M16s. Claymores, booby traps, spider holes, and pungi sticks. That talk was incomprehensible to me then, but I understood the rest of what they said: it was about fighting and fear.

"Do you remember," I heard Dave ask Caputo, "how the nights could be so dark you couldn't see even a foot in front of you, or they could be so light you'd think it was daytime? I hated setting ambush, wondering if you'd been seen or not, being afraid to move."

Sitting on the stairs in the dim hallway, I felt relief and joy, and renewed sorrow when I heard Dave's quiet voice tell how he had seen trapped enemy POWs shot to death because they were burning alive. "They were screaming and turning all kinds of strange colors — reds and grays," Dave said. "Finally, a corporal asked the major in charge for permission to waste them — you know, to put them out of their misery. And the major said yes. Those were the most horrible enemy deaths I saw in Vietnam, because they were the deaths of men who couldn't try to kill us anymore. They were prisoners; the war was over for them, but they died anyway, because of a horrible accident."

I learned how Dave had had to oversee the mass burial of the decomposing bodies of the enemy dead at Hue. "A lot of the bodies were just kids," he said. "We tried to bury them individually at first, but there were too many, and their bodies were rotting fast. In the end we had to get a bulldozer and shovel them in like animals. It made me sick."

And because Dave had at last found someone to talk to, I finally learned how Sam had died. "Another kid from our platoon at Basic School, a guy named Owens, led a relief platoon in the next day, to the place where the firefight had been, and they found Sam's body," Dave said. "The enemy had broken most of his bones — he'd been beaten all over, and for a long time, with bamboo sticks. Owens told me all this months after it had happened, but he was shaking when he told me. I hated hearing the details, but I was glad Owens had someone to tell."

Sam had been dead nearly fourteen years, but I had not known until that night how he had been tortured, the horror of his dying. When Dave finished telling about Sam, I did not stay to hear any more. Oddly and almost unbearably happy and sad for Sam and Dave both, I went up to bed, where I cried in the dark until I heard Dave's footsteps outside the door.

Soon after, he gave up his rented room out west.

Dave's coming home — his true coming home — came with the hard, horrible, rich, and lovely years that followed. In 1982, the Wall was dedicated in Washington, DC, and while I washed the breakfast dishes, I listened to people read some of the names on the television news. A soothing, loving litany of the dead — then, jumping out of the songlike list of strangers: *Kenneth Louis Ouelette.* And they showed the news footage again — the scene of Ken being interviewed at Khe Sanh. *A circle,* I thought. *Life is circles.*

Because we lived in a time zone ahead of Bonnie's, this time I called her: "Guess what? Ken is on the CBS news this morning. And, Bonnie, he looks beautiful!"

And he did. Even on the small black-and-white television in our kitchen, Ken looked beautiful, and young, and alive.

We visited the Wall. That was part of Dave's healing but difficult therapy. We went the first time when the black V was still a new scar in the earth, dark, polished granite dug into the muddy, grassless ground.

"What a waste," Dave said, looking at the bright names on the black monument.

"Not a waste," I said.

"Then it's a tragedy."

"But there are many worse ways to die, Dave. A lot worse reasons to die."

By this time, the boys whose names were on the Wall had become like my sons. The daughter born to me the year they went to war is now the age they were when they died. They would be my age if they had lived, but they did not; and so now, in my heart and in my memory, they are boys, the beloved children of my most brutal, my most important, memories.

We have visited the Wall many more times over the years that have come after. Grass now covers the cloddy ground in front of the monument, and up the hill they have added a bronze statue of three war-weary soldiers and an American flag. And crowds and crowds of people come, waiting in long lines that climb slowly into and out of the small valley of death. I see the lines of people when we go to the Wall: some are veterans or the friends and relatives of veterans, some are too young to remember the war; but many are not, and I wonder at all these others. *Where were you, I think, when these men needed you? When we all needed you? How can you look so long and lovingly on the silent names of these dead when you were so quick to turn your backs on their living faces?*

* * *

Bonnie has just called me. She has called to tell me she is getting married again. I'm happy for her. "Does Libby know?" I ask.

"I can't talk to Libby anymore," Bonnie tells me. "The first five minutes are OK, then she starts in on all that old stuff again. Then you're down for the rest of the night."

"Old stuff?" I say. I think I know what she means, but I want to hear her confess, to hear her tell me she doesn't care anymore. Maybe she never did care the way I thought she did.

Then I remember Bonnie comforting Libby so long ago at Waller Hall; I remember her letters and calls when I felt so alone on this side of the world; I remember the gallon jug of whiskey under her sink — and I see in my mind the lovely redheaded girl who stood half-drunk in the middle of her pretty kitchen, crying out past my eyes into emptiness, "I hate what's become of us!" Then I know that Bonnie knows how much we are missing: how much we lost, how much was taken, and how much was denied us.

She is speaking to me now on the phone — plastic, wire, and cable again; I haven't been in the same room with her for fifteen years. She is confessing. "You know what I mean," she says, "all that war business. You don't want to go over all that again."

"No," I say. "I guess not." And I begin to talk to Bonnie about her new world, the world she is walking into: the place where her husband-to-be, Bob, is, and the place where she and her sons are going. Bright, clean, clear.

"Bob managed to avoid all that war mess," she says. "And I'm forgetting — denying — all that garbage that was my marriage."

Her old life will be put away with the war that surely helped destroy it.

Bonnie has a new life to go to now. And Libby has her

love affair with Ken's death — her way of coping with his dying. Leah has been married to her second husband for twenty years. Sam's baby graduated from college last June, and I wonder if her diploma bears the name I knew, or her stepfather's. She has never known another father. To his own daughter, Sam is no memory at all, unless he is a man in the photographs of the special scrapbook I hope her mother has put together for her. I hope Sam's daughter is unique among her siblings in that she has an album of pictures of a man named Sam Melanson.

Sam, Ken, Dennie. They were all brave boys, good men, and good Marines. But they are gone, and the world has gone on without them. They are the peaceful, young dead, and Jon and Matt and Dave are middle-aged men who have had to learn how to live with bad memories and sad nightmares and the stigma that is the badge they earned for their tour of duty. Still, when I think of them all, I see them young and pure and laughing, in their dress blues at the New Year's Eve Ball, Quantico, 1966. Their own best selves. All of us our own best selves. . . . *"You who . . . will never leave me/ . . . who dance in the sun without stirring the dust. . . ."*

Bonnie is saying something else to me on the phone, and I try to pull myself toward her. But I cannot find the place where she is. I cannot go there because I cannot leave the men.

I hear her tell me that she'll send me her new address as soon as she and Bob know what house they're buying. They hope to be settled by fall.

She tells me to be sure to write.

"Yes," I say. "I will."

We die with the dying:
See, they depart, and we go with them.
We are born with the dead:
See, they return, and bring us with them.

— T. S. Eliot, "Little Gidding,"
from *Four Quartets*